"[Lowell's] recollections of sexual abuse, a disfiguring childhood accident, rampant neglect, and alcoholism—as well as her life-long quest to discover her true paternity—could have made for grim reading, but Lowell's writing remains conversational and refreshingly free of self-pity." —*Entertainment Weekly*

"At its heart, *Why Not Say What Happened?*, whose title comes from one of Robert Lowell's final, bleakest poems, is a portrait of a family in freefall, a mother and her four children floating through a dizzying succession of grand but rotting houses while enduring absent fathers, sexual abuse, mental breakdown, severe injury, alcoholism and the deaths of loved ones. The only thing fending off complete devastation is the author's gleefully black sense of humor." —*The Telegraph* (London)

"With walk-on parts from everyone from the Queen Mother and artist Lucian Freud to film mogul Harvey Weinstein, this book is packed with color. A brilliant memoir." —*Voyager*

"[Ivana] tells her story with verve and wit, and I loved every minute of it." —Ann LaFarge, *Hudson Valley News*

"Shocking and hilarious, this elegantly lucid memoir by Ivana Lowell is that lethal mix of British aristocracy, giant fortunes, huge freezing houses, beautiful women jagged with sophistication, pedophilia, mysterious paternity, cruelty and yes, cocktails. We are reminded of the plays of Oscar Wilde and novels from Ronald Firbank to Evelyn Waugh as we are introduced to a lively and unlikely mix that includes the Queen Mother and Harvey and Bob Weinstein. . . . Lowell is impressive and touching in sparing us none of this tragicomedy, least of all herself." —Mike Nichols

Ivana Lowell

Why Not Say What Happened?

Ivana Lowell grew up in London, Boston, and
New York. She now lives in Sag Harbor with her
daughter.

www.ivanalowell.com

Why Not Say What Happened?

Why Not Say What Happened?

A MEMOIR

Ivana Lowell

Vintage Books

A DIVISION OF RANDOM HOUSE, INC.

NEW YORK

FIRST VINTAGE BOOKS EDITION, NOVEMBER 2011

Copyright © 2010 by Ivana Lowell

All rights reserved. Published in the United States by Vintage Books, a division of
Random House, Inc., New York, and in Canada by Random House of Canada Limited,
Toronto. Originally published in hardcover in the United States by Alfred A. Knopf,
a division of Random House, Inc., New York, in 2010.

Vintage and colophon are registered trademarks of Random House, Inc.

Grateful acknowledgment is made to the following for permission to reprint previously
published material: Alan Brodie Representation Ltd. and Methuen Drama: Excerpt from
"I Went to a Marvellous Party" by Noël Coward, copyright © 1938 by NC Aventales AG.
Reprinted by permission of Alan Brodie Representation Ltd. (www.alanbrodie.com) and
Methuen Drama, an imprint of A&C Black Publishers Ltd. Farrar, Straus and Giroux,
LLC: Excerpt from "Epilogue," "Ivana," and excerpt from "Mermaid" from *Collected Poems*
by Robert Lowell, copyright © 2003 by Harriet Lowell and Sheridan Lowell.
Reprinted by permission of Farrar, Straus and Giroux, LLC.

The photographs reproduced in this book were provided with the permission
and courtesy of the following: Caroline Blackwood by Evelyn Hofer: The Estate of
Evelyn Hofer; Robert Lowell, my mother, and children with rabbits: Fay Godwin ©
The British Library Board; Langton Hall: John Swannell; Daisy, age ten: Christopher Mason.
All other photographs are from a private collection.

The Library of Congress cataloged the Knopf edition as follows:
Lowell, Ivana.
Why not say what happened? : a memoir / by Ivana Lowell.—1st ed.
p. cm.
1. Lowell, Ivana.   2. Lowell, Ivana—Family.   3. Blackwood, Caroline.   4. Mothers and
daughters.   5. Family secrets.   6. Guinness family.   7. Upper class—Biography.
8. Ireland—Biography.   9. England—Biography.   10. United States—Biography.   I. Title.
CT3150.L69A3 2010
973.92092—dc22 [B] 2010018775

Vintage ISBN: 978-0-307-38740-0

Book design by Iris Weinstein

www.vintagebooks.com

*For Daisy
and my mother,
and with love
to
Howard*

But sometimes everything I write

with the threadbare art of my eye

seems a snapshot,

lurid, rapid, garish, grouped,

heightened from life,

yet paralyzed by fact.

All's misalliance.

Yet why not say what happened?

—from "Epilogue," by Robert Lowell

Acknowledgments

I could not have done this book without the many people who have listened, encouraged, and bolstered me over the last couple of years.

I would like to thank my agent, Andrew Wylie, who was there at the start and instrumental in getting me to tell my story. He sent the proposal to Shelley Wanger, who has proved to be the perfect editor—wise, funny, and a joy to work with. I would also like to thank Sonny Mehta and others at Knopf, Chip Kidd, Victoria Pearson, Iris Weinstein, and Ken Schneider, for all their work on this book. In London, my editor at Bloomsbury, Michael Fishwick, has been an invaluable and encouraging force. I would especially like to thank my brilliant friend Steven M. L. Aronson, who read and marked my manuscript with many excellent sug-

Acknowledgments

gestions and who so smartly suggested the title. And thanks, too, to my dear neighbor Jason Epstein, who also went through an early draft and offered up ideas for improvement. I am enormously grateful to Hugo Vickers and Christopher Mason for letting me use their photographs and to Hugo, too, for his indispensable, encyclopedic knowledge. And much gratitude to Pat Sweeney and to my computer whiz, Andrew Skonka, who at any hour was able to rescue me from technological disasters. And to all my friends who have tirelessly urged me to carry on when I felt particularly despondent. In no particular order: Andrew Solomon, John Habich, Christopher Mason, Richard Schurkamp, Elizabeth Cabot, Donna Cohen, Claudie Levenson, Laura Grenning, Karen Easton, Lisa Fine, Francesca Gonshaw, Geordie Grieg, John Holton, Edward Noel, Charlotte and Alex De Cacacci, Bob Weinstein, Kimberley Du Ross, Mercedes and Sid Bass, Kathy and Billy Rayner, Jay Mellon, Ken Butler, Anthony Page, Steven Fayer, Jonathan Moffat and Marguerite Littman. To Evgenia and Sheridan, I would like to say how much I love them, and very special love and thanks to Grace Dudley and Bob Silvers, who have always been there for me, and to Daisy, my daughter, all my love and thanks for bearing with me while I was working on this book. And last but not least, Howard, thank you so much for everything and for never giving up on me.

Why Not Say What Happened?

Prologue

The day after my mother died, I agreed to have lunch with one of her oldest friends at a restaurant on Madison Avenue in New York.

The venue was chosen for its proximity to the Mayfair Hotel, where my mother had spent the last few weeks of her life and where the day before I had watched her jaundiced, cancer-riddled body take its final breath.

I don't remember accepting the invitation or arriving at the restaurant. I do remember thinking that perhaps there was something else I should be doing rather than going out to lunch. But truth was, I didn't have anything better to do. And I really needed a drink.

It's strange when the person closest to you in your life dies.

Everyone assumes you have a million things to do, friends and family to be with, arrangements to make, and tears to shed. But I didn't. The important things were all being taken care of. My brother and brother-in-law were at Frank E. Campbell organizing the cremation, my pregnant sister was back at the hotel resting after the stress of the past few months, and I wasn't ready to cry.

So it was in an unreal state of mind that I turned my attention back to the woman sitting opposite me who asked me the question "Of course, you do know who your real father was. Don't you?"

"My father? Of course I know who he was. It was Dad. Wasn't it?"

She smiled indulgently and shrugged her shoulders. But I was too numb and exhausted to pursue the conversation, so the subject was changed. After lunch I telephoned my grandmother in London, and I told her about the conversation. I had expected her to refute it. Instead she chuckled. "Oh darling, that's such good news. Perhaps that means you are not Jewish after all! Now, Ivana, you must make sure to tell any beaus of yours that you are not Jewish. Because, darling, you will have a far better chance of ever getting married."

I called my sister Evgenia. I told her what had happened. There was a long pause while I waited for her reaction. I thought she would laugh or at least be indignant. Instead she said, "Oh, sweetie, I think she may be telling the truth."

PART ONE

I have recently started going to a new shrink. She is the latest on a list of many. She is British, straightforward, and cozily plump. The sort of woman you want to sit down with, have a nice cup of tea and a bit of a chat. "You have been so bumped and knocked around," she told me after hearing just a little of my history, "that it's a wonder you survived at all."

I certainly don't feel like a "wonder." In fact, I feel that I have fucked up my life. I have spent so long trying to avoid feeling the pain and anxiety that lie so close to the surface of my skin. Alcohol, antidepressants, and stints in rehabs have done little to alleviate the feelings of desperation.

The worst thought I have is that it is too late, that perhaps I am too damaged ever to be fixed. I have spent so much of my life floundering.

Now that I am a mother, however, I have grown up a bit and become brave enough to look back and try to make some sense of the past.

Dysfunctional does not even begin to describe my family and upbringing. Anyway, that is far too easy a word to use—who doesn't come from some kind of dysfunction? But what part of my history has so ill-equipped me to function in adulthood?

"You do know who your real father was. Don't you?" Maybe I had been given a clue to solve a puzzle that I never knew even existed.

ON PAPER IT ALL looks so perfect, so glamorous, so privileged, and interesting. I come from a fabled background. My mother was born into a family that was wealthy, aristocratic, and good-looking. My grandmother was one of three sisters whom the society pages dubbed "the glorious Guinness girls." All three were beautiful, charming, and, thanks to the popularity of the black stout beer whose name they bore, very rich.

They were also spoiled, selfish, and uneducated. They were born during an era when it was deemed unnecessary for a young lady to be equipped with anything other than nice manners and good child-bearing hips. Education was considered unimportant.

My great-grandfather the Honorable Arthur Ernest Guinness was by all accounts an unattractive character. I have heard many stories that illustrate his extravagant and boorish behavior. My mother's favorite was when "Granddaddy" purchased his own private airplane. He knew very little about flying but on a whim one day decided to take the plane out for a little spin. Unfortunately, when he jumped into the cockpit he failed to notice that the plane's mechanic was still working on top of one of the wings. The mechanic was killed immediately after the plane took off, but my great-grandfather ignored this little inconvenience and continued his flight undaunted. Because of his great wealth some of these more despicable acts were labeled as merely eccentric, and as far as I know he never suffered any repercussions or consequences.

At that time he also owned one of the largest yachts ever built. He decided that his girls should see the world, and so he embarked with my grandmother and my two great-aunts on a sailing trip that lasted most of their formative years. Their lives up to that point had been untouched by reality, and the long sea voyage only removed them further from any semblance of normality.

As a young girl my grandmother was waited on hand and foot, a practice that she made sure continued until her death. If she needed to go to the lavatory, a maid would warm up the toilet seat before "Miss Maureen" was allowed to sit down.

When the girls came out as debutantes, they were in possession of cash and good looks, but they needed class to be accepted at the highest level of English society. My grandmother found it in the form of the Marquess of Dufferin and Ava. Basil Dufferin was young, handsome, and eligible. His great-grandfather the first marquess had been viceroy in India and governor general of Canada. He had arguably been Britain's most accomplished diplomat of the nineteenth century. Basil himself had done brilliantly at Oxford and was generally expected to go on to do great things.

The huge society marriage between the dashing young marquess and the vivacious Guinness heiress at Saint Margaret's Cathedral in London was seemingly made in Debrett's heaven.

ALONG WITH HIS TITLE, my grandfather had inherited a large, gray stone Georgian house and estate in the north of Ireland. On a man-made shamrock-shaped lake and surrounded by acres and acres of parkland, Clandeboye House was the childhood home of my mother and her younger sister and brother.

After the three children were born, their glamorous parents continued their exhaustive socializing and entertaining. Both were overly fond of drink (something that is a recurring theme in my family), and they were at the epicenter of the decadent, hedonistic social life of London in the 1930s.

My grandparents and their set cavorted with the fastest, grandest, and most brilliant people that England had to offer, statesmen, royalty, literary figures, and a scattering of talented snobs. Cecil Beaton, Evelyn Waugh, Frederick Ashton, and Nöel Coward were part of their crowd. When Cecil Beaton met my grandmother Maureen and her sisters, Oonagh and Aileen, in the 1920s, he records, "It was disgustingly smart and so dreadfully like the party in a Noël Coward play." In the Noël Coward song "I Went to a Marvelous Party," there is a bit about Maureen:

> I went to a marvelous party
> We played the most wonderful game.
> Maureen disappeared
> And came back in a beard
> And we all had to guess at her name!

While my grandparents were enjoying the high life in London, my mother, my aunt, and my uncle were often left in the austere atmosphere of Northern Ireland. They were looked after by governesses and nannies. My mother would never forgive her mother for her lack of parental love, the loneliness she felt as a child, and the brutal disregard with which she and her siblings were treated. She would never forget this neglect, and in many ways she spent the rest of her life trying to escape the cruel and empty world of her aristocratic childhood.

When England declared war on Germany, everyone's circumstances changed dramatically. The children were considered to be safer in Ireland, away from the blitzing of England, and they spent even less time at the Knightsbridge house in Hans Crescent. This only increased my mother's feeling of isolation.

Even my grandmother did her bit to help out the war effort, joining the Red Cross and consoling wounded young soldiers. She would remind us of this in self-sacrificing tones for years to come. My grandfather Basil, who had been the secretary of state for war in 1935, persuaded the war office to dispatch him to Burma on an operation aimed at demoralizing the Japanese troops who were steadily advancing.

My mother said that he had volunteered partly to prove that he was more than just a privileged aristocrat. But she suspected his real reason was to escape my grandmother. She told me that her father had begun to find Maureen's obsession with royalty and her relentless party giving and socializing tedious. Her father, she said, was a "funny, clever and well-educated man," and Maureen was—"Well, she was the opposite of that, wasn't she?"

It was a dangerous and brave mission for him to undertake and on March 25, 1945, Lord Dufferin was killed in action. He was thirty-five. One of the ironies of his death was that it took place near the ancient capital of Ava, his namesake, and in the country that his grandfather had annexed to the British throne.

His death left Maureen a widow with two young daughters and a son. My uncle Sheridan, aged three years old, was now the Fifth Marquess of Dufferin and Ava and the heir to the Clande-boye estate.

I have a young daughter, Daisy. She was born on the sixteenth of July, the same birthday as my mother. Daisy has enormous eyes. Sometimes it feels as though her eyes are boring into me with uncanny perceptiveness. It is as though she were seeing right into my soul. The look lasts only a few seconds, but it is incredibly disconcerting.

My mother had exactly the same look. My mother was beautiful, but it was her eyes that made her so compelling. They were liquid, pale blue, and huge. Their luminescence only added further to the impression she gave of tremendous sadness and fear. It was as though she was always on the verge of tears or something worse.

By the time my mother was old enough to come out as a debutante in London, my grandmother was harboring hopes of a great marriage for her elder daughter. The highlight of the debutante season was the private coming-out balls given by the girls' parents to show off their offspring. There was no shortage of eligible suitors for Lady Caroline, but my mother found the whole "coming out" process deeply depressing. She was incredibly shy, and her idea of hell was to have to stand with the other debutantes awkwardly waiting to be asked to dance.

The men at these dances would usually be some unattractive duke or earl that she never would have dreamed of dancing with in the first place. She said she became very familiar with the bathrooms of all the large houses in England because she would spend most of her evenings hiding in them.

My grandmother held a coming-out party for my mother at her house in Knightsbridge. The imposing white London house was perfect for entertaining. It had not only a dining room big enough to seat forty for dinner but also a ballroom with a parquet floor where the guests could gather to dance.

My grandmother was determined to give her beautiful daughter a coming-out ball that would rival all the others. Princess Margaret was a debutante the same year as my mother, and she and her sister, the young Queen Elizabeth, attended the event.

The night of her daughter's party, however, my grandmother was so overcome with excitement that she "overserved" herself with champagne. While trying to execute a rather elaborate move on the dance floor, she fell facedown, sprawled inelegantly on the parquet floor. The family's priceless, shamrock-shaped diamond tiara that adorned her head had been broken.

Her behavior in front of royalty left her mortified. The next day she swore off alcohol altogether and never touched a drop again. That one incident was so damaging to her snobbish pride that she was able to overcome the disease that would wreak so much havoc on the rest of us. Perhaps a broken tiara was a small price to pay.

Unfortunately, my mother's alcoholism was to have longer and sadder consequences. And I, too, have struggled with what we politely referred to as "the family problem."

CHAPTER 3

Over the last twelve years, I have been to at least three rehabs. I say "at least" because I have also had a couple of
stays in some rather unpleasant detox facilities. The visits to the rehabs are preceded by a spell of depression and heavy
drinking. Alcohol, of course, only exacerbates my feelings of hope-
lessness and despair. Still I drink.

On two occasions I have ended up in the ER after mixing an
unwise concoction of pills and alcohol. I have never attempted to
kill myself, and actually for the most part, I am very fond of life.

But I would work myself up into a chemically altered state of
morose self-pity, and when I was there, I couldn't really see
much point in or even possibility of carrying on. If living meant
being in that much pain and despair, then oblivion surely was a
better alternative.

I have always overdramatized situations. Perhaps that was the
only way, or at least the easiest way, I could get any attention
when I was growing up. Certainly a drunken late-night phone
call to a friend to tell her you wanted to die—and had already
taken enough pills to see to it that you did—will get a reaction of
some sort.

It is only when you find yourself in the lock down section of
New York Hospital, alone, freezing cold, and violently ill, while
you are puking up the black charcoal vomit-inducing mixture
they force you to drink to pump out your stomach, that you wonder if maybe you have gone too far this time.

The staff in the ER has no time for you. You can see their dis-
dain as you cry into your black pan of sick. They have real emer-
gencies to deal with. Everything bad that has happened in New

Why Not Say What Happened?

York City that night ends up here; victims of accidents and rape, critically ill children, and fatalities. All of them need attention. None of them wanted to be here, but they didn't have a choice. You, on the other hand, did this to yourself, and are a waste of time and space.

REHAB FACILITIES have now become fashionable. They are seen as a quick one-stop shop for anyone with a problem and, more recently, as a convenient place to escape from scandal and bad behavior. Whatever your obsession—sex, drugs, alcohol, porn, gambling, food, or even soft toys (soft-toy addicts who can only achieve sexual pleasure with stuffed animals are fondly referred to as fluffies)—there is a solution for you in rehab.

Most rehabs offer a twenty-eight-day program. This time frame is not based on any medical recommendation. It is the duration for which insurance companies are willing to fork out. While you are in rehab, you attend 12-step groups and lectures and, if you are lucky, you get to see an individual therapist maybe two or three times during your stay. You learn about the nature of your "disease," are introduced to some coping skills and given a discharge plan for when you return to your "normal life."

Because so much of recovery depends on the help and support of others and on the comfort of knowing you are not doing this alone, your fellow inmates are an important part of the rehab experience. Unlikely bonds with total strangers are forged as you share your most painful experiences, your weaknesses.

Everyone is at their rawest and most vulnerable; and, most difficult and most important, without the substance or vice that got them here in the first place.

The rehab experience, I've come to decide, is similar to being put through an automatic car wash. You go in covered with layers of grime and dirt, years' and years' worth of knocks and scratches. After you have been washed, scrubbed, and waxed, you are expected to emerge shining and clean as if brand-new. But nothing can be done about the mileage that you've put on and the rust that still clings to your undercarriage.

After my stays in rehabs I usually managed to remain sober for a length of time. My head would be full of the dangers of relapsing. I had learned enough to know that drinking would only make things much, much worse.

But I was also realizing that just putting down the drink was not enough. Alcohol had been my primary tool for dealing with every aspect of life. If I was to let it go, I needed to find something else to replace it. This idea was so novel to me, so outrageous and frightening, that I didn't believe I could do it.

I had never been taught any other way of living; I certainly didn't have much faith that things would be okay. After all, I hadn't seen much evidence of things being all right in the past. Why should I believe that now things could be different?

CHAPTER 4

B y the time she was eighteen, my mother's relationship with my grandmother had become fairly intolerable. The atmosphere in the London house was tense. My mother was ashamed of her mother's snobbishness, her extravagant lifestyle, and, to my mother's mind, her vulgar behavior.

Maureen was well known and adored in London society for her fondness for practical jokes, her eccentric dress, and her gift for mimicry. She would often arrive at social events wearing a false penis on her nose and a hidden "fart machine" between her legs. She would let the machine rip at opportune moments.

Another of her favorite tricks was to invite an assortment of distinguished guests to dinner at her impressive white house in Belgravia. The house resembled a large carriage house and took up an entire block. The light blue door had three gold doorbells, one marked *visitors*, another *staff*, and a third *tradesmen*. Maureen would open the door herself, disguised as Mabel, Lady Dufferin's drunken, crude Irish maid.

"Lady Dufferin will be down in a minute," she would inform her guests in slurred northern Irish brogue. As Mabel, Maureen dressed up in a maid's uniform, but the normally pristine, starched white shirt and black skirt were wrinkled and stained. Her face would be made-up to resemble that of a woman who had lived an alcoholic's hard life given over to devotion to her mistress. My grandmother would complete the look with a set of yellowing, oversized false teeth. Her normally immaculate bow-shaped, red lipstick–stained mouth was transformed into a yellow, snaggle-toothed grimace. And she would squint through a greasy monoglass that hung from a cheap chain around her neck.

"Will you be wanting to go?" she would ask the perplexed arrivals. The question would be accompanied by a wink and an exaggerated tilt of her head toward the downstairs cloakroom. "If you be needing to go, now is the time to do it," she would urge the guests, shoving them toward the lavatory door.

Sometimes Maureen would carry this act on into the dining room. Mabel would apologize for Lady Dufferin's lateness and insist on proceeding with the soup course. This inevitably would be a disaster, with most of the soup ending up in the laps of the guests.

While these stories of Maureen's outrageous sense of humor and mischievous behavior kept her circle of friends entertained and delighted, my mother just found them excruciatingly embarrassing. She felt suffocated by her background and found her home life intolerable.

MAUREEN CONTINUED to fantasize about an aristocratic marriage and a life spent among the stately homes of England for her daughter, but my mother was becoming more and more determined to avoid such a fate. She was still made to attend the grand parties and dinners that her mother foisted upon her, and most of the time she found them mind-numbingly tedious and pointless.

One hostess, however, held more interesting and eclectic gatherings at her London home. Anne Fleming was the widow of Ian Fleming, the writer best known for his creation James Bond, the womanizing spy. Anne liked to collect people that she found amusing and her soirées would contain a mixture of young writers and artists, as well as society.

At one of these evenings my mother was introduced to a young, intense, and compellingly handsome painter. She already knew of Lucian Freud because somebody had brought him to her coming-out party. He had gotten extremely drunk and while trying to steady himself had tripped over Princess Margaret. The princess had not been amused.

Lucian had escaped to England with his parents from Nazi Germany when he was ten and he spoke with a low, seductive, German accent. Lucian was the grandson of the celebrated psychoanalyst and was just beginning to establish himself as an artist.

My mother was immediately captivated. He was attractive, intelligent, and different from anyone else she had met. He also had all the qualities that she knew would most horrify her mother. Lucian was still married. He was impoverished. And he was Jewish. He was absolutely unsuitable in every way, and therefore he couldn't have been more perfect. He would become her first husband.

CHAPTER 5

My shrink asked me what was my earliest memory. "Being lost," I replied. She asked if I meant metaphorically. No, I was literally lost.

I must have been about three or four and my mother had dropped me off at my preschool in London. This in itself was unusual. Normally this duty would be performed by one of the succession of nannies employed to look after my two elder sisters and myself. That day, however, I said good-bye to my mother and ran up the few stairs to the entrance of the school.

The large red door was locked. When I turned around, my mother had gone. The school was closed. It was a holiday.

I still remember the feeling of absolute terror that took over. I had no idea how to get home, what my address was, or what to do. I just sat on the steps and cried. I must have looked a pathetic sight: a small child sitting alone by a busy road.

Finally, an elderly lady took pity on me and brought me to the nearest police station. I was given milk and cookies while they tried to track down my parents and where I lived. Eventually I was taken home.

But home never felt much safer than sitting alone on those steps. It felt lonely and scary. There was so much chaos swirling around that I always felt some terrible catastrophe was about to befall us.

My mother's marriage to Lucian was not a success. My grandmother had been so appalled by the whole affair that she cut off my mother's allowance. In a letter to Nancy Mitford, Evelyn Waugh wrote, "Poor Maureen's daughter made a runaway match with a terrible Yid." My mother was horrified by her mother's and her friends' anti-Semitism.

"The funny thing," she told me later, was that the viceroy (my great-great grandfather, and First Marquess of Dufferin and Ava) was said to be the illegitimate son of Benjamin Disraeli. "He looked just like him. They had similar dark, handsome looks and Dizzy certainly helped his career." She told me that the rumor was that Disraeli had been to Clandeboye, fallen madly in love with Helen Brinkley Sheridan, and the viceroy was the product. "I love the idea of that," she told me gleefully. "It means that we all have Jewish blood!"

The newly impoverished young couple moved to Paris, where Lucian would paint and my mother modeled for him. She soon discovered that Lucian was a womanizer and a gambler. My mother described to me how depressing it was for her on their honeymoon. If Lucian was not chasing other women, then he was spending what little money they had betting on horses.

Although the marriage was not perfect, the portraits of his wife he painted at that time are astonishingly beautiful. She looks quite sad in them, but that was, she explained to me, because she was so bored. Sitting for Lucian was a long and intense process. He worked slowly and painstakingly. My mother found having to sit still for hours at a time agony. She later commented, "Critics said that he paints the anguish of our age—but he really paints the anguish of his sitter!"

One morning Lucian decided he loved the way the sheets on their slept-in bed were arranged. He wanted to paint the creases on the rumpled pillows and the folds of the blankets. It was only after he had been working for a day on this masterpiece that my mother realized they would not be able to sleep in their bed for months, until he had finished the painting.

Even Lucian got bored during some of the more meticulous parts of the process. "When he was just filling in little bits," as she put it. To entertain them both, my mother read out loud.

While posing for *Girl Reading* she read *The Tragic Muse* by Henry James, and came to identify with the title. These paintings, *Girl Reading* and *Girl in Bed,* were later to become celebrated when they were exhibited at the Tate gallery in London.

While they were in Paris they led a bohemian life, which my mother found refreshing after her stifling upbringing. Lucian introduced her to the artists and writers he knew and respected. He took her to meet Picasso in his studio, a visit my mother found both fascinating and terrifying. "He had the most enormous and disturbing eyes," she told me.

Picasso invited her upstairs to see his doves while Lucian waited downstairs. He proceeded to make "the most terrible pass" at her. He also drew little pictures on her fingernails, which she said was extremely frustrating because they wouldn't last. She couldn't bear to wash her hands until the pictures wore off. For a while she had her very own Picassos on her nails.

In Paris, Lucian and my mother lived in a rather wild hotel called La Lousiane. As the marriage disintegrated, the rows in the hotel between the two of them became more dramatic. A friend of theirs recalled a particularly nasty fight during which

Lucian pushed my mother out of the hotel room into the corridor and locked the door. She was completely naked, but he refused to let her back in. The friend mused, "I am not sure how she ever did get back in. But I suppose she must have eventually."

My mother told me that she finally snapped one night after she had cooked dinner for Lucian and the painter Francis Bacon. She had gone to a lot of trouble over the dinner; tender baby lamb chops with mint sauce, petit pois, and potatoes dauphinoise.

Lucian looked at the food. Without even tasting it, he pushed his plate away, slid it across the table, and lit a cigarette. "I went next door to the bedroom, packed my bags, and left."

AFTER HER MARRIAGE to Lucian ended, my mother moved to America. She had ideas of becoming an actress and studied acting in New York under the formidable coach Stella Adler.

Marlon Brando was in my mother's class. Although fiercely talented in the classroom, my mother confided, he disappointed the adoring girls who tried to sleep with him. All he wanted to do in bed was hug.

Stella Adler felt my mother was too shy and "stuck up" to make it as an actress, but my mother went out to Hollywood anyway. In California she had an affair with an English screenwriter named Ivan Moffat. Ivan was handsome, sophisticated, and amusing. He was also, my mother complained, "not very nice."

Ivan was popular and well connected in Hollywood. He had worked on some successful screenplays, including *Giant* and *A Place in the Sun*. Already playing the part of the English gentleman abroad, Ivan now had the perfect prop. He enjoyed showing off the beautiful Lady Caroline around Hollywood.

Mum would later complain about Ivan's fastidiousness and

cruelty. She told me how he would put her down and attack her appearance. Often, just before they were about to arrive at some important Hollywood event, he would turn on her and tell her how awful she looked. "Why are you wearing that? It makes you look hideous," he would say.

Years later, after her death, Ivan continued to do cruel impersonations of my mother. He took particular pleasure in telling vicious stories about her drinking, which by the time she had moved to Los Angeles had become a problem.

AFTER SHE ABANDONED ACTING as a career, my mother returned to New York. Her affair with Ivan was left open-ended. Someone, I think it may have been Stella Adler, introduced her to a pianist and composer named Israel Citkowitz.

Israel had come to America from Poland as a refugee during the war. He had been a child prodigy and had studied under the brilliant teacher Nadia Boulanger. He had enjoyed early success as a composer, but by the time my mother was introduced to him he was suffering from a creative and mental block.

My mother found him sympathetic. He was, of course, handsome (rather similar in dark moody looks to Lucian Freud) with a cascade of jet-black hair. He also had a vast knowledge of literature as well as music, and unlike Lucian, he was considerate and attentive. He was also much older than my mother and she found him to be a perfect mentor as well as lover.

They were married, and my mother purchased a large brownstone on West Twelfth Street in Greenwich Village. There she embarked upon motherhood.

My mother knew soon after meeting Israel that he would be a good father. He was much kinder and more reliable than either

Lucian or Ivan. He was gentle and sympathetic. He had the chiseled looks that my mother thought would combine well with her own to produce good-looking children.

Looks were always important to her, as they had been to my grandmother. She was determined to do as much as she could to ensure that the genetic lottery swung in her children's favor. Israel and my mother produced three daughters, of which, I had always assumed, I was the youngest.

But by the time I was born, their marriage was long over and my mother had begun a relationship with Robert Silvers, editor of *The New York Review of Books,* who lived with us in the house on West Twelfth Street. Before I was one year old my parents were living apart. For some reason (perhaps just a whim) all of us, including Israel, moved to London, but Bob remained in New York to continue running the *Review.*

My mother bought Israel an apartment in Mayfair, and we purchased a tall house in an Edwardian garden square in South Kensington. The house was divided into four apartments, each with its own front door and lock. My mother took the top-floor apartment and the children and nannies were scattered around the rest of the house.

My mother's idea of decorating was to place as many rickety antiques as could fit in a room onto a comparable number of worn antique rugs. The place was always untidy and unruly. If a television set in our living room broke, the replacement would simply be put on top. I have a photo of me as a small child perched on an old broken sofa next to several defunct TV sets and other pieces of unidentifiable furniture. I look confused and out of place, as though I had just been dumped and left in some builder's scrap yard. It is only when I look closely at the picture that I can tell that I am, in fact, in our drawing room.

Israel's apartment was only slightly more normal. It was dark and smelled of halva and eau de cologne. His piano was in a studio at the end of a dark, long, and narrow corridor. When we visited, he often would lock himself in the room and try to compose his music. All we would hear was the sound of the metronome ticking in an otherwise painfully silent room.

CHAPTER 7

I am not sure of the exact details of how my mother met Robert Lowell. There have been various accounts. She did tell me that she had been seated next to him at some literary dinner, given by Lowell and his wife, Elizabeth Hardwick, and that he didn't say one word to my mother the entire evening.

He was a famous poet with a reputation for being difficult and she found he lived up to his reputation. He was rude, disagreeable, "and a little terrifying." She was therefore surprised when, on his next visit to London from the States, where he lived with his wife and daughter, Robert called. He asked her to dinner.

For me, as a small child, Robert just seemed to appear one day and never leave. I remember them coming back from Amsterdam, where I think they had been on a sort of honeymoon. They presented my two sisters and me with Dutch costumes complete with matching pairs of clogs. It was as if we were being given our own rather strange wedding presents.

I adored Robert. There has been so much written about him, his manic mood swings and difficult relationships. He is often portrayed as a kind of monster—an artistic genius, but still a crazed, self-obsessed monster. I saw a very different side. When I hear or read about him described in those terms, I find it impossible to equate the two men.

He came into my life when I was young, perhaps only four, and to me he was the gentlest, coziest man possible. A tall teddy-bearish presence, he instantly nicknamed me Mischief because I teased him so much.

Robert liked to work lying on his bed. It was strewn with manuscripts, all annotated in his spidery handwriting. My favorite thing was to race into his room, Lulu, my half Labrador–half Corgi, chasing behind. We would run and jump onto his bed and send his papers flying. He didn't seem to mind; actually he seemed pleased by the distraction. He then would read whatever he had been working on that day to Lulu and me.

It didn't matter to him that I didn't have a clue what his poetry meant. He just liked having someone to read to, and I liked the sound of his voice.

ROBERT WAS A VISITING FELLOW at All Souls, Oxford, and held academic posts at several other English universities. My mother bought a redbrick Georgian house about an hour and a half from London, in Kent, and the family decamped there.

The house was called Milgate Park and was surrounded by parkland and sheep and cattle fields. The floors were uneven, cold, stone flags, and it had a huge ancient kitchen complete with hearth and old-fashioned Aga. There was no central heating and everything smelt damp and musty. My mother applied the same decorating sensibilities as she had in our London house.

Although everything was seemingly grand, on closer examination it was shabby and falling apart. The house had a vast entrance hall with dark wood-paneled walls and a sweeping staircase. There was a rather dingy kitchen and living area for the children in one wing. In the other, my mother and Robert had their own studies, kitchen, and drawing room.

There was also a formal dining room but I don't remember its ever being used. In fact, I don't remember our ever eating at all, but I suppose we must have.

Every night, before I went to bed, I would go into Mum and Robert's drawing room and sit with them. There would be a huge log fire burning, and classical music playing scratchily on the

gramophone. I mainly recall hearing Maria Callas's searing operatic tones and the easy music of Grieg, and studying the dusty
record album sleeves.

Robert and my mother would sit alone together for hours talking, smoking, and drinking wine. My favorite thing was to slip in
between them and try to join in their conversation or listen as
Robert read poetry to us.

At an early age I had decided I wanted to be an actress, and as
Robert was working on a translation of Racine's *Phaedra,* we
would read the play out loud, alternating the various parts. He
had a wonderful accent, part New England, part Southern drawl;
it made even the ugliest words sound romantic.

Most nights I was allowed to have several sips of wine from
their glasses. I have since tried to recapture that taste, that feeling of warmth and love, but no matter how expensive or rare the
wine, nothing has ever tasted as good.

When it was time for me to go bed and I was being stubborn,
Robert would threaten me with "Mary McCarthy's spanking
machine." He told me if I did not go straight up, then Mary
McCarthy would arrive, bringing her dreaded spanking machine
with her. I had no idea who Mary McCarthy was, but the idea of
her and her spanking machine terrified me so much that I would
run giggling and shrieking up to my bedroom.

I now know that after we had all gone to bed that picture of
domestic bliss invariably changed. They would both drink too
much, and terrible fights would ensue. A couple of times I woke
up to the flash of an ambulance's lights, and when I looked out of
my window I saw Robert being taken away by men in white
coats. His long absences after these occasions were never really
explained, but I could sense my mother's distress. And her drinking would escalate.

Robert's manic phases were well hidden from me, but for my

mother they were devastating, and on occasion, physically frightening. He would turn from the seemingly sweetest, mildestmannered man in the world into a totally unrecognizable figure. His manic depression would take various forms. One time my mother found him hammering holes into the walls of our London house. He was convinced he was an archaeologist excavating for ancient Roman mosaics. He made enormous gashes in the walls of their apartment. "Honey, I know that there are important artifacts hidden here. I just need time to unearth them." At another time, Robert became obsessed with Civil War uniforms— theatrical ones complete with medals and decorations—and he ordered twelve sets, which his friend Blair Clark had to return.

His behavior could be quite terrifying. One evening he smothered himself with Harpic toilet cleaner, and the strong chemicals severely burned his skin. Another time she found him teetering on the edge of the narrow balcony outside the top floor window. He imagined himself to be Mussolini addressing his troops.

A story my mother loved was that of General Franco lying in bed. He was dying. He heard an enormous roar from outside his window. "What is that noise?" the general asked. "It is the people, General; they are coming to say good-bye to you," his secretary informed him. "Good-bye! Where are they all going?" was Franco's perplexed reply.

My mother always associated Robert's mad balcony rant with General Franco's comment, and it then became a family joke. Whenever one of us was a bit befuddled about what was happening (which in our family was quite often), we would ask in confused tones, "Where are they all going?"

When Robert returned from his lengthy stays in psychiatric hospitals, where he was treated for manic depression, he would be remorseful and ashamed. He wouldn't remember anything he had done. Yet the fact that he had apparently behaved so badly caused him tremendous pain.

I now can identify with some of what he must have felt. Alcohol has a similar effect on me. I have often woken up in a hideous sweat and patted the sheets on my bed looking for clues before I dared to open my eyes. I would have little recollection of what I had done the night before, just a gnawing dread that it had not been good.

For Robert, however, these blackouts were far more disconcerting and frightening. An alcoholic loss of memory can at least be explained. And I am able to choose if I drink or not. For Robert, a manic spell was quite random. As he got older, they became more and more frequent and lasted longer each time.

CHAPTER 8

As children we were given totally free rein. My parents were so absorbed in each other and their work that very little attention was paid to what we were getting up to. My mother and Robert had a son, and whatever parental focus there was, was on little Sheridan.

My mother employed a staff of nannies, handymen, and drivers whose only qualifications seemed to be the ability to dress like hippies and smoke rolled-up cigarettes. At Milgate in Kent, we had several greenhouses at the back of the garden and the gardener and various others of my mother's staff grew their own marijuana. In the evenings mournful music and wafts of herby-smelling smoke would float up from the stables.

My nanny's name was Margaret. I suppose she started working for us when I was about five. She had ratty black hair and wore long flowery skirts and little brown ankle boots. She lived in one of our cottages with her husband, Mike, who performed odd jobs around the house. They had a fierce German shepherd named Lucy.

My bedroom was at the very back of the house, and the easiest route there was by means of the narrow stairs at the end of one wing. I hated going to bed. I was convinced the house was haunted (I still am), and my room was cold, damp, and lonely. Every night I felt as though I was being exiled into some unfriendly and isolated world, away from the main hubbub of the house.

One night I experimented to see what would happen if I screamed at the top of my lungs. After ten minutes of yelling, I realized that no one could hear. Nobody came to my rescue. The only time I remember my mother coming to this part of the house was at Christmas. I had carefully laid out my Christmas stocking at the foot of my bed. I couldn't get to sleep for ages because I was so excited at the thought of Father Christmas paying a visit to our house. At some point in the night (or early morning), I felt a thud at the end of my bed. I looked up sleepily to see my mother drunkenly wrestling with a pillowcase full of presents. She looked at me with huge unfocused eyes. "Shhh! It's just Santa, darling. Merry Christmas."

I think I was about six years old when Mike began to visit me in my bedroom. He would bring his dog with him and tell me if I made a noise or told anyone he would set her on me. He would get into my bed and whisper to me how beautiful I was. He would stroke my chest and kiss me all over my undeveloped body.

He smelt of tobacco and body odor, and his stubble scratched my skin. He made me put my hands and mouth around his penis. He would moan, sometimes cry, and after he had ejaculated he would tell me how sorry he was. It felt peculiar, yet also exhilarating to be able to exert such power over an adult man.

Although I was scared of him and knew what he was doing was wrong, the attention felt good and it also gave me an excuse to stay up later at night. I would wait up for Mike's visits with a mixture of dread and excitement, wondering what would happen if ever we were caught. On the nights when he didn't visit I was disappointed. Like a spurned lover, I would wonder where he was and have jealous thoughts about his wife, my nanny.

When he was finished with me, he would slink out of my bedroom threatening that if I ever told anyone I would be punished and he would make sure his dog would get me.

I didn't tell anyone. I didn't want to—perhaps I didn't want it to end. It wasn't until I was about fourteen that I was able to tell anyone. When I eventually told my sister, she was appalled. But she said that it had happened to her too, with a different handy-man, "Although he just liked to fondle my tits!"

I had been too frightened and also too ashamed about the amount of guilty pleasure I was afforded by our little secret. But at fourteen, I was angry.

The abuse would probably have carried on for much longer had it not been for my accident. One of my many psychiatrists has suggested that subconsciously I wanted it to stop and that I accomplished this in the most violent and efficient way I could.

I REMEMBER EVERYTHING very clearly; it plays in my mind as if I am watching a home movie. It is summer. I know that because I am wearing my school's summer uniform. The uniform consisted of a blue checked cotton dress that stopped a little above my knees.

I had just gotten back from school, and I ran into the house. I had a long-standing game that I played with another of the men who lived on the grounds and did odd jobs for my mother and Robert. His name was Perry, and the game was called Off Ground He.

Every time I saw Perry I would have to run and find some way to get off the ground. As long as my feet were not touching the floor, he couldn't catch me. I loved playing that game and found increasingly inventive places to jump up to avoid getting tagged.

That particular day I saw Perry coming toward me down the corridor, and I ran shrieking and laughing into the kitchen to get away from him. There was a stool next to one of the countertops, and I immediately jumped on it yelling, "Off ground he!"

Somehow my foot got tangled in the cord that was dangling

from the counter. A kettle of boiling water crashed down on top of me. A white-hot pain shot from the top of my stomach down to my knees. I could feel the fabric of my flimsy dress welding to my skin. I looked down and saw layers of my skin peeling away from my body. They resembled layers of wet tissue paper.

There was a lot of screaming and shouting. Someone, my nanny I think, had the foresight to wrap me up tightly in a sheet.

My mother appeared at the kitchen door. She was wearing a tiny towel; she had been in the bath at the time. Her face told me everything I needed to know. It was one of the most frightening and frightened expressions I have ever seen on anyone.

I must have gone into some sort of delirious shock because I remember saying that I didn't want to go to hospital. I would be fine if only I could just stay home and play with my toys.

I was bundled into the back of the car with my mother, now wearing a bathrobe. I still was mumbling over and over again about staying home; maybe I sensed that if we left I might not ever come back. I had lost an incredible amount of fluids, and I soon passed out.

I was taken to the local hospital where they told my mother that there was nothing they could do for me. Fortunately, about two hours away in a town called East Grinstead, there was a famous burn hospital. It had been built during the First World War near an important air force base. Hundreds of pilots who had suffered horrific burns in both world wars had been treated there.

By the time we arrived at the hospital, I was close to death. I had third-degree burns over seventy percent of my body, and I was extremely dehydrated. They told my mother that my chances were not good. She should prepare herself for the worst.

I cannot imagine how she reacted. She would habitually dramatize (and drink over) even the most harmless situation. Now she was confronted with the very real possibility of her six-year-old child's death.

Robert joined her in the burns unit. Together they anxiously watched my heart monitor, waiting for the erratic beat to flat-line. At last, I was officially declared out of immediate danger. The doctors told my mother and Robert to go to a nearby hotel and get some sleep. They both refused to leave. The nurse insisted there was no place for them to stay, but Robert found a small towel and spread it out on the cold hospital corridor floor outside my door. He and my mother lay down on it to spend the night near me.

THERE IS A HIGH RISK of infection with burn patients, and therefore the rooms are kept immaculately clean. The air is pre-cisely maintained at a cold temperature. Only doctors and nurses wearing surgical masks and gloves are allowed in the room.

I had to lie naked on top of the bed so my bandages would not be disturbed. The room was freezing and my plaintive requests for a blanket were denied. I remained in hospital for nine months.

There was a window on the right side of my bed and visitors were allowed to come and peer at me. The only way to talk with me was through a telephone attached to the wall, rather a similar setup to the one for visiting a prisoner in jail. I would lie with my bandaged stomach and legs exposed and try to make small talk.

One day my teacher from the Convent of the Sacred Heart, Sister Mary Sheridan, brought my school class to visit. I will never forget the humiliation I felt, lying there helpless, naked but for my bandages. The nun and twenty of my classmates gawked at me as they recited a prayer.

CHAPTER 9

I finally was able to go home. All those months I had been allowed to see my sisters only through a glass window, and I couldn't wait to give them both big hugs. My mother had been allowed into my room, but she had to wear a white mask, protective coat, and surgical gloves.

The fear of infection was so great that she had been unable to make any physical contact with me. It was almost worse than not being able to see her at all because she was untouchable.

On the day of my release from hospital, I was carried through our front door and put down on the sofa, where I waited for my sisters to come back from school. When Evgenia came through the door, I tried to jump up and run over to her, but my scrawny legs gave way. I fell facedown onto the rug. While I lay in the hospital bed for nine months, the muscles in my legs had become useless. My legs had become two burnt, skinny, charred twigs. They could not support me.

Learning to walk again was difficult. A physiotherapist came to the house every day. She was thin and mean and ordered me about in a loud, sharp, voice. I dreaded her visits. "One two, one two," she recited as she whacked the backs of my legs with a stick. Every step was agony.

There is little more endearing than watching a baby learn to walk. Doting parents smile as they watch tiny, rubbery legs trying to take their first steps. They clap and laugh approvingly at their toddler's unsteady gait. When you are a six-year-old and have to do it all over again on your own, however, it loses its charm.

My physiotherapist made me do all kinds of leg-strengthening exercises. They were boring and hard work, but I knew I had to do them if I wanted to walk again. To this day, I hate going to the gym, because it reminds me of those awful exercises.

EVEN BEFORE THE ACCIDENT, my classmates' parents had looked at me with suspicion. I was the girl who lived in the big, spooky house at the end of the long unmarked driveway. I was also the girl who was dropped off and picked up from school by various long-haired hippies in a beaten-up, rusty, old car. One of my best friends at school was a girl named Nicolette. Her father was also the local wine merchant, and it was no secret just how much alcohol he regularly delivered to our house. In fact, I probably saw more of him than Nicolette did. When my friends' parents allowed them to have playdates with me, it would always be at their houses rather than at mine and always under strict parental supervision.

I was perfectly happy with that arrangement. It was comforting to escape from my house and see how other families lived. I found their houses warm and cozy. They had kitchens whose cupboards were stocked with comfortingly normal kids' food like sliced white bread and Mr. Kipling's strawberry tarts. We would sit down at clean-smelling, polished-wood tables and have good old-fashioned children's food. Things like fish fingers, sausages, mashed potatoes, and to finish, trifle with custard.

Our house was cold and our kitchen pantry contained weird, foreign things—murky bottles of vinegar with tarragon twigs floating about. Solid clay jars of French grainy mustard, which were never opened because of their impossible red wax seals. There was a large array of liqueurs brought back from various holiday destinations that had become sweet, sticky flytraps. My mother adored fresh garlic and would put it on everything, but she didn't have much patience for peeling it. She would take the head of the garlic and with her fingers gouge out the middle of a clove. Our kitchen was littered with lots of half-dug-into bulbs, brown, stale and rancid.

WHEN I RETURNED TO SCHOOL after my accident, I felt as though I was a curiosity, a freak. I walked with a limp and all my friends wanted to peek underneath my bandages to look at my scars. Another by-product of my hospitalization was my cropped hair.

I had always been proud of my hair, and it had taken me ages to grow it long. I had been very resistant to ever having it trimmed, and though I moaned and complained when I had to brush it in the mornings I secretly thought it one of my best features. After lying in the hospital bed for such a long time, however, my locks had become one enormous wild and hairy knot. No amount of Johnson & Johnson's "no more tangles" could help get a brush through it. I was given a Joan of Arc cut and was mortified by my odd new appearance.

Being the class invalid did have its advantages, though. I was excused from PE, which I had always loathed, and the teachers and other girls were told to be especially nice to me. My sister Evgenia said I became insufferable. Because I was perceived to have been through so much, I was able to milk it for all it was worth. I used my invalid status to my advantage and made outrageous demands. At bedtime I would insist that Evgenia come to bed too. She was three years older than me, and this was a demeaning torture for her. I would lie on the sofa and order everyone around. My mother felt so guilty about the accident that she indulged my little reign of tyranny.

After my accident, the molestation stopped. I don't know what happened, but when I returned from hospital Mike was gone, along with my nanny Margaret. Perhaps they were fired because of the kettle, or maybe they just left on their own accord. Whatever happened, another young couple had replaced them.

I have thought about my psychiatrist's inference that somehow I subconsciously orchestrated the whole ordeal to escape the abuse. True, the burnt area of my body is exactly where I was violated. This could suggest that on some subliminal level I wanted to destroy that part of me. But I don't think it was anywhere near as deep or complicated as that. Besides, the burning was far more traumatic for me than the sexual abuse ever was.

CHAPTER 10

I think that my sister Natalya suffered the most growing up in our family. She adored our father and resented our mother's marriage to Robert. Also, being the eldest, she probably was the most affected by Mum's drinking.

Because I was so young and had never really lived with Israel, Robert had wanted to adopt me. Both my sisters felt this would be a betrayal of Israel. "We are Citkowitzes," they told me. I was torn. My mother wanted me to take the Lowell name (for reasons I now understand), and yet I didn't want to upset my sisters. We compromised and I became Ivana Lowell-Citkowitz. It was a real mouthful at school roll call.

Natalya had been my mother's first child, six years older than me and the center of her universe until we came along. Now there were not only two younger sisters but baby Sheridan as well. Her position in the family had been completely usurped. She would do anything to get attention. Many years later, Mum told me that Natalya had taunted her, by claiming that she had slept with Lucian. I never knew whether this was true or whether she had just made it up to upset Mum. It was still disturbing, however.

A lot of Natalya's anger was turned on me. She would tease me relentlessly. I became terrified of her and was relieved when she went to boarding school. I dreaded the school holidays because she would make my life so miserable. Any chance she could get, she would harass me. She threw plates of food at me and chased me around the house with a knife. She did it to frighten me, and it worked.

My mother later told me that she had been worried that

Natalya would physically harm me. She would constantly have to intervene. The result of these interventions was hysterical fights between my mother and Natalya. Then my sister would leave the house and go to London.

I DON'T KNOW EXACTLY when Natalya started taking drugs. The boarding school she went to, Dartington Hall, was famously "progressive." My mother chose it because both Lucian Freud and Ivan Moffat had gone there.

In their day it had been seen as a sort of utopian ideal of education, the total antithesis of the rigorous English boarding schools of that time. There were no uniforms, classes were more or less optional, and a form of democracy ruled the school. The students were able to vote for how they wanted the school to be run and what changes they thought were needed. Ivan told me that when he was there the pupils decided they wanted a swimming pool, and so they simply dug their own.

By the time Natalya was sent to Dartington, the system was breaking down. There were few rules left to break so my sister and her contemporaries pushed harder to find ways to rebel. It was the late seventies, and even in the remotest part of Devon on the edge of Dartmoor it was easy to buy drugs. And they did.

I WAS NINE when I was sent there. The school was divided into two parts, senior and junior, and they were roughly two miles apart from each other. My two sisters were already in the senior school and both were legendary in the lower school.

Natalya, in particular, had a reputation of being very bad. Of course, this meant she was considered "cool." She had managed (and this was no mean feat at Dartington) to get herself suspended twice for doing or buying drugs. She didn't come to visit me in the junior school very often, but when she did she drew a lot of attention.

She was beautiful, like a wild Gypsy, tall, with long black hair and green eyes that she, like my mother, outlined with layers of black kohl. She wore frayed jeans under hippy-ish skirts and smocks. Black Dutch-style clogs were fashionable, and she would clack across the cobblestone courtyard leaving behind a scent of incense and musk oil. She smoked rolled-up cigarettes that she would offer to us, and she usually had some disreputable-looking boyfriend in tow. I think they must have been local boys or friends of hers from London because they drove either motor-bikes or dangerous-looking cars. Natalya's visits to the junior part of school didn't last long, just long enough to intimidate us. My friends thought she was the most glamorous thing they had ever seen. Having her as a sister definitely elevated my own status in the school.

I REMEMBER MY FIRST DAY of boarding school as being embarrassing, nerve-wracking and sad. Inexplicably, I arrived more than halfway through the school term, well into the school year. My mother and Robert came with me to make sure that I got settled.

We took the train from Paddington to Totnes, a journey that was about five hours. There was a buffet car and a bar on the train, and so of course my mother had to have a few drinks to calm her nerves for my first day of school. We took a local taxi from the train station. As we drew up to the school, I began to feel that horrible sense of inadequacy that one feels (or at least I do) when starting something new. I just knew that everyone else had been driven there in normal cars by their normal parents.

Mum and Robert seemed to look particularly odd that day. Robert always had rather wild, mad-looking hair and somehow the journey had made it fluff up more than usual. My mother looked scruffy and nervous and they both lit up cigarettes as soon as we got into the taxi. I knew we didn't look quite right, and part of me resented their presence. Yet I was touched that they were there. I wanted them to go away, but also wished I could run back home with them.

When we arrived at the school, we were told to wait on the bench outside the headmaster's office. The milkman had been by that morning, and two bottles were sitting outside the headmaster's door. While we waited, Robert absentmindedly picked up one of the bottles, put his thumb through its silver foil cap, and glugged down its entire contents. He was just starting on the second bottle when the headmaster popped his head around the door. He glanced at the empty milk bottle and the one in Robert's hand. "Welcome to Dartington Hall," he said at last.

ALL MY CLASSMATES were already used to the school and had formed their little cliques. I felt as though I was never going to be accepted.

That same feeling of discomfort, of not quite fitting in, that I had growing up has stayed with me into my adult life. The only time I ever felt okay, as if I were acceptable, was when I was drinking.

If I had some alcohol in me then I could be anything that you wanted me to be. My friends would tease me, calling me the "performing seal." They would flap their arms and make seal noises. "Arrf, Arrf, Arrf." I was always performing. Depending on the mood, Ivana could be funny, serious, vulnerable, or witty. As I had no sense of who I really was or had any of my own opinions, I would say whatever I felt you wanted to hear. Take away the alcohol, and I was just a damaged body sewn together with stitches of fear and pain.

Although at first I was homesick, I enjoyed my time at Dartington. Being away from the chaos of my home gave me a sense of stability and routine that I'd never had.

Before boarding school, my little brother, Sheridan, and I had been shunted back and forth from Kent to Boston, where Robert was professor of poetry at Harvard. My mother and Robert rented various houses in Brookline, Massachusetts, and I would attend whatever school was nearby for the semester.

At these schools I didn't fit in at all. I had a British accent and had been taught an entirely different syllabus. Even my handwriting was different. "Don't loop your Y's and L's," the teacher would scrawl in red pen over my homework. As for history, I didn't stand a chance. I had no knowledge of American history, and to hide my ignorance I mentioned condescendingly that I thought England had a far more interesting past.

After that, every time the British were mentioned in these rather patriotic Bostonian schools, all faces would turn and scowl at the redcoat in their midst. My accent was mimicked constantly. And while some of the teachers may have been impressed by Robert Lowell's reputation as a poet, my classmates just thought my family was weird. One semester we rented a particularly gloomy, dark brown clapboard house. My classmates called us the Addams Family.

MY NEMESIS AT SCHOOL that semester was a boy named Rory Gallagher. He was from a rough Irish Catholic family, and for some reason he developed a maniacal crush on me. He followed me everywhere, talking in an atrocious British accent. He would even follow me home from school.

One day during a gym class, I was doing a handstand against the wall. As I was coming down from the handstand, Rory pushed a steel mat holder under my legs. I hit the metal hard and broke one of my legs. Having a broken leg was wonderful. I was the invalid again. It guaranteed a long period of bed rest, reading, and watching American TV.

Still, my school's principal demanded that Rory and his parents personally apologize to me. They came to our house and stood in the dark hallway looking petrified. All his bravado had vanished. Rory said a terse sorry to me, to my mother, and to Robert. His parents, who had a reputation in the school of being hard, criminal types, were blithering wrecks. Rory's dad was big and tough-looking, but in the presence of Robert he became cowed. He insisted on shaking Robert's hand and said humbly, "I'll see to it nothing like this ever happens again, Mr. Lowell." Rory never bothered me again.

EVEN THOUGH MY SCHOOL LIFE was a bit of a trial, I loved America—so many channels on the television and a wonderful variety of junk food. We even had a family station wagon that suited my suburban sensibilities perfectly. But since neither my mother nor Robert had a license (nor should they have had), we hired Harvard students to take us around and do our errands.

Robert would take me to Harvard Yard, to the bookshop, where he would buy me heaps of books on birds, fish, and butterflies, any subject that he was particularly obsessed with at the time. I still have them all and look through them with my daughter. The best part of our outings together for me (maybe for both of us) were our visits to Friendly's, where we ate enormous chocolate fudge ice cream sundaes.

I wish I had been old enough to appreciate more of the adult life that was happening around me, to recall the many people who came to the house and what they discussed. I just remember a lot of cigarette smoke, a lot of alcohol, and lots of talking late into the night. I do remember that the poet Frank Bidart was a great friend of Robert's and a very kind and gentle presence in the house. The Southern writers Peter Taylor and Bill Alfred were also regular visitors, and the house was always filled with Robert's students from Harvard.

My mother and Robert seemed happy, and during that period I felt as though I was experiencing what it might be like to be part of a family.

AT DARTINGTON I was able to settle into the life of a normal nine-year-old. History, English, and drama were my favorite subjects.

I particularly liked drama and was tapped as the class actress. I was given the lead in the school play, *The Girl with a Million Wishes*. I was so proud when my whole family came to see the play. My mother and Robert made the long trip from London bringing little Sheridan, and both Evgenia and Natalya came to watch me, too. It was one of the few times that the whole family was together. And, as it would turn out, also the final time.

The last time I saw Robert was at the end of the summer holidays in 1977. I spent every school holiday in Ireland, at Castletown House, the stately Palladian home that my cousin Desmond Guinness had restored for the Irish Georgian Society. My mother was taking me back to boarding school and, as the taxi went down the long cypress tree–lined driveway, we both turned and waved.

Robert was standing on the stone steps of the vast house. He looked particularly tall and handsome, dressed in his usual uniform of loose Irish wool cardigan and baggy corduroys. He wore soft brown leather slippers. He clutched little Sheridan's hand and waved good-bye to us. "See you in two months," I shouted.

After we had left, Robert, I later found out, had taken Sheridan for a long walk around the grounds of Castletown. They headed through the woods and across the fields to the river that bordered the land.

Robert loved water and had a lifelong fascination with fish. Both images appear frequently throughout his poetry. One of the last volumes of poetry he wrote and dedicated to my mother was called *The Dolphin*. The poem in it called "Mermaid" is a very personal account of their life together.

> *I see you as a baby killer whale,*
> *free to walk the seven seas for game,*
> *warmhearted with an undercoat of ice*
>
> .   .   .   .
>
> *One wondered who would see and date you next,*
> *and grapple for the danger of your hand.*
> *Will money drown you? Poverty, though now*
> *in fashion, debases women as much as wealth.*
> *You use no scent, dab brow and lash with shoeblack,*
> *willing to face the world without more face.*

When the Irish poet Seamus Heaney came to visit, he and Robert would spend hours talking and absently fishing by the river. On that last day in Ireland, Robert was able to share his passion with his young son.

IT WAS BEFORE LUNCH, and I had just got back to my bedroom at school after morning classes. "Ivana, Alice needs to see you in her sitting room." Alice was my housemother, and she and her husband, Steve, presided over the house I lived in at Dartington. The pupils never were allowed into Steve and Alice's part of the house, and so I had an immediate feeling of dread. What had I done now?

Alice and Steve were sitting down, and they both wore the same awful, slightly embarrassed expression that I had seen before on my mother's face. "Ivana, we have some bad news." Plunge, my heart fell into my stomach, and I felt my whole body flush with dread. "Robert is dead."

There was delay in the time the words were spoken and their actually reaching my brain. During that small instant he was still alive, and everything was okay. And then he wasn't, and I felt nothing was ever going to be all right again.

They explained that they had thought it best to tell me themselves; it was on the news, and they didn't want me to find out from "another source."

I thanked them for telling me and said I would like to go to my room. I wasn't so much sad as furious. I was furious at Robert for leaving us and furious at God. Every night I had prayed to Him that nothing else bad would happen to our family. It took me a long time to say my bedtime prayers because I asked God to bless everyone I knew, and I named everyone individually. Sometimes I skipped the name of one of our cats or a cousin, and I would feel very guilty, thinking I had condemned them to some ghastly fate by my omission. But I always made sure to ask Him to look after Robert. I knew that if Robert were to die, our whole family would fall apart. He was the closest thing to a rock I had ever known.

Robert had died in New York. He had flown from Dublin, and was in the back of a taxi going from JFK airport to see his ex-wife, Lizzie, and their daughter, Harriet. He suffered a massive heart attack. The cabdriver couldn't wake him when they arrived at Lizzie's apartment, so he got out and rang her bell. He thought Robert was drunk and had passed out. When Lizzie reached him, Robert was already dead. In his arms he was clutching a Lucian Freud portrait of my mother, *Girl in Bed*.

EVGENIA AND I took the train back to London. "How do you think Mum is going to be?" The question was unnecessary. We both knew that she was going to be "really bad."

The house in Redcliffe Square was more disheveled than ever. My mother was not only drunk but sedated. People were milling about trying to make arrangements. I went to my little brother's room. He was curled up in his bed. He looked young and confused. No one had bothered to tell him what had happened, or maybe they just couldn't face telling him.

"Your dad is dead." I had no idea how to explain death to a six-year-old. I was twelve. I just repeated what other people had told me when Israel had died and tried to sound reassuring. It must have got through to him, though, that something very sad had happened. We lay on his bed, snuggled, and cried.

There were to be two memorial services, one in London and one in Boston. The funeral was to be in Boston. Natalya took me shopping to buy something smart and black for the occasion. We went to Harrods.

I enjoyed that shopping expedition. I had Natalya's undivided

attention, and she was being sweet. I bought a hideous black cor-
duroy skirt, black V-neck sweater, and clumpy black orthopedic-
looking shoes. I didn't mind what I looked like. Natalya and I
were together and having fun, albeit in a morbid sort of way. After
shopping she took Sheridan and me to see *Lady and the Tramp*.
The movie has lots of sad bits so we were all able to cry
unashamedly.

The memorial service in Boston was huge. The church was
packed with the great and good of literary America. I remember a
lot of somber readings and watching my mother, her face crumpled under her black hat, her body shaking. Her cheeks were
streaked black with rivulets of eyeliner, and she smelled of
brandy.

After the service Bob Silvers took Sheridan and me to see *Star
Wars*. We were allowed as a special treat to have the giant-size
popcorn buckets with extra butter. Two days later I returned to
Dartington.

CHAPTER 12

D amaged people are different," writes Josephine Hart in her book *Damage*.

As I grew up and into my late teens, I was considered pretty. I had big eyes (although not my mother's huge ethereal blue orbs), a pertly turned-up nose, and a pleasant smile. I went on dates and my suitor would tell me how beautiful I was. Instead of accepting his flattery I would be thinking, If only you knew. If only you really knew how hideous I am underneath my clothes, you wouldn't be chewing your penne pesto with such a lecherous look.

If I liked my date and knew how the evening was inevitably going to end, I couldn't concentrate on anything. I would be wondering when to tell him. Do I tell him now just as he is about to bite into his tiramisù? Do I casually announce, "By the way, I am burned and have scars and you will hate me when you see me naked"? Or do I wait until we are fondling on the sofa, and he has gotten past my breasts and is moving toward my stomach?

It happened that way a few times, and the reactions were varied. When I waited for them to find out for themselves, there would be terrible moments of awkwardness. Sometimes they would pretend that they hadn't noticed anything was different, yet they'd discreetly try to remove their hands from the offending area and go in a different direction. Another mistook my burns for some terrible lumpy rash and wanted to know what I had been bitten by or if I was allergic to something. Others told me I was much more lovable because of my burns, that they made me who I was and that they wouldn't want me without them. Liars.

One boyfriend told me he knew the best plastic surgeons in

the world, and said he would pay for the operation to remove them. I tried to explain that when seventy-five percent of your body is scarred, no amount of plastic surgery can remove it.

IN FACT, my mother had already taken me to the best plastic surgeons in the world. It became a sort of pastime for us. We would hear of some amazing breakthrough in the burn world and we would get excited. We would sit nervously in the waiting rooms and look at the other people. We had a game in which we would try to guess why they were there. Nose job? Breast augmentation? Eye lift? Or just your run-of-the-mill face-lift?

On one visit a particularly unattractive woman sitting in the waiting room wouldn't stop looking at me. Finally she asked, "Excuse me, did Dr. Radcliffe do your nose? Because I want one just like it." That cheered us up enormously.

These visits invariably, though, would have the same depressing outcome. The doctor would examine me, make the usual tut-tutting noises, admire the work that had been done at the burn hospital in East Grinstead, and announce that there was nothing he could do.

"You're a very pretty girl and you're lucky it's not on your face." I knew that, but it wasn't what I wanted to hear. I then would feel dreadful that I was not more grateful that my face was not disfigured. I knew that thousands of people would give anything to have their scars where mine are. I still wanted mine to be gone.

We were told of one doctor in Boston who had a brilliant new technique for scar removal, a breakthrough in the burn world. We eagerly went to see him. He told me I could have two balloons inserted into each of my thighs. The balloons would be pumped-up to stretch the skin to its full capacity, and after the balloons were removed, the two pieces of stretched skin would be pulled over to meet in the middle, and then sewn together.

My mother nervously asked, "And how long would she have to wear these, um, balloons?" He told us a minimum of three months, but probably more to get a "really good stretch."

After the visit my mother and I went and had an expensive lunch. We became more and more hysterical with laughter as we thought of my "balloons." What happens if one pops in a public place? How on earth does one get comfortable at night in balloons? Can you accessorize balloons?

Long after we had decided against the procedure, we were told by yet another plastic surgeon that the balloon technique is a complete sham. Not only is it expensive, time-consuming, and painful, but the scar left behind from the stitching of the skin is just as bad, if not worse, than the original one.

These rather gloomy trips to the doctors brought my mother and me closer. We were good at gloom, and they gave us an excuse to go afterward and have a boozy lunch. We had an expression we liked to use jokingly when things were a bit grim: "It's too bad, even for us!" This expression would take on a whole new meaning when my mother became ill.

MY MOST HUMILIATING EXPERIENCE regarding my burns was my pubic hair transplant. I was in a serious relationship with someone, but he said he couldn't get past the fact that I did not have any pubic hair; all my hair follicles had been burned away so I was unable to grow any in that region. He complained that my lack of hirsuteness in that department was off-putting because it made him think of a young child, even one of his daughters.

I was so insecure and eager to please that I agreed to have an operation to try to remedy my flaw. The procedure is not only embarrassing but extremely tiresome. Individual follicles of hair from your head are removed and then planted, like seeds, into the requisite area.

I had the operation at a small clinic on the Upper East Side and was put under general anesthetic. I was told that I would need to have someone pick me up afterward, as I would be too groggy to go home alone.

My boyfriend (whose inspired idea this was in the first place) was to come and collect me. But about half an hour before I was due to go under, he informed me that something urgent at work had come up. He couldn't do it. My mother reluctantly agreed to come and pick me up, although she thought the whole thing demeaning and distasteful and was furious at my boyfriend for even suggesting I needed it.

The transplant took about two hours. After coming out of the recovery room I waited to be picked up. I waited and waited, but no one arrived. Eventually I called my brother, and he came and took me home. My mother apparently had found the idea so upsetting that she had got drunk and passed out.

In the end, the hairs never took, except for a few lonely sprouts.

CHAPTER 13

Almost a year after Robert's death, I had returned from a school camping trip and was told my sister Evgenia was waiting for me in my housemother's sitting room. The all-too-familiar pained expressions and looks of pity were on everyone's faces. I knew what was coming. I just didn't know the details.

There are a few seconds between the time when you know you are about to be told something devastating and the actual telling of it, a moment when you can still pretend everything is all right. These moments don't last very long, but at the time they seem infinite. As if reality had been suspended.

My immediate thought was that something had happened to my mother. I lived in fear that she would do something to herself. Often when she was lying passed out, drunk, I would check to see if she was still breathing. She also made threats. She would say she didn't want to live, that there was no point, that her life was over anyway.

The threats were so regular that they had become tedious. Once I was lying in bed in my apartment in the house trying to get to sleep. My mother had been on a particularly bad drinking spree and there had been tears and arguments. She had finally gone upstairs to her apartment to go to bed, but she came back down and started hammering on my front door, which I kept locked. I told her to go away and shut up, but she kept screaming and knocking, insisting that she was hurt.

Finally I stomped to the door, annoyed, and ready to tell her to fuck off. When I opened the door, her hair was a tangled ball of blood. She had fallen down the stairs and hit her head on one of the steps. As we waited for the ambulance to arrive, I felt guilty. But how was I to know that for once she had been telling the truth?

But now Evgenia was sobbing. "Natalya is dead." That didn't make any sense at all. My mother, yes. But not Natalya. She was strong, beautiful, and, to me, invincible.

She had overdosed on heroin. She was eighteen. My mother told me later that Natalya was booked to go to a rehab the next day. She was excited to be going. She wanted to get well. She was optimistic that she was going to be able to beat her addiction. She had probably decided to have one last hurrah.

I know that whenever I had to go away, into "a place," I would get really drunk as a send-off. After all, it would be the last time. I wanted to make it count.

Natalya had asked one of her friends to get some drugs. He had given her the "hot shot" that had killed her. They found her in the bathtub.

I DIDN'T GO to her funeral. My mother thought it would be too upsetting for me. I would be better off staying at school with my friends. The funeral service, she said, would be "too traumatic." But I knew the traumatic part would be seeing my mother trying to cope with so much pain and guilt. I knew that we wouldn't recover from this. I stayed at school.

"GUINNESS CURSE STRIKES AGAIN. DEATH OF GUINNESS HEIRESS." The newspapers in England were full of accounts of my sister's death. A few months before a distant cousin of ours, Lady Henrietta Guinness, had jumped from a bridge to her death. She was young, had a great deal of money, and she left behind a seven-month-old daughter.

We never even knew of her existence until the newspapers linked the two deaths and gleefully attributed them both to the "family curse."

My mother said that there were a number of reasons why our family was considered cursed. One was that Lord Dufferin, when he was viceroy to India, had arrogantly refused to remove his shoes when visiting a sacred mosque. For this sacrilege, the viceroy and his entire family had been placed under a terrible spell.

Another possible reason the family may have been cursed was that the same Lord Dufferin had taken, or arguably stolen, a significant amount of furniture and important artifacts from India. The booty that he brought back to Ireland was considered unlucky.

Clandeboye is still filled with mementos from the viceroy's reign. The walls of the vast entry hall are lined with all kinds of ancient weapons and armory. Some 6,000-year-old Egyptian burial ropes hang forlornly among the swords and daggers. A stuffed bear and the heads of other ferocious animals add to the cold, museum-like atmosphere.

Of course, well-known families are often said to have a "curse." It is a handy way to excuse generations of entitlement, self-indulgence, and general bad behavior. It is also much easier to attribute alcoholism, madness, and suffering to something supernatural. If I am "cursed," then I am not responsible for my own fuck-ups.

AFTER ROBERT AND MY SISTER DIED, we never tried to get back any semblance of normal family life. I was somewhat insulated at my boarding school, but school holidays in Ireland were hell.

My mother's drinking had gotten worse, and she spent most of the day alone in the part of the house she had shared with Robert. Castletown no longer seemed the magical and romantic place it once had been. It was open to the public during the day, but at night the front door would be locked and all the lights turned off. It took on the desolate, inhospitable feeling of a museum after hours or a school during vacation.

If we wanted to visit (or check up on) Mum at night, my brother and I had to go through the back door in the stable yard and then navigate our way along the cold, dark corridors to the third-floor landing, where she lived. To add to the spookiness of the journey, Castletown was famously haunted. There were many tales about the ghosts who roamed around the estate. By the time I reached my mother's rooms I would be completely on edge. The idea of an encounter with the storied spooks was one fear; the prospect of having to confront a specter of a different kind, my mother, was another.

When I couldn't face dealing with my mother, I would hide in my room and try to escape through books and my own fantasy life. I befriended a strange girl whose family rented one of the flats at Castletown. Karina had wild dark eyes and tangled black hair. She looked like a little Gypsy girl and spoke with a thick Irish accent.

We would take the bus from Celbridge into Dublin and steal from the fancy department stores. Karina was shameless and completely fearless about stealing. We would go into the makeup department of Switzers, and she would pretend to choose a lipstick for her mum's birthday. In her most posh and genteel accent she consulted with the cosmetic saleswomen at the same time as she stuffed little pots of eye shadow and blush down her trousers. The feeling of daring and the terror of being caught were exhilarating, and after our thieving we would reward ourselves with hot chocolate and cream-filled meringues at Bewley's Café.

My friendship with Karina finally ended when I discovered her personal stash of stolen goods. She had been stealing not only from stores but from my mother's bag, my jewelry drawer, and even from my little brother's piggy bank.

WHILE SHE WAS MARRIED to Robert, my mother had begun her own writing. Her first book was a collection of short stories inspired by her childhood in Ireland. She relished finding the worst in everyone and everything, and her descriptions are brilliantly funny and cruel.

For some unfounded reason, I have always been an optimist. Perhaps that is what has prevented me from going totally insane. But my mother always predicted, and deeply felt, impending disaster. She had a disarming habit of suddenly gutturally exclaiming "Oh God!" as though something awful had happened, or was just about to. We could be doing something perfectly innocuous like shopping or driving along in a car when the voice of doom would strike her and she would let out one of her Oh God's! It was really unnerving and would make me jump. "Shut up, Mum," I would say crossly. But we both would remain unsettled. That same darkness carries on into her writing. It is one reason why her books are sometimes so uncomfortable but so compelling to read.

Life in Ireland after the loss of Robert and Natalya became too lonely, and we soon moved back to the house in London. My school life at Dartington had also been tainted by the death of my sister. I was now in the senior school, where there were very few rules. I no longer had the cozy feeling of a surrogate family that the junior school had given me.

Evgenia had left and was going to a prestigious day school in London. I told my mother that I was worried that Dartington was too druggy, and academically, well, the school was not up to much. I said that if I stayed it was unlikely that I would pass any of the Oxbridge exams. I am not sure how much truth there was in that. I think I had just had enough of the place.

Looking back, I can see the same pattern that has defined my life. When I start to feel uncomfortable or don't like something or some place, I leave. In AA they call it "doing a geographic." You hope that if you move to a different school, relationship, or country, then your life will get better. Of course, it doesn't. The same old miserable you is still there, just in a different setting.

I left Dartington.

CHAPTER 14

The setting of my new school was beautiful. Cranborne Chase was a boarding school for girls in Wiltshire. The surrounding countryside is known as "Hardy country" because it was where Thomas Hardy set many of his romantic novels.

The school itself was a white Palladian house named Wardour Castle. The grounds were meticulously manicured, and dotted with impressive yew trees and topiary. It was perched on a hill overlooking a valley, and from our dormitory windows you could see into the distance to the ruins of the old Wardour Castle, four miles away. The building had a domed rotunda with frescoes of cherubs and angels. We had chapel there every morning, and I loved singing our daily hymn because the echo from the dome made my voice sound so resonant and pure.

My mother and I had chosen the school because we had been impressed by the look of the place. But once I got there it was just another school, with all the same horrid school-food smells, sounds of bells, and feelings of dread and homesickness.

I arrived in the middle of the school term (again), and so all the girls (again) had already formed their bonds and cliques. The first day I arrived I was shown into my class common room. I was immediately surrounded by a group of curious fourteen-year-olds who began interrogating me. "Where do you come from?" "What bands do you like?" "Do you smoke?" "Grass or hash?" I asked back. The girls stared back at me with a new respect. "You really smoke dope?"

At Dartington in the senior school we had been allowed to smoke cigarettes, so of course we found smoking pot more fun. I never had liked it; it made me tired and paranoid. But I had become an expert at rolling joints. Actually, I think that was the only useful thing I did learn at Dartington. That, and knowing when you are about to receive some really bad news.

Cranborne had the reputation of being a fairly lenient school, but after Dartington it felt like Dartmoor Prison. Although there wasn't an official school uniform, we still had to wear grey skirts, grey sweaters, and white shirts. We slept in dorms (I had always had my own room at Dartington) with the lights turned out by the matron at nine every night. And there were no boys.

I already had had many crushes and flirtations with boys by the time I got to Cranborne. I was surprised to see that the girls at my new school, deprived of contact with the opposite sex, formed crushes on each other. Some were openly lesbian, while others had secret longings. Little notes and gifts would be swapped among the lockers or found on pillows, and after lights-out, bed-hopping was routine.

The first night I was there I went into the next-door dormitory to share some of the food, or "tuck," that I had brought with me from home. The matron burst in on our midnight feast and shined a torch in my face. "New girl, you're on the walk starting tomorrow morning."

The "walk" was the most tedious of all the punishments doled out at Cranborne. It entailed waking up at six in the morning and walking two miles to old Wardour Castle and then back. The walk was supervised by two school prefects. Fortunately, the icy morning of my punishment the prefects who had to accompany me were as disgruntled and lazy as I was. We went only as far as a large oak tree that shielded us from view. We hid behind it long enough to make it seem plausible that we had walked two miles. During my so-called walk I decided that this school was definitely not for me. I also realized how good I had had it at Dartington.

At Dartington I had also discovered what was to become my favorite pastime of all—drinking. The part of England where Dartington is situated is famous for its very strong, very rough apple cider known locally as scrumpy. It tastes revolting, like rotten apples mixed with gasoline. But it has a high alcohol content and it is cheap. My friends and I would fill big plastic petrol containers with it, and on the weekends we would drink as much as we could stomach.

I suppose I should have had some warning that my drinking was different from everyone else's. I would always drink the fastest and the most, become violently ill, usually vomiting into the bathtub, and then I would lie on my bed with the room spinning until I passed out. When I woke up, I was eager to do it all over again. I liked the feeling of being drunk. I was able to talk and act the way I wanted to without self-censorship. It was the only time I ever was able actually to feel anything. I could release some of the emotions I kept stuffed down deep when I was sober. I invariably would become maudlin and start crying, telling my friends how miserable I was and how much I hated life. I would become sentimental and self-pitying. My biggest complaint was how awful it was to have a mother who drank so much.

RUNNING AWAY FROM BOARDING SCHOOL entailed meticulous planning. I first had to plant the seeds of doubt about the school in my mother's head. I needed her to be sympathetic. If I was going to go to all the trouble of running away, I couldn't have her sending me straight back.

We had one ten-minute pay phone call a day. I used every minute begging my mother to let me come home. I cried and cajoled and moaned about how homesick I was. I made up stories and said that the other girls teased me mercilessly. I told her they mocked my burns. It was true that I wasn't getting on with my classmates, but that was because I had made up my mind that I wasn't going to stay at the school. I had made no effort to make friends. I told my mother that I had been nicknamed Streaky Bacon because of the way my scars looked and that I was too embarrassed to shower or wear gym clothes. I knew the best way to get pity and to manipulate the situation was by using my accident. It was the one thing that would guarantee sympathy, especially from Mum, who still felt responsible for what had happened.

I also had to plan my escape for a time when it would cause the least suspicion. We had Thursday afternoons off, and we were allowed to go into town for shopping. For safety reasons we had to sign out of the school in groups of at least two or three.

The day of my breakout I didn't confide in anyone. I was lucky because another unpopular girl also wanted to go to town. She happened to be the daughter of the headmistress, so we were signed out without question. I had a small briefcase, which I filled with as much of my personal stuff as I dared. If I was stopped and asked where I was going, I'd explain I was on my way to the town library to work on a project. I would say that all my research papers were in the case. I had saved enough money, about twenty-five pounds (hidden under my mattress), to pay for my train ticket and taxi once in London.

The town of Tisbury is about four miles from the school along one straight flat road with tall hedges and rolling fields on either side. The countryside, normally so reassuring, seemed menacing as I made my way toward the train station. The walk seemed endless. I was terrified and sick with nerves. The rules and authority of boarding school seem all-powerful when you are a pupil; the idea of breaking them was nearly inconceivable.

Why Not Say What Happened?

I felt exposed and conspicuous as I walked to the station clutching my little case; a young, thin solitary figure trudging along an empty road. I was convinced that every car driving past held a teacher or staff member out to catch me and thwart my plan. I felt as though there was a neon sign over my head with the words *runaway schoolgirl* glowing in bright letters.

The station was empty when I finally arrived. The grumpy man behind the desk gave me a suspicious look as I asked for a single, one-way ticket to London. I prayed that there would be no one on the platform to recognize me. I was in luck. It was deserted.

It was dark by the time I reached our house in Redcliffe Square, and I felt that I had done something heroic, daring, and monumental. I spoke to my mother through the intercom: "It's Ivana, and I have run away from school." I felt so relieved to have actually made it home that I burst into tears.

I had hoped that my mother would recognize the enormity and pathos of the situation. But she didn't seem at all surprised or fazed by my arrival. "Oh, darling," she said when I came upstairs, "I am just going out to dinner. Why don't you have something to eat and we'll talk later."

I never went back to Cranborne Chase. Thus ended my formal education.

PART
TWO

CHAPTER 15

B y the time I arrived back home after boarding school, my mother had become part of the bohemian London art and literary worlds.

Although undisciplined and vague in most aspects of her life, in her writing my mother was sharp and focused. She would sit for hours with a school notepad on her lap, totally immersed in the longhand pages she was scrawling. Her attention would be diverted only long enough to light an untipped French cigarette, which she would smoke while pacing around the room. There was never an ashtray handy, so she would always be vaguely wandering around the house in search of one. But watching her, you knew that she had no idea what she was looking for. Finally she would pace back to her chair muttering something to herself and use her coffee cup to extinguish the flame.

She was well respected by other writers, and her books were praised by the critics. She won prizes for her novels and was in demand as a journalist.

Friendships were also important to Mum, and she put a lot of energy and time into them. She would spend hours on the phone relishing the gossip and listening to the woes of others. She was wonderful at offering her insights and giving advice. She would read her friends' manuscripts and take ages thinking about how to improve them.

One of my mother's great friends during this period was the painter Francis Bacon. Mum had gotten to know him well through Lucian, although by this point the two great artists were feuding. But she had first met Francis at a ball.

She was then eighteen, and was invited to a formal London

ball given by Lady Rothermere, who was to become Mrs. Ian Fleming. Princess Margaret was among the guests, and she immediately spotted her on the parquet floor wearing a crinoline. My mother said Princess Margaret was being worshipped by her adoring set, who were known at the time as "the smarties." She was revered and considered glamorous because she was the one "Royal" who was accessible. Princess Margaret smoked and she drank and she flirted. She went to nightclubs, and she loved show business and dancing to popular music. My mother said that Princess Margaret used to send out confusing signals. At times she seemed to want to be treated as an ordinary racy young girl. But other times her need for "ordinariness" made her behave in a manner that was rather embarrassing.

In order to put them at ease so that they could forget they had a royal figure at their table, she would pick up strings of spaghetti in tomato sauce from her plate and make loud sucking noises as she ate them with her fingers. This was her idea of "normalcy." Yet it was confusing for those around her. They never knew how she expected to be treated.

She encouraged familiarity and then, without warning, drew herself up to her full, small height and administered chilling snubs in which she reminded the socially inept that they had offended the daughter of the King of England.

Toward the end of the ball given by Lady Rothermere, after much champagne had been consumed, my mother noticed Princess Margaret seemed to be seized by a desire to show off. She grabbed the microphone from the startled singer of the band and instructed them to play songs by Cole Porter. All the guests who had been waltzing under the vast chandeliers instantly stopped dancing. They stood like Buckingham Palace sentries called to attention in order to watch the royal performance.

Princess Margaret knew all the Cole Porter lyrics by heart but she sang all his songs hopelessly off-key. Nevertheless, she was given encouragement by her audience. All the ladies in their finery and all the gentlemen penguin-like in their white ties and perfect black tails clapped for her. They shouted and they roared, and they begged for more.

Princess Margaret became a little manic at receiving such approval of her musical abilities and carried on. Just when she had embarked on a rendering of "Let's Do It," a very menacing and unexpected sound came from the back of the crowded ballroom. It grew louder and louder until it eclipsed Princess Margaret's singing. It was the sound of jeering and hissing, of a prolonged and thunderous booing.

Princess Margaret faltered mid-lyric. Mortification turned her face scarlet, and then it went ashen. She looked close to tears. Her smallness of stature suddenly made her look rather pitiful. She abandoned the microphone as a crowd of flustered ladies-in-waiting rushed off the stage and out of the ballroom. The band stopped playing and there was an awkward silence. There was a buzzing of furious whispers as Lady Rothermere's guests started to take in what they had witnessed.

"Who did that?" my mother asked the nearest white-tied and black-tailed man who happened to be standing next to her. His face was red; rage had turned it apoplectic. "It was that dreadful man, Francis Bacon," he said. "He calls himself a painter, but he does the most frightful paintings. I just don't understand how a creature like him was allowed to get in here. It's really quite disgraceful."

My mother said that later when she was married to Lucian Freud and had got to know Francis he once referred to the incident.

"Her singing was really too awful," he said. "Someone had to stop her."

Mum told me that one of the reasons she adored Francis was that he had an anarchic fearlessness that was unique. She said she could think of no one else who would dare to boo a member of the royal family in a private house. Among all the guests assembled in Lady Rothermere's ballroom, more than a few had been secretly suffering. But they suffered in silence, gagged by their snobbery. Francis would not be gagged. If he found a performance shoddy, no conventional trepidation prevented him from expressing his reactions. Sometimes his opinions could be biased and perverse and unfair, but he never cared if they created outrage.

He could be outspoken and crushing if provoked. She remembered him being pestered in a bar by a very bad and irritating artist who was trying to make Francis come to his studio to look at his work. The artist said he had the feeling that Francis only refused to come and look at his paintings because they threatened him. Francis replied that he didn't feel in the least threatened by the man's paintings. "I don't want to come to your studio because I've seen your tie."

My mother loved those stories about Francis because she shared his attitude toward snobbery and the mediocre. I think she wished that she had had the nerve to boo along with him.

CHAPTER 16

My sister Evgenia was attending St. Paul's girls' school in London, and she had also started modeling. She had her own apartment on the ground floor of our house. My little brother and I shared the middle apartment with a nanny. My mother had the top two floors.

After I had run away from school, I was sent to what is known as a "crammer." These are places where you literally cram for the required O level exams. You study the syllabus, go through old test papers, and are taught exam techniques. The classes are made up of wealthy dropouts and foreign students. My house was close to the crammer, and it quickly became the hangout for all my friends.

As a mother, in the nurturing and maternal sense of the word, my mother had not been the best. But in her relationship with teenagers, particularly the troubled ones I befriended, she was wonderful. She allowed us to smoke and drink and swear. She never seemed to know—or for that matter care—whether we were meant to be in class. She doled out advice and sympathized with our troubles. And she spoke to us about sex and relationships. "Sex is the best feeling ever," she told us. "Absolutely the best."

But she also warned us about men. For someone who had had three marriages and many intense love affairs, she had a cynical view of men. She often despised them and took great pleasure in finding and pointing out their weaknesses. "Some men," she told me once when I was trying to get rid of a particularly ardent suitor, "are put on earth just to be in love with one." I found that remark quite disturbing.

Introducing her to my boyfriends was a nightmare. She set daunting criteria for them to live up to. They had to be handsome, intelligent, well-read, and funny. And they had to "get us." "Getting us" meant tolerating the squalor of the house, her drinking, her often cruel sense of humor, and her fierce interrogations of all of them. It also entailed accepting the fact that if you wanted her daughter, then she came along with the package. She was my best friend, my drinking buddy, the person whom I loved and whose love I wanted most in the world. It was difficult for a mere man to try to come between that.

ONE NIGHT, JONATHAN, a friend of mine, who had amorous feelings toward me, snuck out of his London boarding school to come and visit. I had Melissa, one of the daughters of the Earl of Dudley, living with us. For some reason, my mother had taken a dislike to Jonathan even though he was the son of her old screenwriter friend Ivan Moffat. I hurried Jonathan into the apartment, and just as all three of us were all about to watch a movie, I heard my mother tipsily trying to get her key into the front door lock.

Melissa and I quickly shoved Jonathan into the closet in my bedroom. "Mum will freak if she finds you here," I warned.

He had been left in the closet for some time, while in the next room Mum—in one of her expansive, let's talk about the world and everything moods—held Melissa and me captive. Then, full of mischief, we encouraged Mum to have a look in my wardrobe. She seemed confused at the suggestion, eager to carry on with the conversation, but did as we asked.

The first thing that Jonathan saw were my mother's eyes, first wide with surprise, then ablaze with fury. "How dare you hide away in cupboards . . ."

Why Not Say What Happened?

Jonathan was arraigned forthwith in the drawing room by my mother's new very young poet-lover. He had been ordered by Mum to chastise the young intruder. It was a role that was quite alien to him. Yet he dutifully explained that Caroline did not take kindly to having men hiding in her daughter's bedroom.

It was agreed that Jonathan could spend the night on the sofa. Later on that night, as if Melissa and I had not inflicted enough on Jonathan, we encouraged him to drink a large glass of vodka. I asked him whom he fancied most, Melissa or me? He hesitated, trapped, angry at the question and, I think out of spite, chose my friend. Fate, we would only find out much later, had dealt a kind hand.

We left him to pass out on the sofa. When Caroline woke him the next morning, he was feeling lucky to be alive after having been violently sick in his sleep. Inducted into the ways of Redcliffe Square life, he stumbled blurrily back just in time for morning roll call at Westminster School.

OCCASIONALLY, my mother would decide to throw impromptu cocktail parties in her flat. She served what she called a Champagne Cocktail—*méthode champenoise,* brandy, a sugar cube, and a splash of Angostura bitters. It actually tasted quite good, but it was lethal. She put out some peanuts and occasionally a little bit of cheese. A few days before the party she would sit by the phone with her tatty and ancient black leather address book and invite everyone in it. The guest list was a nice mix. There'd be painters—Bacon, of course, Michael Wishart—dukes and duchesses—Devonshire, Marlborough. Sometimes even my grandmother was invited, very last-minute with the hope that she wouldn't come, but to my mother's dismay she invariably did. Lady Diana Cooper and the Duchess of Argyll and my grandmother would sit in the center of the drawing room holding court with a crowd of sycophantic admirers at their feet. Of course there were writers, Ian McEwan, Beryl Bainbridge, and an assortment of journalists. She would also invite all our Guinness relatives for a bit of crack, as the Irish call it.

The five flights of stairs up to my mother's flat were uncarpeted and steep. By the time the guests reached the top, they were panting and hot. My mother heated the house as though we were growing orchids. I think because she had grown up in such freezing homes it was one luxury she really enjoyed. The perspiring guests were greeted by my mother, who immediately pressed one of her specialty cocktails into their hands. They were never offered an alternative, and there wasn't one for them anyway.

Because the "champagne" she served her guests wasn't very good, my mother feared it would give her a bad hangover. In the kitchen, she kept a supply of what she called "the good stuff," which she and a few favored guests would secretly help themselves to all night.

Of course everyone would get drunk. Even normally temperate people (not that there were very many at her gatherings) would become caught up in the bacchanalian atmosphere and behave uncharacteristically badly. Embarrassing passes were made, offensive arguments took place, and there was an unpleasant amount of vomiting in the bathroom.

My mother presided over all of this with glee. On these occasions she herself would remain quite sober. She enjoyed all the dramas and intrigues far too much to miss them. She would rush up to me to tell me who had gotten "really bad." It was my responsibility to try to persuade them to go home. I would get their coats and call them cabs. But it is hard to get a drunk person to do anything, especially if you are a fifteen-year-old schoolgirl and they are fully grown, cantankerous adults who are determined to stay.

Once the Duke of Devonshire got "so bad," insulting the other guests and shouting obscenities, that my mother decided he really had to leave. He was a rather large man and put up quite a fight. In the end a crowd of us had to push him physically out of the front door. He fell most of the way down the five flights of stairs and landed awkwardly on the stone tiles of the entrance hall. We all peered nervously over the balcony, and my mother declared that he must be dead. But with a dignity in keeping with his aristocratic status, he picked himself up and yelled a good night and thank you up the stairs. As though nothing abnormal had happened, the Duke walked unsteadily out to his car and driver.

EVEN THOUGH MY MOTHER was often incapable of behaving in the way one would expect of a mother, I felt loved by her. Not in the carpooling, making sure you brushed your hair and teeth kind of way. But she was honest with us, and her love was palpable. She would suddenly grab me and kiss me violently. She would exclaim, almost as though she were in pain, "Oh, I love you so much."

We would talk about death. I asked, "Isn't the thought of death made easier knowing you live on through your children?"

"No. It makes it far, far worse because I will miss you all so much. How will I know that you are all right?" One of her closest friends, the writer Alice Thomas Ellis, said to me after Mum had died, "I miss Caroline so much it makes me cross." That is how I feel.

When something really awful happens, I still think, Oh, Mum would have loved that. There was always some new obsession about something being "really bad." After Chernobyl, she refused to drink Russian vodka because it was "radioactive." Out went the Smirnoff and in came Finlandia.

Then there was a rumor that traces of antifreeze had been found in white wine. After that we were not allowed to drink any white wine at all. If anyone ordered it in a restaurant, she would scream, "Stop! That's pure antifreeze you are ordering."

My mother was also very strange about money. She was oblivious most of the time about what things cost, but could develop obsessions about things being too "expensive." We never had a nice car. When I complained about the shabbiness and unroadworthiness of our car, she said, "No one has cars anymore!" Therefore, we had only secondhand cars of unspeakable decrepitude.

Long-distance telephone calls were also deemed a luxury only for the truly rich. Perhaps it was a throwback to wartimes, but Mum was convinced that long-distance calls would bankrupt her. "It's five pounds a minute!" she would hiss over my shoulder if I was on the phone to a friend who lived anywhere other than where she considered "local." "Mum, Helena lives in Surrey. It's not bloody Australia," I would try to explain. But she never got over it. Still, if I asked her for some cash to buy a magazine or something else cheap, she would give me far more than I needed.

Because we never had any home-cooked meals, she had an account at the food hall of Harrods. We could order whatever we wanted from the assortment of precooked delicacies on offer. They would arrive in a Harrods van, neatly packed in green-and-white boxes secured with green "Harrods" ribbon. There were boxes filled with smoked salmon, caviar with blinis, kedgeree, and lobster salad. And Harrods' own label champagne would arrive by the case.

We also had an account at the closest Italian restaurant, Pontevecchio. My sister and I ate there, and entertained our friends there, nearly every night. We signed the check using our mother's name. Sometimes she would be dining at another table with a friend or lover, and we would pretend not to notice.

WHEN MY SISTER WAS MODELING and had become a well-known face on the London social scene, I would tag along behind her to all the fashionable parties. I think she enjoyed showing off her rather naïve younger sister.

I was fifteen, and it became a game among my sister's friends to try to corrupt me. I still hadn't developed a taste for alcohol but liked the effect. I drank a sweet sickly concoction called a Tequila Sunrise. After a few of those, I would become confident and, in my view, entertaining. I thought I had a good singing voice, and for some reason I am able to retain the lyrics to songs after hearing them only a couple of times. So, goaded on by my sister and her friends, I would belt these out unashamedly, rather like Princess Margaret but without the royal admiration.

My mother seemed not to notice what her daughters were up to. She was with a young Oxford don named Andrew Harvey. Andrew was one of the youngest men ever to have been offered the distinguished position of Fellow at All Souls' College. He was half Indian, attractive with a mass of black, unruly hair, and he wrote poetry. He moved into my mother's upstairs apartment and quickly made himself invaluable to her.

I enjoyed his presence in the house; it was a relief to have someone else looking after her and also to be the main focus of her drunken attacks. He was always cheerful and polite, and best of all, he did all my homework for me.

Their affair broke up soon after Andrew returned from a trip to Ladakh in the Himalayas. My mother couldn't bear the fact that when he came back he had "become all spiritual." He tried desperately to share his newfound enlightenment with her, but she just thought that his trip had "made him creepy and disingenuous." She mercilessly mocked and trivialized what he believed to be his spiritual awakening.

Andrew Harvey went on to write several books on spiritual enlightenment, but shortly after their breakup he published a book of poetry called *No Diamonds, No Hat, No Honey.* The female character in these poems is clearly based on my mother. She is a cruel and cynical tormentor named Lydia, who humiliates the long-suffering Fernando, obviously based on the author himself. In poem IV of the long and intense book, Lydia—or my mother—describes the kind of books she likes to read:

> *"In the stories I love,"*
> *Said Lydia,*
> *"The wicked stay wicked."*

The entire book goes on in this vein with my mother becoming progressively more demonic and evil. She cruelly tramples on all of Fernando's dreams and beliefs and tries to crush his spirit.

Andrew sent her a copy of the book signed with a gushing and intimate inscription. She read the book intently, and when she had finished she put it down and rolled her eyes. "God, he really is an awful poet, isn't he?"

CHAPTER 17

Those cozy evenings spent with Mum and Robert, all of us reading poetry to each other, had instilled in me a love of language and performing. We also would read plays out loud and alternate the parts. My mother had wanted to be an actress, and Robert had a natural flair for the dramatic, so we took our roles very seriously. I loved doing comedies—Oscar Wilde, Sheridan, Shaw, and Coward. Robert preferred heavier material with large universal themes, particularly the Greek and Roman tragedies. My mother liked the "depressing plays," as I referred to those by Chekhov, Ibsen, and Strindberg. "I am in mourning for my life," she would exclaim, and she was completely convincing.

Being able to make someone else's words come to life and to tell a story was exciting. I also liked the fact that I could be someone else for a while. I think all three of us enjoyed escaping from the prisons of our own minds.

Robert's translation of Racine's *Phaedra* was given a professional production in London. The lead part was played by a beautiful Maria Callas look-alike and I was completely starstruck. Robert allowed me to sit in on the rehearsals and would sometimes ask my advice about words or sentence changes. The actress often came over to our house, and I ran through her lines with her. After that I was hooked. I decided I had to become an actress. My mother encouraged my thespian ambitions. Because she had been too shy to pursue her own acting career, she was very excited at the thought of mine.

In England, drama schools take themselves very seriously. The courses are full-time, and you may graduate only after three years of regular attendance. There are about four or five schools that are considered good, and they are notoriously difficult to get into. As every aspiring actor knows, the audition process is rigorous and intimidating. You are asked to prepare two monologues—one classical, i.e., Shakespeare, Webster, Jonson, or Marlowe; and one contemporary.

For my modern piece my mother and I cobbled together some excerpts from Sylvia Plath's *The Bell Jar*. We included a particularly harrowing description of electric shock treatment. I wore a long black overcoat to my auditions and manically puffed on one of my mother's unfiltered Gitanes. As Plath, I described the electricity running through my body and let out a piercing scream, "Wheeeeeeee! Every jolt drubbed me till I thought my bones would break and the sap fly out of me like a split plant."

It seemed to go down well with the various judges, and I was accepted by two of the schools I wanted to attend. I was narrowed down to the last five at RADA (Royal Academy of Dramatic Art), which involved being called back and called back. They also made me do my speeches (for my classical I had chosen a Shakespearean piece) in various different ways. I think my attempt at doing Cressida as a Russian tightrope walker was my downfall, and to my fury I was rejected.

I eventually settled on what was then called the Guildford School of Dance and Drama. Guildford is a middle-class, rather bleak suburb of London. But it does have a wonderful theater where many shows destined for London's West End have their tryouts. The drama school is attached to the theater, and graduating students were often picked to be in the professional companies. I was excited.

By the time I got to Guildford I had lofty, rather grandiose ideas about acting and about my talent. I had been in a couple of plays at the Edinburgh International Festival and had somehow managed to attract the attention of a well-known agent, so I thought I was only a few parts away from a theatrical dame-hood.

The program at Guildford was punishing. I knew that it had a reputation for being strong on musical theater, but I hadn't realized to what extent. The days seem to be spent running from one form of grueling dance class to another: ballet, tap, jazz, classical, Laban (too tedious and inane to explain), and character. In character, we learned those dances that you see (and yawn through) in every production of Shakespeare or in the "ballroom" scenes of period adaptation movies.

I HAD ALWAYS ENJOYED DANCING until I got to Guildford. But something happened to me there, and I developed a complete block. I felt the same humiliation that I had when I was trying to learn to walk again. I felt that my legs wouldn't cooperate with the rest of my body, as though my burns had somehow caused them to rebel. I couldn't pick up any of the dance routines during the jazz classes. I had no rhythm or coordination in tap. In ballet I was completely graceless. I hoped that if I smiled and put on meaningful expressions no one would notice what the rest of my body was doing, but that didn't work for long. I was placed in the bottom group for all the movement classes. I was usually the only girl dancing with all the clumsy boys.

At Guildford I became anorexic. I think I thought if I was really, really thin, then at least I would look like a dancer. As most of our time was spent in exercise clothes in front of full-length mirrors, our bodies were under scrutiny all day.

I ate ridiculously tiny amounts. During our lunch break, I would avoid going to eat with the other students. At night my gourmet meals consisted of weird combinations of low-calorie items available at our local deli. A sliced tomato drenched in vinegar and hot sauce with maybe a pickled onion or gherkin on the side.

There was another reason to starve myself. Since my burn accident I had developed a loathing of my body. I was ashamed of it. I tried to disassociate myself from it, and by reducing my size I felt I was shrinking my scars. The only fattening thing I did allow myself at the end of the day was alcohol. I had developed a taste for Stone's Ginger Wine, a very sweet and warming drink.

For the duration of my acting course I rented a three-bedroom mews house. The house was undistinguished apart from its name, Dove Cottage. For some reason my mother found the name hysterical. She would telephone me and ask, "How is life at Dove? Perhaps you will find love in Dove."

I rented the spare bedrooms to two girls from my class. At the end of the exhausting day I would hide in my bedroom and dissolve my woes in ginger wine. My main concern was how to consume as few calories as possible and to calculate how much alcohol I could drink without suffering from a hangover the next day.

Before I went to Guildford I had never considered myself privileged. At the schools I attended everyone came from the same kind of background as mine, as did my friends in London. In fact, my three best girlfriends were daughters of earls and like my mother used the title Lady in front of their names, but their upbringings had been even colder and lonelier than mine. For them the house in Redcliffe Square had become a refuge and, oddly, a place where they felt at home.

I didn't know how out of touch I was. I thought that I was worldly and sophisticated, but I had no idea what the world was like. I suppose I still have trouble dealing with reality. At Guildford, however, I became aware of how different my upbringing had been and how oddly sheltered and yet at the same time unprotected I had been.

Because money was such a big issue among my fellow students, I did my best to disguise the fact that I had some. I had never had to deal with money before. If I wanted any, I would just ask Mum. She would rummage around in her grungy bag. After digging up broken cigarettes, cloves of garlic (she bought her own to restaurants as "they never put enough in"), or foreign bills from countries visited long ago, she would unearth fifty or a hundred pounds and give it to me.

My friends at drama school priced every café, sandwich shop, and pub. One of my first roles at Guildford was to learn to act as though I was frugal.

The first time I went on one of our group theater outings, I arrived at Waterloo Station with the other students and immediately headed for the taxi stand. "Where are you going? The tube is over there." I was nineteen and had never taken the underground. I had no idea what line or district I was meant to be traveling. Everyone else had little folders with their student ID cards and their bus and tube passes. Red-faced, I kept everyone waiting while I found a ticket booth and boldly bought my ticket.

My friends looked at me uncomprehendingly. "Did you only buy a single? It's much cheaper if you buy a season ticket. Why didn't you use your student card?"

"Oh, I usually take the bus," I muttered. "I hate being underground. I get really claustrophobic."

Another lie I had to remember. Once again I felt out of place, different, and humiliated. I didn't even know how to take public transport.

WHILE I WAS AT GUILDFORD I met and started dating a friend of my sister's. He was about fifteen years older than me and one of my first grown-up relationships.

Peregrine was from an old, grand Scottish clan, complete with tartan, coat of arms, and crumbling estate. The family had one of those wonderful, eccentric-sounding titles after its name—Of that Ilk—meaning "from that moor or hill." The Moncreiffes' wealth had dissipated over the years, but Peregrine was determined to prevent the house and land from having to be sold. He became a banker and made enough money to buy the estate from his older brother.

While I was dating him, Peregrine became one of the first bankers in England to command a million pounds a year in salary. One morning I went into the student common room and found everyone crowding around a newspaper article. Spread over the two middle pages was a large photo of Peregrine and me with the excruciating headline, "The Big Banger and the Guinness Heiress." The newspaper had dug up a photograph of us at some black-tie event and we both looked particularly smug and odious. That was the end of any street credibility I may have had at drama school.

My relationship with Peregrine ended as a result of my drinking. It was the first significant consequence that alcohol had caused in my life. In Scotland, New Year's Eve, or Hogmanay, is celebrated in grand style. There are balls where all the clans, wearing their appropriate tartans, get together. The girls wear sashes; the men, kilts; and bagpipers play music to which reels are danced. The reels are taken very seriously, and the true Scots are familiar with them all. When the first chord is played, ears prick up. "Oh, it's the Duke of Firth," and the dancers collect into neat lines and begin the reeling.

I had never danced a reel before. I also still had a phobia about my dancing from being so embarrassed at Guildford. I had started drinking whiskey early on in the evening, and by the time the dancing began I was horribly drunk. I turned the reeling into a fiasco. I stumbled around tearing my dress, tripping my partners up, and whooping along with the bagpipes.

Peregrine drove me home in ice-cold silence. I knew I had fucked up, but I couldn't let it go. "I hate Scotland," I slurred. "Hate everything about it. Stupid country. Stupid music. Stupid traditions. Ireland and the Irish are far superior!"

The next day I was hungover and mortified. But I didn't want Peregrine to know how embarrassed and how frightened I was by my own behavior. Rather than admit that my drinking was starting to be a real problem, I pretended that I had been completely aware and in control of my actions. Even though I could barely remember what I had said, I acted as though I stood by my comments.

Back in London two days later, Peregrine wrote me a formal letter officially ending our relationship.

I LASTED ABOUT A YEAR at Guildford. I kept waiting to be given a big, juicy tragic role to show off my acting ability. But instead, I became more and more frustrated at the emphasis that the school put on musical theater. My fear of dancing had gotten worse, and I had started finding excuses for why I couldn't do the classes.

I also was becoming ill; I was coming down with mononucleosis. Now the looming prospect of performing in the end-of-term showcase was horrific.

I didn't mind the pieces of straight theater we were scheduled to perform, but there was one dance routine that gave me nightmares. It was choreographed to some Indian-sounding music. We had to do a belly dance type of movement with our hips while our arms reached over our heads, palms of hands placed together framing our faces. At the same time, you had to move your head from side to side without moving your neck or shoulders. I just couldn't get it. For some reason, my neck and shoulders wouldn't stay still and I ended up wiggling my entire body manically in the hope I would achieve the same alluring effect.

The dance teacher and the other girls in the routine were convinced I was deliberately trying to sabotage the performance. They couldn't believe anyone could be so clumsy and uncoordinated.

One girl was an exceptionally graceful and gifted dancer; she had been doing ballet since she could walk. She had been given a solo to perform during our Eastern routine, and she made it clear that she despised me. I think she thought that I was trying to prevent her from having her moment. But I really was trying. I spent hours at home practicing in front of the bathroom mirror, only to wind up crying with frustration.

It all came to a head during one of the dress rehearsals. I had been placed at the very back behind one of the tallest girls in the group, as out of sight of the audience as the teacher could manage. Yet I was determined to get it right this time, and I had worked myself up into a mental frenzy.

The music started, and I jerked my head enthusiastically toward my left ear. As I did, I felt and heard a loud snap. A bolt of pain shot up the left side of my neck, and I yelled out in shock.

By the time I got to the chiropractor in London my neck was actually feeling a lot better. But I was taking no chances. I had found my perfect escape. I told him I couldn't move my head at all, that I was in constant pain and I was suffering from dizzy spells.

"Whiplash," he diagnosed. He fitted me with a hideous orthopedic neck brace, and instructed me to wear it at all times. Any form of exercise was forbidden.

I gleefully left the Guildford School of Dance and Drama shortly afterward.

CHAPTER 18

One of the first questions you are asked in rehab and in the standard questionnaire issued by Alcoholics Anonymous is, "Have you ever suffered consequences as a direct result of your drinking?" Your answer is meant to determine whether or not you are an alcoholic. The fact that you are even filling in the questionnaire is a pretty good indication of the answer. But looking back at my drinking history, it is astounding how dishonest I was in my answers.

The dreaded and overused word, *denial*, a word which appears so often when talking about addiction, comes to mind. I honestly didn't realize how much and for how long alcohol had been slyly running my life. As with the Peregrine debacle, it had made decisions for me that I would never have made had I been sober. Alcohol determined the fate of my relationships, my career choices, where and with whom I lived, and how I felt about myself.

In AA, of course, one of the first suggested steps toward your recovery is the admission that you are powerless over alcohol. I realize now that I was powerless over alcohol long before I ever had my first drink. If you have the gene, predilection, disease, or whatever label you prefer to put on it, alcohol is a terrible and all-powerful adversary. My mother found that out, as did so many other members of my family.

It is hard to admit to being powerless. From very early on we are taught to think positively, to believe we can do anything, and never to give up. I am proud of the fact that I was tough and strong-willed; the fact that I am sitting here today is testimony to that.

I think that is why it is so difficult for me (and for so many of us) to admit defeat when it comes to alcohol. We don't want to feel that we are weak. We believe we should be able to beat it. I have come to realize, though, that where alcohol or any other illness is concerned, just wanting to beat it is not enough.

I weigh about 114 pounds. If I entered a boxing ring with a professional opponent twice my size and with Mike Tyson's punch, however much I wanted to prevail, I would still get the shit beaten out of me.

Yet with drinking, even when the blows got harder and the consequences more dire, I kept going back into that ring. It seems so unfathomable, insane actually, that I would continue to go back for more. Back for more sickness and more misery. Back again to cause worry and shame, to hurt my relationships and alienate my friends.

But when the bruises healed and the guilt subsided a little bit, the memory of the last hospital visit, the stench of the bloody vomit, the terrible shame, would fade. A voice would start to whisper in my ear again. "This time will be different. This time you can outthink and outsmart the monster. It wasn't *so* bad. You just weren't prepared. You were just going through a rough period. This time you'll know better." And back I would go for another horrendous bout with Mike.

The paradox that I have to accept is that the only way I can become free from alcohol is by the rather deflating admission that I am utterly defeated by it.

CHAPTER 19

While I was at drama school, my mother had bought and (sort of) moved into a rather mad house in Leicestershire in the middle of England. My mother and I had always suffered from what we called *Country Life*–itis. We would drool over copies of *Country Life* magazine, study the front section filled with beautiful photographs of expensive houses and estates for sale, and we would imagine ourselves already living in them. "Charming Georgian rectory, in the picturesque village of Little Codsdale. High ceilings, five bedrooms, walled garden, etc." We would excitedly choose which bedrooms we would have and how we would change whatever decoration we could see in the photos. If we knew someone who lived nearby a particular house, we would really go into high fantasy.

In reality, my mother did want to spend more time out of London. She had always loved the country and, as she put it, "just wanted to get away from it all." I think she also felt that if she had a nice country house, her children would all feel as if they had a proper home to return to. We had always been scattered, and now my sister was living in New York, my brother was at boarding school, and I was in Dove Cottage. So, in her mind, the dream house idea practically made sense.

Through an ad in *Country Life* we found a company called Property Vision. This was run by two handsome, well-spoken, and well-bred young men who specialized in finding buyers for the perfect country house. We had wasted a great amount of boring time looking for houses on our own. We would travel for hours by train and then cab to look at the "exceptional eighteenth century listed country house with lovely views" only to discover it also was directly under Heathrow Airport's roaring flight path. Or that the "extensive modernization" so glowingly described meant that all the charming historic details had been ripped out and replaced with hideous faux features.

Now the nice men at Property Vision vetted the houses for us. When one met with their approval, they drove us there themselves, and then took us for a nice pub lunch on the way back.

My mother had particular ideas about what her house should and should not have. As she had grown up at Clandeboye, she had to have high ceilings, large well-proportioned rooms, lots of big (preferably bow-shaped) windows, and uninterrupted views. There also had to be a walled kitchen garden as well as some sort of water on the land. She drove Property Vision mad, and in the end she found the house herself.

"I think I have found rather a dream," she announced when she called me early one morning. "In fact, I am in the house right now."

I had seen her the day before at the wedding of one of our Guinness cousins in Northampton. The wedding had been inevitably raucous and boozy. I had to get back to London for some reason and left my mother up north to stay for the night.

"A man at the wedding told me he was selling his house and as he lives nearby he invited me over for breakfast. Darling, I think it's rather wonderful."

The man turned out to be Bobby Spencer, a cousin of Lady Diana, and also, as we came to learn later, a bit of a black sheep. Langton Hall was a neo-Gothic, dark grey stone pile. Fields and fields of sheep and cows flanked an impressive, winding driveway and led to a dark portico.

When I arrived to meet my mother for my inspection of the property, I felt like I was in a Hammer Horror Dracula movie. I stood dwarfed by a huge wooden front door and pulled on the ancient bell. The huge doorway opened into an enormous wood-paneled great hall complete with cold flagstone floors and a gigantic fireplace.

The house was freezing and the hall pitch dark. The walls were covered with gloomy portraits of Bobby Spencer's ancestors. Over the fireplace and along the walls of the staircase were musty and desiccated tapestries. There were also some large animal skin rugs scattered around. It felt as though no one had lived there for centuries. Bobby Spencer welcomed me with great enthusiasm.

I had been promised a late lunch and was starving by the time I arrived. I was ushered into a small back kitchen. Formica on the countertops and green linoleum covered the floor. There was a squat rusty fridge and a double burner electric stove.

Bobby pulled out a can of tomato soup from a dusty cupboard and from the same cupboard produced an old saucepan. While the soup was heating, he left us to "nip down to the cellar to fetch us a nice little treat." He returned carrying an ancient-looking bottle of red wine. The label had molded off but he declared, "This will be absolutely delicious."

We ate the soup seated around a food-stained and rickety kitchen table. The first sip of wine remedied everything. Bobby was right: it was delicious. We finished my tour of the house, glasses in hand. By the end of the visit we were certain that the house was, indeed, "rather a dream." My mother agreed to buy it.

THE HOUSE HAD SEEMED sparsely furnished when Bobby Spencer had inhabited it, but after he had moved his few things out it seemed cavernously empty. We had thought we had a lot of furniture, but the scale of Langton Hall swallowed the pieces.

The day we moved in my mother and I sat opposite each other on the two Knole sofas we had thought would look so perfect in the hall. We huddled in our overcoats and made elaborate decorating plans. As the afternoon light faded, so did our enthusiasm. The prospect of sleeping in our damp, unwelcoming beds was grim. We telephoned for a taxi and checked in to the nearby inn, Langton Arms.

Although we continued to fantasize about how marvelous it was going to look once we had decorated, we never actually moved into the main house. Directly behind the house, next to the walled kitchen garden my mother had always dreamed about, was a large cobbled courtyard. Surrounding it were a clock tower, stables, and three cottages.

My mother moved into East Cottage and I took the one opposite, West Cottage. Both the cottages were well heated and cozy. The bedrooms were wallpapered in pink and purple roses, and carpeted wall-to-wall with matching pink wool. We made endless fun of East and West cottages, and continued to make grand plans for when we moved into the "big house." Secretly, though, we were thrilled with our eccentric arrangement.

One of Bobby Spencer's businesses had been as a wine merchant. Langton Hall had a vast wine cellar and Bobby stored wine there for some of his clients. The "cellar" was not climate controlled or damp-proofed; in fact, it was just a creepy damp basement. But he charged cellarage rates.

Still, there were fabulous bottles of wine, vintage champagnes, and valuable port stored down there. It was so musty that all the labels had peeled and rotted away, and although I am not much of an oenophile, I knew the wine was not being kept as it should have been. I don't think Bobby had a clue what was there or to whom it belonged. After he sold us the house, he had nowhere to put all the bottles, so he rather unwisely left them behind.

We didn't think of it as stealing; "possession is nine tenths of the law," my mother liked to remind me as we tried to decipher the labels on the bottles we had chosen to accompany our evening meal. We would send my brother down to the cellar with a flashlight and a shopping bag, and it was potluck as to what he would bring back. Sometimes the wine had turned and was pure vinegar. But more often it was a sensory delight and surprise. The fact that we had no idea what we were drinking only enhanced the guilty pleasure.

The house also had a large well-established kitchen garden. And there was a greenhouse where the hot, spicy smell of yellow and green tomatoes and hairy, prickly, penis-shaped cactuses loomed. Outside, hard-to-establish asparagus, tiny new potatoes, lettuces, carrots, cabbage, and every kind of herb were planted. There were the makings of a vegetarian feast.

Life at Langton Hall suited my mother. She could be lady of the manor without the responsibilities that usually accompany that title, and she was able to write. There was also enough distraction so that she wasn't lonely. In fact, the location of Langton provided Mum with the material for her next book.

THE TOWN OF MARKET HARBOROUGH is in the heart of fox-hunting country. It is where the Melton Mowbray meets the Quorn, two distinguished hunts. Our house had land where the two meets converged and so it was necessary that they had our permission to use the fields.

Both Masters of Foxhounds paid a visit to my mother. They assumed that because she was titled and had bought such a (from the outside at least) grand house she would be amenable to hunting. Watching or listening to hounds braying, horses galloping, horns sounding, and the flash of black and red flying across the fields is thrilling and beautiful. It was only when you realize that the object of the chase and fanfare is a small, terrified fox running for its life that this vision paled. Oscar Wilde famously described foxhunting as "the unspeakable in full pursuit of the uneatable."

I had my first and only hunt and "kill" in Ireland. The hunt was a renegade affair that met outside our local pub in County Kildare. I was mounted on an enormous wild-eyed mare that I had never ridden before. My cousin Desmond Guinness thrust a large stirrup cup (the name given to the ludicrously alcoholic beverage drunk for Dutch courage) into my hand. "Just hold tight and follow me," he advised. "If you fall off, let the horse catch up with us and we will meet you back at the pub."

I drained my stirrup cup and shouted, "Tallyho!" The next couple of hours were a blur. Apparently the hounds picked up a scent immediately, and we were off. I lost any semblance of control over my horse and just prayed she wasn't suicidal.

We galloped through fields and fields of maize and peat, jumping over everything in our path. I vaguely remember streams, ditches, barbed-wire fences, and one huge stone wall. My hat fell over my eyes. I lost both my stirrups and my grip on the reins. I clung to my horse's mane and tried to make myself as flat as possible. Maliciously, she seemed to want me off her back and veered toward the trees with the lowest branches. It was a miracle I wasn't decapitated.

Suddenly we stopped. There was tremendous noise and commotion. The fox had been caught. The hounds and the huntsmen were ecstatic. As it was my first kill, the Master of the Hounds made a great show of bloodying me. He smeared the revolting mix of blood and fur all over my face, and then congratulated me.

There was very little left of the fox, its sad head and his majestic tail had been taken away as trophies. I felt sick.

Back at the pub there was huge rejoicing. A number of riders and horses had been badly injured, but this was treated with ridicule and hilarity. One famous story attributed to that hunt (and I am sure many others) is of two huntsmen riding past the same fallen and crushed horse and rider. "I could see that they were alive, and so I carried on," the first one bragged. "I was sure that they were dead, and so I just carried on as well," guffawed the second.

WHILE MY MOTHER WAS LIVING in the heartland of foxhunting, she became fascinated with the subject and wrote a book, *In the Pink*. It details the enormous amount of passion the blood sport inspires, not just in those for whom hunting is a way of life but also for those who oppose it. My mother tried to take a wide-eyed and innocent view about her subject. She adopted the hunting community's platform. She discussed what abolishment would mean to those whose livelihood depended on the sport. She detailed what would happen to all the land that was preserved specifically for hunting. And she remarked upon the sadness of the demise of yet another English tradition.

But although she tried to put forward the argument of the hunter, she clearly felt the cruelty to the animal outweighed all other considerations. Mum and I would secretly plot ways in which we could save the fox. We thought that perhaps on a hunting day we could stand innocently by an open gate in one of our fields, and when the fox had passed, quickly shut it and then run and hide. Or maybe we could catch the fox ourselves and smuggle it safely away before the hounds could get at it. But we realized both these ploys would be useless. The zealous horses and riders would just soar over the fence. Besides, how could we ever catch a fox?

Why Not Say What Happened?

While she was researching her book, my mother became fascinated by the "antis." She was impressed by their zeal, but also she was horrified at the lengths they would go to in order to sabotage a hunt. They would break into the kennels and poison the hounds' food. They would try to maim the horses prior to a hunt. They would spook them by rattling tin cans as they raced over the fields.

THE BOOK WAS NOT POPULAR in the hunting community, and as that constituted most of our neighbors, neither were we. I thought the book was fair. Like my mother, I tried, and almost succeeded, in seeing both sides. In the end, however, neither of us could condone it. For all its pageantry and often splendid images of horses and hounds, man against beast, or however you care to justify it, foxhunting is an inhumane, bloodthirsty, and revolting sport. And yet England is a country with peculiar traditions.

Of course foxhunting has now been banned in England and Ireland. It continues, however, illegally. For a sport that is so conspicuously noisy and flamboyant it is ironic that it manages to have a life "underground."

After the publication of my mother's book, we felt a definite chill toward us in our little community. My mother had never played her lady of the manor role according to expectations. Apart from the fact that she had never actually moved into the big house, there had been no fetes, garden parties, or teas to introduce herself to the locals. No appearances at Sunday church or at the Market Harborough Woman's Institute. And now she had published a book that seemed to mock the most important aspect of the area's country life.

It was the middle of July, and my mother and I were sitting on the stone terrace that opened out from the drawing room's French windows. We had made a Pimm's Cup with all the fruit, borage, and mint that the summer cocktail requires. Dark ominous clouds loomed over us and a chilly, grey, hazy fog began to descend. We stared down at the green topiaried avenue toward the ha-ha and pulled our raincoats up to prevent the drizzle from spotting our necks. "In the summer this will all be so marvelous," we agreed, ignoring the fact that it *was* July. "We will have such delightful picnics." And then we retreated back to our centrally heated cottages.

PART
THREE

W e are much better suited to the American climate," Mum declared. "At least they have proper seasons over there." And that was that. The dream of Langton Hall had ended. My mother rather sadly sold it to some developers with plans for a hotel and conference center, and we moved to New York.

Mum had always maintained her American life. Apart from our shivering summer at Langton Hall, our summers had mostly been spent in rented houses on Long Island. Her friends from when she had lived in New York and L.A. would visit.

One of her most enduring and important affairs had been with the influential *New York Review of Books* cofounder and editor Robert Silvers. During her marriages to Israel Citkowitz and Robert Lowell, they had maintained a close friendship. Bob was and still is one of the most important men in my life. An enormous figure in my childhood, he always seemed a wise and sane presence amidst the madness. I adored the times when I was able to see him.

When I was at Dartington, huge packages from the *Review* would arrive containing all the books he thought I should be reading. As someone who cared so much about education, he took an enormous interest in our schooling, and I think he was puzzled by Caroline's laissez-faire attitude toward it.

Bob had been a lifeguard in the summer in his teens, and when he came and stayed in Sagaponack he would spend hours in the ocean. His daring and his lack of concern for the size or ferocity of the waves always impressed me.

I thought him most heroic. He taught me how to judge the tide, catch a wave, and ride it to shore. Bob also seemed to know everything about everything. Best of all, he was a patient teacher. No subject was too childish or too boring to interest him. The latest children's fashion, the last movie I had seen, the book I just had read—all seemed to intrigue and amuse him.

He was handsome and kind, and I often wished he were my father.

MY MOTHER MOVED INTO an apartment in a modern building on the Upper East Side of Manhattan. The building was very unlike her with its glitzy health club and white-gloved doormen. But it was streaming with light and had a wonderful view of the river. Life in Condo, as we named the apartment, suited her in a funny way. She was particularly gratified to find that you could have everything delivered.

I stayed in London to pursue my acting. I was living with my boyfriend Kim in his house in Notting Hill Gate. Kim was also trying to become an actor. The relationship was ill-conceived, even slightly incestuous. He was my second cousin. His father was the son of my grandmother's sister, the beautiful and frail Oonagh.

His father, Gay Kindersley, was a charismatic and celebrated figure in horse racing circles. Having attended Eton and Oxford, Gay became a passionate amateur jockey and racehorse trainer. He owned a string of steeplechasers and kept them in his stable in Lambourn Valley, the heart of England's racing country.

Gay was a fearless rider. He was too tall by usual jockey standards, but he managed to win the title, under national hunt rules, of Britain's leading amateur jockey. During his riding career he broke nearly every bone in his body, but still his one ambition was to ride in the Grand National.

In March 1965, Gay, wearing his own colors of green and mauve, finally did ride in the Grand National. Unfortunately his horse, Ronald's Boy, fell at the third fence. But Gay's passion for racing never abated. Gay was also well known for his capacity for drink. After a few pink gins he would entertain whomever cared to listen with bawdy Irish songs.

I think that whether consciously or not, both Kim and I felt some kind of compulsion to live up to our family's reputation for eccentricity. We certainly acted that way. Our relationship was based partly on the fact that we were Irish and Guinnesses and, therefore, were expected to behave badly.

We drank constantly. We caused terrific scenes in public. Kim would get (or seem) slightly drunker than me, and so I would act the part of the long-suffering and victimized girlfriend. Shouting, in streams of tears, I must have stormed out of every fashionable restaurant and nightclub in London. Or so I remember.

As Kim had grown up in the same kind of environment as I had, the craziness and chaos felt familiar and normal to both of us. There was nothing either of us could do to shock the other, and so we just kept pushing the boundaries. My mother liked Kim because he was a member of the family and he "got us." He wasn't fazed by any drunkenness or rude behavior because he had experienced it all before at home.

When we were invited out, it was often, I came to realize, purely for the amusement of others. We would provide the evening's entertainment. They knew we would get drunk and have a hideous row. We became something of a sport, like bear baiting. "Let's have Kim and Ivana over and watch them fight. See who kills the other one first."

We once went to a cousin's wedding in Dublin for a weekend and didn't get home for two weeks. Egged on by our relatives (and the barman of the Shelborne Hotel), we were always too bad to make it to the airport.

We had a terrible argument in the hotel and I threw my shoe at Kim. Unfortunately, the stiletto heel caught the corner of his eye. There was a tremendous amount of blood and he required six stitches. The doctor kept asking if he wanted to press charges against me, but Kim said he couldn't understand what all the fuss was about.

At the time I thought we were behaving so glamorously, a modern-day Zelda and Scott Fitzgerald. But now I realize that I—both of us really—were probably in the early stages of alcoholism.

Alone and lonely in London, I missed my mother. Evgenia had also moved to New York. She was working for Farrar, Straus and Giroux publishers. I felt left behind.

I was acting in a production of *Pride and Prejudice* in London, playing the part of young Kitty Bennet. My mother and I decided that once the run was over, I should move to New York and try my luck at acting over there. I was fortunate that I had an American passport, but Kim was unable to secure a green card and had to stay in England. We tried to do the transatlantic thing for a while, but, inevitably, the relationship fizzled out.

BOB SILVERS KNEW Irving "Swifty" Lazar and arranged for me to go and meet Swifty at the agent's apartment on Fifth Avenue.

Swifty was legendary. He had famously shaped the careers of many movie stars and although he was getting on in years, when I went to see him he was still powerful and charismatic. He had a large bald head and he wore huge thick, pebble-lens glasses.

He came up to my chest. I was extremely nervous but he couldn't have been sweeter.

He was full of energy, almost frantic, as he buzzed around his apartment. I was standing at the picture window looking out onto the magnificent Central Park view when he approached me. He looked up at me myopically and declared, "My, you are a beauty!"

Swifty had retired from the movie business and into the literary world, negotiating outlandish contracts for his clients. He called an old contact of his at William Morris and ordered the underling to take me on. At William Morris the slick agent instructed, "The first thing you have to do is get rid of your speech impediment."

"My what?" I have always prided myself on my clear pronunciation and Queen's English. I certainly have never felt impeded in any way.

"Your British accent! It's gotta go."

I was furious. Every time I opened my mouth in America I was complimented on my charming accent, and now I was being told to lose it. I was sent to a voice coach and spent hours practicing talking with a slack jaw and flattened vowels. I was learning a Queens accent but this one was Flushing rather than royal.

There is a wonderful scene in the movie *Singin' in the Rain* when the blonde bimbo, in order to succeed in the "talkies," is trying to learn to speak properly. "I cayn't stand 'im," she cries nasally. That is how my American accent sounded. "I cayn't stand 'im."

My agent at William Morris arranged a lot of auditions for me and, ironically, I did a number of voice-overs in my "impeded" accent. He also sent me up for a daytime soap opera. A part was open for a British bitchy diva. I was offered it.

I was so naïve and grandiose. I thought that because I was a trained "classical actress," nothing less than Shakespeare or Chekhov should ever leave my lips. I scoffed at the "sides" I had been given to act. Looking back, I realize that I was a fool to have dismissed such an opportunity.

CHAPTER 21

The same night I turned down the soap I met my friend Don Boyd for dinner at Elaine's restaurant in New York. Don was a well-respected movie director and producer. He had cast me in small roles in a couple of his films, including one as a nurse in the life of Ian Fleming. It was Fleming's widow, of course, who had introduced my mother to her first husband.

As I picked at my Caesar salad, I moaned to Don about my dilemma. "I don't think I could bear to sign a two-year contract! I think I will miss London. And what about Kim? I can't leave him behind." These were genuine concerns, but I was also frightened. This was a real job with real responsibilities. It was the real world, a place I was not accustomed to.

I was carrying on with my self-absorbed rantings when a bottle of Dom Pérignon arrived at our table. "From Harvey Weinstein," the waiter informed us. Don and I looked down to the end of the restaurant where an ill-shaven man sat. He was wearing a rumpled shirt splattered in pasta sauce. He acknowledged our glances with a wink; and then raised his glass of Diet Coke in a salutation.

Harvey and his brother Bob's company, Miramax, had just produced one of Don's movies. The film's distribution hadn't worked out so well but Don, although still smarting from what he felt had been some neglect on the Weinstein brothers' part, appreciated the champagne gesture. Harvey came and joined our table. The three of us talked for hours. Miramax was beginning to be a player in the then small independent movie world. They had just had a success with *Sex, Lies, and Videotape,* and Harvey was on a roll.

Even then, I had heard the Weinsteins had a complicated and cantankerous reputation. But on that first evening Harvey was quite charming and very intelligent. He had a voracious, if uneducated, intellect and a need for knowledge. He grilled me on all the books I had recently read and plays I had seen.

After our dinner at Elaine's, he persuaded me to come downtown the following day to "learn everything you need to know about the movie business." But what he really wanted me to do, I soon learned, was to help him in the publishing world. He had a dream of starting his own publishing company and he saw me as someone who had contacts in a world unfamiliar to him.

He soon convinced me to work at Miramax, and I was given the wonderfully ambiguous title of Vice President of Creative.

It seemed a dream job. I was paid not only to read but also to go to movie screenings in the middle of the afternoon and offer up my comments. The job entailed courting young writers; we were always on the lookout to publish and secure movie rights to the next hot novel.

Miramax Books was a most outrageous and renegade affair. Harvey felt that the screenplays of some of the movies he was producing should be published. He thought that they could be of wide interest not just to a select group of film students but also to a general readership.

In the beginning, when Miramax was still independent, we had no distributors for the books. But Mort Janklow was one of the few literary agents who believed in the enterprise. He arranged for us to meet with the heads of some of the largest publishing houses to try to secure a book distribution deal.

I remember entering the hushed and pristine conference room of one prestigious publishing house. The executives were dressed in suits and ties, immaculately groomed and polished.

Harvey swaggered in, and my co–vice president Francesca (a beautiful former actress and my friend) and I trailed in his wake. The conference table was laid out with little water bottles, and there was a secretary poised to take the minutes of the meeting. Neat business cards were given to us, but we had none with which to reciprocate.

Harvey plonked himself down at the head of the table, cracked open a can of Diet Coke, and lit a cigarette. "So how soon can you get this published? I need it to coincide with the movie's opening."

"Well, Mr. Weinstein, we don't think you fully understand the nature of the book publishing world. We need a long lead for our catalogue, and, quite honestly, in our professional view screenplays don't sell."

Harvey went ballistic, and the meeting ended in shambles. Fortunately Disney purchased Miramax soon after, and the books were put out under their publishing division, Hyperion. Harvey was proven right. The screenplays of *Sex, Lies, and Videotape; Pulp Fiction;* and *The Piano;* as well as some novelizations of Miramax films, were extremely successful and set a new standard not only for film scripts but for movie-book tie-ins.

I KNEW ABOUT HARVEY'S REPUTATION as a womanizer; tales of his trying to seduce every young actress in town were infamous. However, I wasn't quite prepared for being on the receiving end of his onslaught. He would call me into his office under some pretext, and before I could scream *Sex, Lies, and Videotape* his office door would be slammed shut, and he would be playfully chasing me around his desk as though we were in some Feydeau farce. I was always too quick for him, and I don't think he would have done anything anyway if he had ever caught me, but it made for an interesting work experience.

Late one evening I was in my apartment gossiping with Francesca. She was staying with me while she was over from England working on a Miramax book project. At the time, I was in between apartments in New York and had temporarily rented a tiny furnished apartment in an upscale white-glove apartment building. It was on a high floor with wonderful city views but it had only two rooms. There was a small living room with a kitchen at one end, and a bedroom and bathroom leading off it.

Francesca was sleeping on the sofa bed in the living room and we inevitably would stay up for hours late into the night, girlishly discussing our woes, plotting our lives, and drinking wine.

This particular night we were talking as usual about our boyfriends. I was dating an Englishman named Geordie Greig. Geordie was an energetic, clever young journalist living in New York and working as the New York correspondent for the London *Sunday Times.* He was from an old, prominent upper-class Catholic family and had attended public school and Oxford. He was ambitious, worked hard, and lived downtown in a grungy walk-up building above Joe's Pizzeria. We made a strange couple, but I liked his intelligence, his humor, and, for want of a better word, "spunk." My mother liked Geordie; she respected his curiosity and tenacity as a journalist and she also felt he "got us," and in a funny way he did. He later went on to become editor of *Tatler,* that glossy magazine focused on the English upper classes, and is now the editor of the London *Evening Standard.*

Francesca was in a volatile relationship with the rock star Peter Gabriel. It was on and off, and then more off than on, and our favorite thing at night was to lie on the sofa bed and dissect our relationships.

We were onto our second bottle of wine and both in our most comfy clothes, T-shirts and knickers, when there was a bang on our front door. We were startled. It was a doorman building and visitors were always announced, especially at two in the morning.

I raced to the door and peered through the little glass peep-hole. I could see the distorted but unmistakable face of Harvey blinking impatiently back at me.

"Oh God. It's Harvey," I shrieked to Francesca. "Quick, let's hide."

We both started giggling uncontrollably and I tripped over the sofa bed as we scrambled to the tiny bathroom and locked ourselves in. But once we were inside we decided we were just being silly. "He knows we are here. And look, there's two of us. What can he possibly do?" Francesca said.

We hastily pulled on our jeans and I went and opened the door. As casually as I could I feigned surprise at seeing him.

"I've just come to check up on my girls. See what trouble you're getting into," he growled.

"Oh, you know us, Harvey. Just working away as always, thinking about book and film projects for you," I said cheerfully.

The living room was small, made smaller by the sofa bed. There was nowhere for him to go. He seemed large, and out of place, and he didn't seem to know what to do with himself. The only place for him to go was the bedroom, so he went and sat on the bed. Francesca and I both awkwardly edged away.

He lay down on the bed. "I am so fucking exhausted," he groaned. "Which one of you girls is going to give me a back massage?"

The scene was comical: Harvey lying spread-eagle, dwarfing the bed like Gulliver pinned down by midgets, and Francesca and I laughing nervously, still edging as far away as possible.

I said as flippantly as I could, "Oh Harvey, you know you hire us for our intellectual and literary abilities."

He laughed, relaxed, and for the next hour or so proceeded to complain about this "schmuck" and that "fucking moron," all well-known people in the movie industry. They were all "fucking him over," and he was going to get his "fucking revenge." Francesca and I sat there listening to his litany of grievances, fascinated but not quite sure how to respond.

Eventually we had had enough and started yawning. "Well, we really should call it a night, Harvey, big day tomorrow," I said. He looked tired but reluctant to leave. It was well known and a common complaint among overworked employees that he survived on very few hours of sleep. Finally he got up. "Be good girls, I love you the most, and sell millions of copies of our fucking books," he growled, and disappeared out into the night.

I never understood how he was allowed up to our apartment. He probably bribed the doorman, but of course he has always been extremely persuasive.

HARVEY HAS AN EXTRAORDINARY, almost photographic retention for everything he has seen or read. Five minutes before a meeting with an author or literary agent, you only needed to give him the briefest summary of a book.

Late one afternoon he called me up. A famous director was interested in doing an adaptation of Dickens's *Bleak House.* "Read it and give me a synopsis; we are meeting him tomorrow morning, and I want to seem as though I've read the fucking book." I had read *Bleak House* but not for years and certainly couldn't remember it well enough to précis it for him. This was the time before everyone had access to computers and search engines; no easy click to do my research for me.

Clandeboye, where Maureen and her sisters grew up,
in Bangor, Northern Ireland. It was built by a pupil
of Sir John Soane in 1801 for the first marquess
of Dufferin and Ava, incorporating
the original 1674 buildings.

My mother with Maureen, c. 1930s

Maureen with her debutante daughters, Caroline and Perdita,
at a coming out ball, c. 1940s

The wild and free-spirited poetess and actress Iris Tree, photographed by her husband Curtis Moffatt in 1933

Ivan Moffatt in Europe at the end of World War II

*My mother with her first husband, Lucian Freud,
on their honeymoon in Paris, c. 1949*

*Caroline modeling
in the 1950s*

*Caroline photographed by
Evelyn Hofer, c. 1950s*

Israel Citkowitz looking rakish on the rooftop of MoMA, c. 1950s

Also on the roof of MoMA, Citkowitz, left, talking to James Dean, center, and Leonard Rosenman, who was writing the score for East of Eden

*My eldest sister, Natalya, giving flowers to Princess Margaret
while Lord Snowdon looks on. Maureen is on the left.*

*A side view of Milgate Park, in Kent, the Georgian house
where we lived from 1968 to 1974*

*Robert Lowell, my mother, Evgenia, and me holding our
pet rabbits on the hallway stairs at Milgate, in Kent, 1972*

Natalya, Evgenia, and me, at age five, with a monkey

My sister Natalya, age fifteen, with monkeys in the 1970s

*My brother, Sheridan, Mum, and Robert
in the drawing room at Milgate*

Caroline and Robert in the drafty drawing room at Milgate

Langton Hall, in Leicestershire, where my mother and I lived in separate cottages behind the main house in the courtyard—one of our more eccentric living arrangements

*The front of Castletown, the Palladian house restored by
Desmond Guinness, in County Kildare, Ireland. Caroline
and Robert lived in the main house, and the children
lived in the right wing in the late 1970s.*

*Caroline walking in the garden of Castletown with Robert.
It was 1978 and the last time any of us would see him.*

*Maureen going in to dinner with the Queen Mother, "the Cake,"
at Maureen's house in Hans Crescent*

*Neal Levinson-Gower with the glamorous Guinness girls at another
Cake dinner. He is talking to his grandmother Eileen Plunkett.
To the right, her sisters, Oonagh and Maureen.*

I am trying to talk to a bored Alec Guinness at one of Maureen's dinners.

*Maureen arriving at Claridge's, with my brother-in-law Julian Sands,
for the Tiara Party Evgenia and I gave her in 1996 on her ninetieth birthday*

Evgenia and I had a sofa set among Maureen's favorite white Casablanca lilies, so she could receive her guests in splendor at her Tiara Party.

*Robert Silvers holding Daisy at her christening
in New York, 1999*

Daisy, age ten, in Long Island

Why Not Say What Happened?

I rushed out to my nearest Barnes & Noble and bought a copy. It was a thick, heavy tome. I got home and desperately tried to skim it to glean all the salient points, but it was Dickens, for Christ's sake, and there were so many plotlines and characters. I knew that even if I stayed up all night reading I would never be able to do the book justice.

I called my brother, Sheridan. "Sher, you've read *Bleak House* right?" Of course he had; my brother has read everything and, like camels with water, he retains everything he has read.

"'Course I have," he replied as though I were an imbecile for even asking.

The next morning I arrived at the Miramax office with a beautifully written (by Sheridan), detailed synopsis of *Bleak House*. Harvey read it in about two minutes and swanned into the conference room to meet with the producer and director. During the meeting, not only did it seem that he had read the book several times himself, but, more impressive, he would put his own spin on the material and give incisive suggestions on how it would work cinematically.

One morning I was late for a meeting in his office with a group of America's top book publishers. While they waited, I learned later that Harvey had turned to the assembled group and joked, "Yeah, Ivana will probably arrive in a gown straight from some fucking ball!" He was constantly asking me to invite Royals to his movie premieres even though I had told him a million times I hardly knew any, and that I doubted the Queen Mother was going to fly over for the event.

In the beginning, while I was working in the book division, I had no contact with Harvey's younger brother, Bob. I was a little frightened by the idea of him. He was said to be the brains behind Miramax and a genius at the financial side. I had the impression that he thought the book division was a waste of time and money. Whenever I passed his office, right next door to Harvey's, I would scuttle by hoping he wouldn't notice me and question what I was doing there.

Harvey telephoned me at about nine o'clock one evening. "Meet me and my brother at Elaine's in half an hour. Bob wants to learn more about Miramax Books." Oh no, I panicked. He's going to want to see numbers and projected profit margins, and God forbid if he asks for receipts because I never kept any. I gathered up the latest mock book jacket and our "list" for the fall catalogue and then raced over to Second Avenue to Elaine's.

Harvey and Bob were sitting at the same table where I had been sitting the night we had first met with Don Boyd. Bob looked extremely uncomfortable as Harvey introduced us, and I noticed he had kept his black overcoat on as if to make a quick getaway. As I sat, Harvey announced he had to leave immediately; he had an important meeting. Bob looked horrified. And I gave Harvey a desperate look. "Don't go," we exclaimed in unison. But he was already out the door.

We sat in silence for a few minutes, and then I began nervously babbling about the book division and how well it was doing. I was convinced he was about to tell me that Miramax Books was not a viable proposition and that my services (such as they were) were no longer required. But he just let me rattle on and seemed, if anything, rather perplexed by my hard sell. Eventually he told me that he had no interest in the book division. "That's Harvey's thing," he said. "Have fun with it."

At last I realized why Harvey had summoned me. It wasn't to talk about books. Bob had just come out of a difficult divorce. He had been living in hotels and had just moved into a luxury rental on the Upper East Side. He was feeling displaced and lonely. Harvey thought because I was "social" in New York I would be good for Bob to know. Perhaps I could introduce him to some new people.

Once we had a few drinks, and I realized I was not on a job audition, I relaxed. Bob and I started to form a genuine friendship. We were total opposites, but our differences only seemed to cement our friendship further.

Bob was funny and smart and modest about his great success. One thing we did have, though—and our friendship remains intact to this day—is a similar sense of humor and of not quite fitting in. He "got me." And I in a strange way got him.

I called Bob from JFK soon after our first meeting to tell him I was going to London for a few days.

"What are you up to over there, Iv?" He liked to shorten my name, although it's not really that long.

"Oh, just seeing friends and things. And tomorrow night I'm going to my grandmother's for dinner with the Queen Mother." Bob responded immediately with a chuckle. "Okay. You're having dinner with the Queen Mother, and I'm having dinner with my mother from Queens. That pretty much sums us up doesn't it, Iv?"

CHAPTER 22

Every year Maureen gave a black-tie dinner at her house in Knightsbridge for her old friend the Queen Mother. I had been going to this event since I was about thirteen, old enough to know how to conduct myself properly.

And every year the format was almost exactly the same. The only thing that changed was the guests—the deaths during the year of one or two of Maureen's older friends would inconveniently call for a slight reshuffling of the cast. One or two fresher faces from Britain's establishment would step in to replace the deceased.

The worlds of ballet (Sir Frederick Ashton, Dame Antoinette Sibley), theater (Sir Alec Guinness, Sir John Mills, Derek Nimmo, Moira Lister), politics (the infamous John Profumo, Norman St. John Stevas), and the aristocracy (running the gamut from Honorable to Duke)—all convened to pay homage to the Cake, as the Queen Mother was fondly known among her contemporaries. She had been given the nickname after she had attended some grand wedding, and when they announced that the cake was about to be served she had shrieked excitedly, "Oh the cake! The cake!" The name had stuck.

Although she was ostensibly giving the dinner in honor of the Cake, Maureen was competitive with her and envied her royal status. I think my grandmother would have adored nothing more than to be addressed as "Your Majesty" or "Your Highness" and to be constantly bowed and curtsied to. Maureen was also miffed and resentful that the Queen Mother did not reciprocate her generosity with as many invites back for dinner at Clarence House as she would have hoped for.

Why Not Say What Happened?

Every year my sister and I would arrive early, supposedly to help Maureen get ready. But it was really to allow Maureen to inspect us. She needed to make sure our appearances were suitable for the royal gaze.

Once we had passed muster, we would wait in her overheated bedroom while she readied herself for the great evening. Her bedroom was decorated in hand-painted silk wallpaper from China. Tropical birds flew over multicolored fields of flowers, and this design was echoed in the chintz on the curtains and bed fabric. Maureen would sit at her mirrored Art Deco, kidney-shaped dressing table and put on her face. There'd be a slash of red lipstick, a dab of loose face powder. She'd then comb her polar-bear-white, bobbed hair into a silver clip shaped like a hand, and she was done.

Maureen had great style. Perhaps it might be best described as Drag Queen Meets Aristo. Although she had some "good stuff," my grandmother far preferred gaudy fake jewelry. Usually she chose something amusing and slightly risqué—earrings festooned with monkeys in questionable poses, large peacock-shaped brooches, and enormous necklaces strung with colorful glass balls. She wore these all together over bright Chinese silk pantsuits or vintage Hardy Amies taffeta ball gowns.

Wherever you went with my grandmother, she would unfailingly be noticed. People always knew she was a "somebody." She had to be in order to carry off that look of hers with such confidence.

She loved to tell a story about when she was visiting New York in the 1960s. She was staying at the Plaza Hotel and had spent the day on Fifth Avenue shopping. "I had a car and chauffeur, of course, but when I tried to return to the hotel there were crowds and crowds of people and police barricades. They were refusing to let anyone near the hotel. I ordered my driver to pull up as close as he could. We were stopped by a young police officer and I rolled down my window. He told me no one was allowed through because the popular band the Beatles were staying there. 'Young man,' I said as I peered at him incredulously through my spectacles, 'I am the Beatles' mother!' He was so in awe, he whisked me right in."

MY GRANDMOTHER had bright blue eyes that were sharp and unforgiving. She hid these behind her signature blue, cat-shaped diamante eyeglasses. The spectacles covered up most of her heart-shaped face and were tinted just enough for her to see out but shielded enough for her keen, penetrating gaze to go unnoticed.

She always carried a large bag. Her favorite, of which she owned several in different colors and patterns, became her trade-mark. It was shaped like an upside-down lampshade. "The bucket" was studded with pear-drop rhinestones that formed animal shapes; I remember an owl, a horse, and a snake.

You never knew what she was going to pull out of the bucket, but once she began to rummage inside, you knew some kind of practical joke was about to emerge. It was a habit she continued late into life.

On the night of the Cake dinners, once her preparations were complete she would give her Pekingese a slobbery kiss on its mouth, then we would descend the five flights of stairs down to the front hall to await Her Majesty's arrival. The hall, normally dark and depressing, was lit up with candelabras and decorated with enormous floral displays. Maureen's faithful American sec-retary, Sally, fussed around excitedly, taking photographs and peeping out of the front door to see if there was any sign of the royal Daimler.

Why Not Say What Happened?

Finally the car would pull up and the Queen Mother, accompanied by the Duchess of Grafton, would enter. My grandmother would curtsey elaborately and the two women would exclaim over each other's outfits. "Ma'am, you remember my granddaughters Evgenia and Ivana." Down we would bob.

"Of course, aren't they charming," she would gush each year.

Then came the highlight of Maureen's evening—alone time with the Queen Mother. She would grip the Cake's arm territorially, and steer Her Majesty up to her dressing room for a little tête-à-tête. I have no idea what they talked about, but every year the ritual lasted exactly half an hour.

My sister and I would join the other guests in the main drawing room, where the usual cocktail hour banter was taking place. All eyes were kept on the door in anticipation, but Maureen was not going to let her moment of glory go unnoticed. The two grand old ladies would pause for several minutes in the doorway with requisite drama before they made their entrance.

They both were small in stature, nearly the same size, but as they came into the room their combined presence was enormous. My grandmother looked radiant, her expression always triumphant as she clung to her prize.

Maureen had already decided whom she was going to favor that year, and once she had settled the Queen Mother comfortably in an armchair she would grab the chosen one and lead him or her up for an audience. Every year she would warn whomever she was introducing, "If I see Ma'am looking distracted for one second, I will swoop in and bring up someone else. You mustn't be greedy with her!"

My mum found the evening to be simply ghastly. She couldn't bear to watch her mother's sycophantic behavior and blatant snobbery. She also loathed being back under her mother's forever disapproving eye, once again being transported back to the world she had been so determined to escape.

As she grew older, the Queen Mother seemed to take on even more importance in my grandmother's life. It was the high point of her year. She became increasingly hysterical about planning the evening, making a million calls about arrangements. She would phone our house endlessly to check on what we were going to wear and to warn us about tardiness. "You know you absolutely cannot arrive after Ma'am," she would lecture for the millionth time. "Her Daimler has special parking privileges in the front spot outside of Number Four. If you arrive late the police will simply turn you away!" As if I hadn't heard that before.

My mother, in the end, just refused to go. Her relationship with Maureen had never been "all right," as she put it. But now it was impossible. My mother also resented the fact that I would go. "You are just sucking up to her because you are as snobbish and repulsive as she is," she told me one year just as I was leaving the house. "Don't think that she loves you. She isn't capable of any love but self-love."

She would make up improbable-sounding excuses as to why she couldn't attend, and each year they would become more implausible. One year she said she had contracted "parrot fever." Her "symptoms" began about a week before the dinner. She said she had a high temperature and felt absolutely ghastly. She complained she felt weak and lost her appetite for everything except (funnily enough) vodka. I knew my grandmother was relieved. Her worst nightmare was that my mother would get drunk at one of these dinners and disgrace the family.

The Queen Mother was always charming and seemed to enjoy herself at these dinners. If she realized that she was there mainly to quench my grandmother's never-ending thirst for attention she didn't appear to mind. Her own more literal thirst was sated by her vigilant attendant. She had a fondness for a particular cocktail, gin and Dubonnet, which she would imbibe throughout the evening. When she required replenishment she would simply give a gay little laugh and tilt her empty glass slightly over her right shoulder. In an instant her man would appear with a cocktail shaker and, as though performing a subtle magic act, discreetly refill her glass.

Throughout the dinner everyone's eyes would dart toward where the Queen Mother was sitting. If she turned and began talking to the partner on her right, protocol required we all follow suit, even if we were caught in midsentence. When she turned, a sea of black ties and tiaras would turn with her; it was as if we were watching an absorbing tennis match at Wimbledon. Often I would be happily chatting away, and my dining companion would roughly nudge my leg. "Turn," he would hiss, and I immediately had to start fresh with whomever was on my other side.

One year I was next to Sir Alec Guinness. He was very prickly to talk to, but I was absolutely starstruck. He was, after all, one of the greatest actors of his generation. I had watched *Kind Hearts and Coronets* many times, in awe of his performances as the various scheming family members battling to get their inheritance. My grandmother had sweetly seated him next to me in the hope that he could "help get you a part in acting."

Alas, while Ma'am seemed entertained by whomever was seated to her left, Sir Alec seemed excruciatingly bored by me. His wonderfully droll expression, used to such effect on stage and in the movies, didn't seem half so amusing when it was directed at me. We were uncomfortably between courses, and I couldn't think of anything else to say to Sir Alec. He seemed intently focused on his bread roll.

"So, how are we related, Guinness-wise?" I finally asked, hoping some bright familial banter might cheer him up.

"We are not," he snapped. "I am not that type of Guinness!"

After that I gave up. I quaffed another glass of wine and wondered how long it would be before dessert was served.

Sometimes, if my sister and I weren't in Maureen's good graces that year, if we hadn't written a thank-you letter for something, or gone to tea with her enough times, we would be invited only for after dinner. Various friends of hers would give their own dinner parties around London, and then everyone would converge at her house about 11 p.m. I actually preferred these dinners. They were more relaxed, and the wine and food was better and more plentiful. Maureen, even for royalty, was never a generous hostess. But these alternative dinners were definitely meant to be a downgrade.

The first year my brother, Sheridan, was invited (as an after-dinner-only guest), he was about fifteen. As usual the ladies left the men to enjoy their port and cigars at the long Louis Quatorze dinner table, and Maureen would accompany Ma'am back to the drawing room, where the after-dinner-only guests would be waiting. This enabled my grandmother to make her second entrance arm in arm with Ma'am.

Sheridan was the first person she introduced Ma'am to after dinner, and he became completely flustered. He didn't know whether he should shake her hand, bow, or curtsey. So instead he kissed her. A proper, full-on kiss. My grandmother was horrified, and there was a moment of absolute hush in the room. His strange behavior was tantamount to treason, practically a hangable matter.

The Queen Mother reeled back a little and then dissolved in a giggle. She turned to Maureen. "Charming!" she announced, and then she moved on looking a little flushed.

CHAPTER 23

One particularly annoying aspect of being sexually abused or traumatized as a child is that everyone wants you to talk about it. "The only way to get over the trauma," my psychiatrist said, "is to relive both the burning and the abuse. Talk about it as though it were occurring at this precise moment. That is the only way you can come to understand that it wasn't your fault."

"I already know it wasn't my bloody fault," I said. "And why on earth would I want to go through something again that was so horrible the first time?"

Anyway, the one good thing about pain—I mean the deep, searing pain that I experienced when I was burned—is that you cannot reproduce it. It is a memory of agony, but not a physical one. It would be intolerable if one's nerve endings and memory were in tune.

As an adult I do recognize that what happened to me wasn't my fault, yet guilt and shame were still part of the fallout from that accident. And, like my burn scars, they are almost impossible to remove. But someone else's pain is almost harder to bear.

I WAS STILL LIVING in London the first time my mother became ill. She was staying in a hotel in Holland Park when she started having ghastly stomach pains. "I think I may have something rather serious," she told me weakly over the phone. My mother, like so many of us, hated going to the doctor, and so she rarely went. She was of the school that, if you don't know about it, it doesn't exist. So when she made the appointment with our old family doctor I knew there must be something really wrong.

A series of tests revealed she had cancer. So far it was mostly in her bladder, and she would need to have an operation to have the organ removed. After that, she would have to wear a catheter and urine bag for the rest of her life.

She took this news quite calmly. She had never had much vanity, and so, although she thought this sounded fairly undignified, it wasn't the end of the world for her. I checked her into a private room in a hospital in Charing Cross to await her operation.

As soon as she was sedated I hurried out as fast as I could. I had such a loathing of hospitals, having spent so much time in them, just the smells and the sight of all those brisk white coats everywhere made me feel ill. I told her I would come back straight after the operation.

The next day I called the hospital to see what time my mother could be visited, but I had a hard time getting information. There seemed to be confusion as to what ward she was recuperating in. Finally I just went over. There had been some kind of mix-up. After her operation she had been taken to the National Health ward. This place was quite a different story from the expensive part of the hospital where she had previously been. No clean private rooms with en suite bathrooms and bouquets of flowers. She was in an overcrowded ward packed with moaning patients. The noise and smells were intolerable.

I eventually tracked her down. She was lying crumpled under one of those small and scratchy hospital-issue blankets. She looked so tiny and frail. Next to her was a stainless steel post and hooked onto it was her urine bag. The sight was so pathetic. I wanted to cry, but I didn't want to let my mother see my shock.

"I don't know what's happening." Her huge eyes looked up at

me sad and frightened. "No one has been near me for hours. I haven't had anything to eat and I am freezing. I think I have been forgotten." I went searching for her doctor but the place was so chaotic; no one seemed to know anything or where to find him.

After sitting alone with her for what seemed an eternity, I had had enough. I felt we were both getting ill just by being in the place. "That's it! Come on, Mum. I am getting you out of here!" We managed to unhook her tube and bag half-filled with urine from its steel rod, and I got her dressed. Fortunately she had been wearing blue velvet leggings that fitted loosely over her bag. Her bag dangled down the side of her right leg.

I was terrified as we tried to walk nonchalantly out of the ward. I felt as though I was running away from school all over again. But no one seemed to care or to try to stop us as we left the hospital. We stepped out into the rain and drabness of busy Charing Cross Road. Mum was cold, hungry, and frightened. I hailed a black cab and told the driver to take us to Soho.

We went straight to Wheeler's, her favorite fish restaurant in London. It is where she had held her wedding reception after her marriage to Lucian. It was under much different circumstances that we arrived this time.

The maître d' greeted us in his usual effusive manner. "How lovely to see you, Lady Caroline." He pretended not to notice, but we must have looked such a sight as he escorted us to our table.

I gripped my mother's right arm and supported her. Slowly we made our way past the tables of well-dressed diners tucking into their oysters, potted shrimps, and dressed crab. The restaurant is a great favorite among the English upper classes; they feel at home with the wood-paneled walls and reproduction paintings of Stubbs's horses and hunting prints.

We didn't mind that we were attracting rather a lot of strange stares from the other customers. The room was warm and cozy and delicious smells were wafting from the kitchen.

We ordered a bottle of champagne and lobster thermidor. As we settled into our red velvet banquette, a peculiar look appeared on my mother's face.

"I think my bag needs emptying," she whispered. "It would be too awful if I had an accident in here. Don't you think?" I agreed that it would.

We hobbled down the stairs to the ladies' room. In the small toilet cubicle decorated in floral Laura Ashley wallpaper, we struggled with her bag. It had complicated valves, which we had no idea how to work. At last I opened the right valve, but it took me by surprise and urine came squirting out all over us.

By this time we were laughing uncontrollably. Grand ladies were coming in and out of the bathroom to powder their noses. Their presence just made us laugh even more. What must they have thought of the guffaws of laughter coming from behind our toilet door? We could only imagine. "This really is too bad, even for us," my mother giggled. "We are such a couple of clowns!" But in the end we managed to get the job done and with great satisfaction returned to our champagne and lobster thermidor.

There we sat, hiding from the world, drinking to numb our pain, pretending that everything was going to be all right. And knowing that it wasn't.

CHAPTER 24

Ⅎll my visits to rehab blur together. I have been to the poshest and to the grungiest. In the fanciest one I was housed in an Italianate villa overlooking a beach in Malibu. We had a personal chef who would prepare healthy meals catering to our individual tastes. Fresh juices would be squeezed to order for us and two daily massages were required as part of the program.

We had flat-screen TVs in our rooms and were allowed to keep our cell phones, to go shopping, and even sometimes to go out to dinner, although we would be with a friendly young supervisor from the rehab to make sure we didn't order any alcohol with our meal. There was a gym with a trainer on hand at all times and the luxurious living room was equipped with a movie screen. Each evening the "guests" could choose what film they wanted to watch.

A celebrity client who was there while I was even brought her nonaddicted boyfriend with her to keep her company. She used a phony name, which was ridiculous as everyone knew exactly who she was, and she never came to the in-house AA meetings or to group therapy. I don't know why she didn't just check into a fancy hotel. I suppose the point was that there was no liquor on the premises, and it would be a bit more difficult than usual for her to have her cocaine dealer come round.

The philosophy of that particular rehab was that addicts and alcoholics are spiritually and mentally sick people. They should be treated with dignity, not punishment.

Of course while I was there I embraced that philosophy wholeheartedly. Far better to play with horses (equine therapy) and have acupuncture than to sit through endless boring lectures on the physiology of alcoholism.

At the opposite end of the rehab spectrum, you are infantilized and treated like a prisoner. Five or six inmates to each grim dorm. Every moment is accounted for. You are summoned to lectures, groups, and meals by bells and an infuriating loudspeaker system. "Meeting time!" it screeched three times a day, and we would all line up single file and trudge to the auditorium. Beds had to be made and rooms kept immaculate at all times. The dorms are inspected daily, and if your bedspread is out of place or a piece of rubbish found in your wastebasket, you are "pigged." The "pig's" name is written up on a blackboard, and you have to pay a fine.

Telephone calls are made on a pay phone and restricted to three ten-minute calls per week. The phones are on timers, and if you go over the allotted ten minutes your call is automatically cut off. This is horrible, especially when you are on the phone to your uncomprehending five-year-old daughter. "I love you, Mummy. When are you coming home?" CLICK!

Everyone is assigned a unit and you are allowed to talk only to those on your unit. Of course fraternizing with the opposite sex is out of the question; it is a crime that results in immediate dismissal.

You would think that being expelled would be a relief. But it's not like that. By the time you get to rehab, most people are desperate. They have done so much damage back home. Robert had a line that my mother and I liked to use—*"You have burned your boats, and now your boats are burning."* Everyone is sick of you. Nobody trusts or believes you anymore. And your own self-respect has disappeared a long time ago.

By going to rehab you are showing a willingness to change. It is a sign of good faith. It is a chance for you to begin to rebuild some of the relationships you have so brutally destroyed through your drug or alcohol use.

People want to see you do your time. They want to see you punished, not rewarded by spending a month in comfort. The tougher it is the better, as far as they are concerned. "You put us through all that suffering and worry. You selfishly chose alcohol or drugs over us. Now you suffer. Lock her up and throw away the key!"

No. Being kicked out of rehab is not an option. Just do as you're told, say all the right things, don't question the rules, and pray that your counselors don't recommend "extended care."

Although the accommodations and food quality differ from place to place, the message is the same. Don't drink; get a sponsor, which is an AA mentor; and go to AA meetings. It sounds so simple and I suppose it is, but it takes at least a month away from the boozing for your mind and body to heal enough to absorb even the simplest messages.

The rules of the rehabs change from place to place. Each facility has its own set. Every rehab searches your luggage and takes away "contraband." Razors, mouthwash, and even your perfume are locked up.

I once was checking in while a young inebriated man (last hurrah) was having his bag searched next to me. He was very affable and cheerful as they went through his belongings. It was only when they discovered in his duffel bag a large ziplock bag full of assorted painkillers that he seemed to sober up. "Hey! Those are mine. Can't I keep those?" he slurred. The technician shook his head and headed to the bathroom. "But I get them back when I get out of here, right?" The young man's voice began to rise in panic. When he heard the sound of the toilet flushing, he suddenly seemed to comprehend the situation. He dissolved into hysterical tears.

A young female "client" passed by and shook her head sadly. "I hid my pills in my diaphragm when I got here. They lasted about a week until they got too soggy," she commiserated.

The places that offer treatment for sex addiction, for instance, are very strict on dress code. No spandex, no low-cut tops or short skirts and shorts. Nothing really that could trigger a sexual urge or fantasy. At one of the places I went to, we all wore color-coded badges that signified what group we were in. The male sex addicts were made to wear signs saying *men only,* and the women, *women only.* This ensured that no one from the opposite sex would try to sit next to them at meals or talk to them.

My first day there I was lost and lonely and I tried to engage another patient in a friendly conversation. He looked furious, pointed to the colored badge on his chest, and marched off in the opposite direction. I felt totally rejected until later when all the codes were explained to me.

As much as patients love to grumble and complain about treatment centers, there is something oddly comforting about being in one. Perhaps that is why I have been to so many. There are some very angry and hurt people outside waiting for you, and for the time that you are in treatment you are able to hide from them all. Your furious spouses, children, debt collectors, disgruntled drug dealers will just have to wait until you are recovered enough to deal with them.

For this reason, the no or very little phone policy makes total sense. In one facility the little telephone cubicle was referred to as the "pain booth" because everyone came out of it either in tears or in an apoplectic rage.

You think that because you are locked up and presumably getting "better," everyone back home will be just thrilled to hear from you. That a few weeks in Minnesota or Arizona or wherever the hell you are can "poof," like some Harry Potter spell, make things all right again. Wrong! Jobs are still lost, marriages over, custody of kids gone, and jail sentences still pending.

A phrase you hear often in rehab is "If you throw enough shit up in the air, some of it is bound to come back down and land on you." While you are away in treatment, you are pretty well sheltered from all the crap you have tossed up. Another one is "Rehab is your bridge back to life." The problem is that the life you are crossing back to doesn't seem all that appealing. No, far better to pull up the drawbridge and stay put.

I was good at being in rehab. Rather like boarding school, it felt safe and uncomplicated. Whether it was high-end or fairly basic, I felt that at least for the time I was there I was okay.

Life didn't seem quite as frightening.

CHAPTER 25

After my mother's operation she returned to New York, and to life in "Condo." But she felt claustrophobic and I think overwhelmed by the city. The streets seemed crowded and manic, but high up on the thirty-sixth floor of Condoland, it was unreal and lonely.

One of my mother's close friends was the successful art dealer and poet Stanley Moss. He had a beautiful house in Water Mill, on Long Island, surrounded on all sides by water. Off-season, we would often spend weekends with him and his wife, Jane. Stanley was an avid fisherman and kept a boat in the nearby old whaling town of Sag Harbor.

My mother didn't care much for boat life. The bouncing and jolting bothered a back injury she had sustained in a car accident many years before. This same spine injury, she claimed, was also what prevented her from being able to drive a car. She said that the driving position was agony for her.

I never believed that. I think she was just nervous about driving. Anyway, the fact that she never drove was a blessing, given the amount of alcohol she consumed.

I too am a bit phobic about driving. If I don't have to, then I'd rather not. This also is a good thing. I have seen too many people's lives ruined (practically everyone in rehab has a horror story) by the lethal combination of automobiles and alcohol.

Mum never wanted to come out on the boat with us, and instead she wandered around Sag Harbor. It had the feeling of a quaint old English village, and she liked the eccentric combination of Gothic Victorian, Italianate, and Greek Revival architecture. It also felt manageable to her. She liked visiting and admiring the ocean views of her friends' houses in more remote locations of the Hamptons, but "Sag" felt safe and cozy. And there she didn't need to drive.

While we were out on the boat, my mother went to real estate agents. She quickly found a broker and she was off. It didn't take her very long. I knew by the tone of her voice as soon as she called me from a real estate office in Sag Harbor that she had found a house. "I think it's rather wonderful!" That sounded familiar. Once we got off the boat, Sheridan and I drove over. The proximity of the handsome house to the main street of the village was also convenient. It was a five-minute totter (or trudge as she called it in the winter) down to the grocery and liquor stores.

While my mother settled into her new life in Sag Harbor, I continued (in a rather vague capacity) to work at Miramax. Once I had begun seriously dating Bob Weinstein, Harvey treated me warily. In fact he hardly came near me. "You're Bob's problem now," he growled when I asked him what he wanted me to do. Bob was equally unhelpful. "I don't have anything to do with the book department; that's Harvey's thing."

Then one day Harvey stopped me in the corridor, "I want you to do a *Like Water for Chocolate* cookbook," he barked. "We are bringing out a special-edition DVD of the movie, and I want to have a book to coincide."

"Okay." I was thrilled to have been given something to do, even though I had no idea how to do it.

Like Water for Chocolate was a wonderful movie based on the popular book by Mexican author Laura Esquivel. Both the book and the film explored the passionate aspects of food, the cooking and the eating of it. Whatever emotion the cook felt while preparing the food is experienced by whoever eats it.

In one memorable scene in the movie, the lead character is

preparing a banquet. She is deeply unhappy while she cooks, and her tears flow into some of her dishes. When the guests eat the food she has prepared, they too become overcome with sadness. The feast dissolves into a mass of men and women hugging each other and sobbing inconsolably.

I had loved the movie, and the idea for a cookbook seemed like a terrific one until I looked at a copy of Esquivel's book. It was described as "a novel in monthly installments, with recipes." The book was divided into twelve sections, one for each month of the year, and each section began with a recipe.

I went back to Harvey with the bad news. "It already is a cookbook," I told him. He flew into a rage. "I don't care if it's already a fucking cookbook! Write another one. Call it a sequel! I want a Miramax book to tie in with the movie. You're in charge of Miramax Books so make it happen." It is pointless to argue with Harvey so I dutifully agreed.

My initial response was panic, but the project turned out to be really good fun. I like to cook, although, of course, I had never written a cookbook before. But my mother, of all people, had. In the 1980s, with a friend of hers, she had had quite a success with one. *Darling, You Shouldn't Have Gone to So Much Trouble* was a collection of very easy recipes that take less than fifteen minutes but seem as though they had taken hours to prepare.

She had written to her friends and asked for their favorite "cheat" recipe, and she had had a surprisingly good response. The resulting book was an amusing and useful little collection, peppered with funny anecdotes and wry illustrations. Lucian had given her his recipe for tomato soup, about which he said that although it did take quite a bit of effort, the end result turned out to taste exactly "like a can of Heinz tomato soup." And Francis Bacon contributed a really revolting recipe for something he called "Workhouse Stew."

I thought that perhaps I could use the same format. I also realized that as I am really disorganized, I would need help. I enlisted my friend Lisa Fine to come and work with me. Lisa is an energetic and stylish Southerner who had worked in magazines and had helped put together several coffee table books. And most important, Lisa loved to cook, and, like me, she loved to eat and drink. She also lived a few floors below me in "Glittery Towers."

We decided that as the movie was all about food and passion, our book should be an aphrodisiac cookbook. We started out using Harvey's showbiz connections and we asked all the celebrities he knew for their recipes. The response was disappointing and we realized that most celebrities don't eat, let alone cook.

Our next approach was far more satisfying and provided us with hours of culinary pleasures. We asked the chefs from restaurants considered the most romantic in the country to give us their sexiest, most "aphrodisiac" recipes. They were more than happy to oblige, and, of course, Lisa and I wherever possible had to go to the restaurants to try their dishes.

To our great delight our favorite (and often the most expensive) foods turned out to be aphrodisiacs. Lobster, caviar, asparagus, artichokes, chocolate, and, famously, oysters are all considered to be foods that put you in the mood for love. Of course, alcoholic beverages of any kind, as Shakespeare said, loosen inhibitions and "provoketh the desire." The Bard also added the caveat that it "taketh away the performance," but no one listens to that part.

Lisa was brilliant at organizing all the recipes and shaping the book, and I had great fun finding quotes about food and love and placing them next to recipes I thought appropriate. We gave the recipes titles such as Hedonistic Hash, Always Game Stew, and (named for my mother) Lady Caroline's Lamb with Three

Byronic Sauces. We ended up with an eclectic little book, which turned out to be quite successful.

AFTER THE BOOK WAS FINISHED, I didn't have much to do, but I still enjoyed going to the Miramax office in Tribeca. I looked forward to the cab ride down the FDR in the morning. As I sped along with all the other New Yorkers going to work, I felt that I had a purpose and a place in the world. The hubbub of the office was also comforting. My cubicle was in the middle of the publicity department and I would listen to the frenetic calls the PR girls made as they organized ad campaigns and press junkets.

I kept myself busy on the phone. I talked to my mother a lot. Then I made my usual round of phone calls to my friends in the city to find out what everyone had done the night before and get all the good gossip. I would arrange to meet someone for lunch and try my best to drag them down to Tribeca.

When Bob had a lull between his meetings or screenings, he would buzz my office, and we would go for something to eat or a Diet Coke. Sometimes I would be buzzed to meet him in the screening room, and I would sit with him and Harvey and their acquisitions or marketing people and watch some movie they had just bought or were contemplating buying.

I remember one grey afternoon, midweek, settling into one of the comfortable velveteen seats in the screening room. Bob was in a good mood sitting next to me and we were joking and laughing about something. As the lights went down and the movie began I thought, I must have the best job in the world.

THE MONTHS AND WEEKS leading up to the Academy Awards were the most frenzied and exciting time of the year at Miramax.

The studio became famous for its brilliant and exhaustive Oscar campaigns. The publicity department worked literally around the clock badgering Academy members, sending them not only movie screeners but books and posters, basically anything they could to get them to pay attention and to vote for a Miramax movie.

The first year I began dating him, Bob invited me to go with him to the Academy Awards. I was excited and flattered that he would want me to go to something so public with him. He had been divorced for a couple of years now but was still very private about our relationship. I didn't get to meet his two daughters until we had been seeing each other for a long time.

Going with him to the Oscars was a big deal. The Miramax film *The English Patient* was nominated for several awards that year, including the big one for Best Picture, so it was an exciting time to be a part of the company.

I went with one of my girlfriends to Bergdorf Goodman to buy a dress for the great occasion. The saleswomen in the evening wear department were thrilled to help me pick out something for such a glamorous event. I think they hoped I might wind up on TV or at least photographed on the red carpet wearing one of their dresses. I tried on about ten dresses; I wanted to get it just right. Not too sexy, as that would look like I was trying too hard. And not too flamboyant. No, I wanted to look sophisticated and elegant in a classic, English way.

In the end the saleswomen, my friend, and I decided that a black dress—although it could be construed as "boring" and a little too "safe"—if original enough, was permissible.

I finally tried on the perfect dress. John Galliano, a fellow Englishman, beloved by the fashion cognoscenti, had designed it. It was made of black organza with a bow neck that draped in a cowl halfway down my back, leaving my skin exposed until just up to the top of my behind. In the front, the dress clung in a flattering hourglass silhouette down to my ankles where it then (Galliano's stroke of genius) fishtailed into a pool of fabric over my feet and onto the floor. I admit I felt wonderful in it, the movie star I had never gotten to be.

The dress was incredibly expensive, but I told myself that this was a very special occasion and that the dress was timeless, something I could wear again and again.

Bob and I stayed in separate suites at the Peninsula in Los Angeles. He used the excuse that he needed to take meetings and have conference calls in his room, but I think he just wanted to have his own space, away from me.

There was something a little off about our relationship; we never seemed able to be totally relaxed and comfortable with each other. I don't know quite what it was, but something always felt forced and uneasy.

Therefore, the separate-room arrangement suited me as well. I was able to order up room service and have my friends to my suite whenever I wanted. I also had sole custody of the minibar.

The days leading up to the actual Oscars are extremely busy for everyone involved in the nominated pictures. There are endless breakfasts and lunches, press conferences, and industry parties to attend. I tagged along with Bob to some of them, but I was happy to be left to my own devices.

I had a few friends in L.A. and once people caught on to the fact that I was Bob's date I suddenly had a million more. People I hadn't heard from in years started calling me at the hotel asking me to get them invited to the Miramax Oscar party. I had never felt so in demand.

The day of the actual awards I went to Bob's mother's room to get ready. Miriam was a fixture at all the Miramax events; she was devoted to her sons, and they adored her.

She had a hairdresser coming to her suite. We decided I should have an Audrey Hepburn, circa *Breakfast at Tiffany's*, swept-up hairdo. I wore very exaggerated black kohl eyeliner, dark grey eye shadow, and bright red lipstick. To complete the outfit, I wore a pair of long ruby and diamond earrings that my grandmother had given me, with a matching tennis bracelet.

I was nervous but excited as I knocked on Bob's door, thinking that I looked pretty fabulous. I waited for his rapturous response.

"What the fuck do you think you look like?" he screamed. "You look ridiculous! You look like an old lady. Your hair looks terrible, and you have on too much makeup. And what the fuck is with that dress? It's much too long! How are you meant to walk down the fucking red carpet in that dress? Didn't they tell you in the store that it was too fucking long? You are not wearing that!"

For a second I thought he was joking, and then I realized he wasn't. I felt sick. It was as though I was Cinderella and the clock had just struck midnight; all my finery—the baubles and the fancy clothes—stripped from me with one cruel stroke. My big moment was desecrated.

I couldn't have felt more exposed if he had physically ripped the dress off and rendered me naked.

I started crying and tried to defend myself. "But it's the design of the dress," I sobbed. "It's how it's meant to look." But Bob was already on the phone. "Get me housekeeping," he screamed to the front desk. "Send someone up right now. And tell them to bring a pair of scissors!"

Two timid-looking Mexican women appeared at the door. "Do you see this dress?" Bob roared at them. "It's too long. Fix it!" Still crying, I just stood pathetically as they tried to hem the dress. But there was too much fabric. "I so sorry," the younger one said to me. "I think we gonna have to cut it." My initial shock was beginning to wear off, and the reality of the situation was seeping in. "Since when did you become such a bloody sartorial expert?" I screamed at Bob. I took the offending gown off and threw it at the ladies. "Here! Take the damn thing! I'm not going anyway." The women hurried off with the dress, and I stormed back to my room wearing a hotel bathrobe. "Enjoy the fucking Oscars," I yelled over my shoulder.

I was shaking when I got to my room. I went to the minibar and opened a split of champagne, which I glugged down from the bottle. I was mortified. And then I became furious. "How dare he? How the fuck dare he?"

My phone rang. "Iv, don't be so silly. Of course you're coming. Hey, I'm sorry. Listen, the dress is back. Please come and try it on." I thought about refusing, I half wanted to tell him just to piss off, but then I thought of the alternative. Staying behind alone in the hotel, watching it all by myself on TV?

Reluctantly I went back to his room. I put the dress on. It looked awful. About four inches of fabric had been cut off from the bottom. It now hung sadly, like a shapeless black pillowcase, down to just above my ankles. The whole point and glory of the dress was gone.

I took the hairpins out of my hair and let my once immaculate chignon down. There was so much spray in my hair it now looked like brown straw. My eye makeup and lipstick were smeared from all my crying. I went to Bob's minibar, took out another bottle of champagne, and said, "Okay, I'm ready. Let's go."

I HAD INVITED my mother's old boyfriend Ivan Moffat to the hotel for lunch the next day. Over the years my mother had kept up a friendship with him and whenever he came to London or New York, or if ever we were out on the West Coast, we would meet for lunch or dinner. I always looked forward to these occasions.

Ivan seemed glamorous and sophisticated. He had wonderful stories about old Hollywood. As a young man he had been part of a group of filmmakers assigned by General Eisenhower to promote the war effort and improve film coverage of the war. The great film director George Stevens was in charge of this unit, the Hollywood Irregulars.

I met him in the hotel restaurant. "You don't look very good," he said with his characteristic bluntness.

I probably did look pretty awful. I was extremely hungover and still full of resentment about the dress. I told Ivan the whole story. He loved it and kept stopping me to press for more details. He seemed to be enjoying the whole thing a bit too much, I thought.

As he laughed at my plight, I remembered my mother telling me how cruel he had been to her when she first arrived in Hollywood, constantly nitpicking at her about her clothes and her appearance. I realized there was a similarity between Bob and Ivan, two men who seemingly couldn't be more different: Ivan, the grandson of the legendary theatrical impresario Sir Herbert Beerbohm Tree, elegantly turned out in his bespoke Savile Row suits and Lobb shoes, and Bob, who wore Yankees caps, T-shirts, and sneakers to the office. Just the night before, Bob had seemed so uncomfortable in his tuxedo, pulling and scratching at his collar like a dog with an itch in some unreachable spot.

Of course it wasn't really about what my mother or I wore or looked like. It was their own deep-rooted insecurities, their own feelings of being "less than." Ivan did a much better job of masking it than Bob. He always seemed charming and supremely confident. And yet even at the height of his career, when he was winning Oscars and being feted by Hollywood royalty, he remained an outsider. The consummate Englishman abroad. He may have been writing screenplays for Elizabeth Taylor and James Dean, but he was still just a writer and therefore very low on the voracious Hollywood food chain.

And Bob should have been basking in the glow of success. *The English Patient* did win Best Picture that year. But instead of enjoying the moment, he focused on what awards they hadn't won and how he "could have done better." Nothing was ever enough.

Throughout our lunch Ivan was critical of everything and everyone. He expressed his disgust at the current movie industry and the "vulgar people" who ran it. He sneered at the hotel I was staying in—"Couldn't you have chosen somewhere chicer than this?"—and complained about his food. "The hamburgers are much better and cheaper at Hamburger Hamlet," he grumbled; his apparently was undercooked, although I heard him ask for it rare.

His bitterness was palpable and he seemed angry and resentful that I had somehow swanned my way into a world that had once been exclusively his. I no longer needed him to show me around Hollywood and introduce me to people. It seemed pointless to remind him, as I was picking up the bill (well, Bob was actually; well, Miramax was; well, Disney was), that he could at least try to be a bit more gracious.

Ivan only cheered up when he told stories of the old Hollywood, a time when he had flourished both in his career and as a man about town. He told me that he had taken my mother to the Oscars the year *Giant* had been nominated for several awards. He said she hadn't really fitted in and that he had felt uncomfortable bringing her. I wanted to stop him and say that perhaps she just didn't want to fit in. I couldn't imagine my mother wanting to impress, or being impressed by, people in the movie industry.

He told me how painfully shy my mother was and that, although part of her wanted to become an actress, the process of auditioning and having to schmooze to get parts was too much of an ordeal for her.

Ivan also told me how, while she was in Hollywood, my mother had volunteered to be a part of a six-week, medically supervised experiment with LSD. She had been introduced to this "treatment" by Cary Grant, who claimed that he had been helped enormously by it. My mother also seemed to have benefited from it. Although she said the hallucinations and dreams she experienced were "hellish," they somehow opened her up and afterward she seemed less self-conscious and introverted.

I told Ivan that I had had a disastrous experience the one and only time I ever took acid. While all my friends were floating around exclaiming how "intense" the colors were and how beautiful everything looked, I sat petrified and frozen in my chair.

I was convinced I was Chinese takeaway. I felt I was suffocating, trapped inside one of those little white cartons. My "trip" seemed to last forever, and I never understood the attraction of mind-altering drugs. Of course I was also scared of drugs after what had happened to my sister Natalya.

Ivan recounted a story—whether to compete with my own or for a more altruistic purpose I didn't know—about his own experience with drugs. Many years ago, while staying at Blenheim Palace, he had taken LSD before dinner. During this grand dinner party, he removed his black tie, announced to everyone in too loud a voice that he was in fact a rat, got under the table, and proceeded to gnaw at the ankles of each guest in turn, before passing out at the Duke of Marlborough's feet, or so he said.

Throughout lunch there was an uneasy feeling. Although Ivan

acted in his usual suave, sardonic way, I felt there was something we both were avoiding talking about. Something that perhaps was just not ready to be aired. I knew that Ivan and my father, Israel, used to play chess together, and suddenly I felt I was involved in a very complicated game with him. I don't think either of us really understood the board on which we were playing and neither one of us was ready to make the next move.

After lunch with Ivan, I flew back to New York. Bob stayed on to do some more business, but I was pleased to be getting out of there. I had had enough of Hollywood.

CHAPTER 26

I was sitting idly at my desk in the Miramax office when my mother called me from her house in Sag Harbor. Her voice sounded faint and weird. "Darling, I am afraid it's back." It was about eleven in the morning and at first I was annoyed, thinking she must be drunk already. "What, Mum? What's back?" I asked impatiently. "My thing. You know. My illness. I thinks it's come back." Suddenly I felt sick. It had been two years since she had had the operation and we had all managed to sort of put it in the back of our minds. We never dared talk about "it," as if acknowledging its existence would somehow give "it" new life.

"I'm sure it's nothing, Mum. It's winter and freezing. You have probably got some kind of fluey cold."

"No. I am afraid not. My doctor out here wants me to see a specialist in New York. He's already sent him the results of some tests he's done on me."

"Don't worry. I'm sure it's nothing. The doctors always do this just to cover themselves so you won't sue them." I didn't know what I was talking about, just babbling; because she sounded so frightened I knew I had to act strong. "Just come in for your appointment and afterward I will take you out for a really good lunch. We can try the new Côte Basque."

My mother had kept her Manhattan apartment but she used it less and less, preferring to hide out in Sag Harbor. She found coming into New York stressful even for fun things, and this trip did not seem like it was going to be fun.

Evgenia was living in Los Angeles so I telephoned Sheridan and told him to meet us at the hospital on the appointed day. He met us at New York Hospital in the waiting area for all the gastrointestinal and pancreatic-type specialists.

Sheridan had been living in the city attending classes at Columbia University. He had become an ardent socialist and was quiet and intense. He looked just like his father, with Robert's square jaw, and he even wore the same kind of eyeglasses. Today he was wearing his usual Marxist student uniform of black beret and leather coat, and he carried some manifesto on socialist reform. It felt comforting to have him there.

We were kept waiting a long time, and all three of us were nervous. You could tell because our jokes were even sillier than usual: praising the "beautiful décor" of the hospital, making fun of the other gloomy patients who were waiting, and giggling every time the foreign voice made yet another completely incomprehensible announcement over the hospital loudspeaker system.

Mum looked scared, almost childlike. The black velvet leggings she had taken to wearing since her bladder operation appeared even baggier than usual, and her hair seemed thinner and whiter.

I remembered the countless times I had sat with her while she held my hand in rooms just like these, waiting to hear bad news about my burns. Now I had become the mother, trying to be reassuring and comforting.

By the time she was actually seen by the doctor we had almost forgotten why we were there in the first place. Sheridan and I waited outside and the doctor called us in just as Mum was putting her shoes back on. I can't even remember exactly what he told us. It seemed the cancer had come back in her stomach and it had metastasized. She was going to need a nice cocktail of radiation and chemotherapy.

What he was saying was all sounding very doctorish and

unpleasant, but he said it in a calm way. When I looked over at my mother she seemed not to be taking it too badly.

He ended his talk by saying, "I am afraid all Lady Caroline's naughty years of smoking and drinking have finally caught up with her." A flash of anger appeared in my mother's eyes.

"Yes," she said. "And I *really* enjoyed them!"

As the doctor was saying good-bye he turned to Sheridan and said, "I was a great fan of your father's work. I studied him in college." Sheridan's only reply was a look of bemusement.

We were almost out the door when the doctor called me back. "Ah, Miss Lowell, I need to talk to you for just a minute. Your mother and brother can just wait in the waiting area." I sat back down again and this time he looked at me with a grave expression. It looked practiced; he must have rehearsed it in front of a mirror—they probably teach it at med school. "I believe in telling it to the family members straight. I don't believe in giving them false hope. Then I leave it up to them to decide how much they want to disclose to the patient. Okay?"

Oh no, here it was again—that same ghastly inescapable moment between the world's seeming fairly all right, and its becoming a total nightmare. I wanted to tell him to shut up and quickly run out of his office before he had a chance to say anything else. But he had already continued. "I'm afraid what your mother has is terminal."

It had now become a scene in a movie, one that we have all watched a thousand times. "Oh, and how long does she have, Doctor?" "A year. Perhaps two, with aggressive treatment, but what we are looking for now is quality of life. We want to make sure that the time she has left is as comfortable and easy as possible."

Mum and Sheridan both looked nervously at me when I came

out of the doctor's office. "What did he say? Was it really bad?" I felt so odd, so guilty. Why did I have to have this knowledge? I didn't want it. Why couldn't I have been lied to as well?

"No, Mum, it was about your insurance. All these people want is to make sure they get their money. He was worried because you didn't have your insurance card. Typical you. Now, let's go and have lunch."

AND THEN WE WERE in the world of the ill. A place where the only things that seem to exist are doctors and hospitals and people who have gone through the same thing. Concerned friends ask stupid questions: "Have you got a good doctor?" You are tempted to make some facetious reply: "Hmm, a good doctor. Nope, never thought of that one. We just thought we would use the local vet."

Suddenly everyone becomes an expert, everyone has a miracle cure. "There's a bark that's only found on certain trees in the Amazon jungle. If you extract the sap and make tea out of it, it completely gets rid of all the cancerous cells in your body."

My mother adapted to the role of dying patient rather well. She achieved a Zen-like calmness and listened to every piece of advice she was given. She refused the chemo and radiation. "Darling," she told me, "it might give me a little more time, but what's the point if I am going to feel absolutely ghastly?"

It was November in New York and we were having terrible blizzards. The snow made it hard to get around and impossible to get cabs. I would struggle over to her apartment on the East River to pick her up to take her to yet another doctor or specialist for more opinions. We often had to walk long blocks in the snow with the wind whipping our hair and burning our faces.

By the time we arrived anywhere, our faces were wet, our black eyeliner smudged from our tears. The weather gave us a good excuse for our wet faces, although we both knew our eyes were streaming from despair.

I don't remember who introduced Cathy Guccione to my mother, but after they met my mother's medical care changed completely. Cathy was the dynamic wife of *Penthouse* magazine founder Bob Guccione. She was South African and had been a dancer. She had helped Bob start up *Penthouse,* and she also ran some health magazines, one of them ironically titled *Longevity.*

A year and a half before, Cathy had been diagnosed with stage three breast cancer. She had been told she had only a few months left to live. Not being one to give up easily, she had fought it with everything that her connections and money could get her.

Cathy had become an advocate of a non-FDA-approved drug, hydrazine sulfate. Cathy had been taking hydrazine for the last year and felt that the fact that she was still alive and seemingly doing well was because of it. She had published numerous articles in *Penthouse* about the drug, and she was convinced that there was a conspiracy among the big drug companies to keep this drug underground because it was cheap and apparently so effective.

CATHY ADOPTED MY MOTHER and took up her cause. I was so exhausted I didn't mind handing over the reins. Cathy was not only full of suggestions and ideas and solutions, she also had a car and driver, which made our lives much easier. Endless packages of food and vitamins and gift bags filled with things designed to pamper oneself, such as body lotions and massage gloves, would be delivered to the apartment. All things my mother wouldn't use in a million years, but I liked them.

Cathy immediately persuaded my mother to change hospitals

and go to her doctor, the appropriately named Dr. Payne. The first thing he said was "I am God. I am here to manage your life and death—I can make sure that you will never have any pain." We loved hearing the no pain part, although the God bit was alarming.

My mother had been feeling worse and worse. Her stomach was completely distended and she was hardly able to eat anything. She couldn't even drink alcohol except, as we had discovered over a Japanese lunch, a small amount of sake. What was more disconcerting for those who knew her well was that she didn't even want to drink. I bought her cases and cases of the fattening and nutritious vanilla-flavored Ensure. She loathed it but tried to keep it down.

Cathy was hooked up to a portable morphine machine, which she carried around with her everywhere. It made funny whirring noises and whenever she needed another shot she just pressed a button and received an instant boost. Dr. Payne fitted my mother with the same machine, which she adored. She was quite proud of it and was endlessly giving herself little fixes.

Once, Cathy was sitting on the bed next to Mum chatting away. They both had their little boxes sputtering away beside them. I noticed my mother was getting agitated and looked in pain. She started pressing her button more violently. Cathy meanwhile seemed to be getting loopier and more expansive. I suddenly burst out laughing. "Mum, you're pressing Cathy's box!" All three of us dissolved into fits of laughter, the kind you have only in the most macabre situations.

WE MANAGED TO HAVE one last Christmas together as a family. We spent it out in Sag Harbor: my sister and her husband, the actor Julian Sands; Sheridan; Mum; and me.

Why Not Say What Happened?

The weather was particularly beautiful and my mother's beloved garden was coated in a thin layer of snow. For once, there was no quarreling about the food or her drinking. She was unable to eat but made a valiant attempt to participate in the ritual. She didn't, though, try to play Santa that year.

My sister was pregnant, and that made my mother happy but also a little sad. She really hoped she was going to be able to meet her first grandchild yet was doubtful that she would. She had always said that she wanted to hear "the pitter-patter of tiny feet" around the house. I felt guilty that I hadn't had a child yet. It suddenly seemed incredibly important.

My mother now wore a startled expression, one of disbelief. She looked youthful and beautiful again. Her enormous eyes were far clearer than they had been for a long time and her manner was sweet, almost apologetic.

All Christmas long I kept trying to make the most of every moment. I wanted to be able to cherish the seconds, hoping that I could somehow suspend if not thwart the inevitable. Every so often Mum would take Evgenia's hand or Sheridan's or mine and just grip it. She still wore her gold wedding ring and Robert's gold wedding ring and a silver ring I had made her in jewelry class when I was about twelve. She never took them off. Our last Christmas, in a strange way, was one of the best Christmases we ever had. It was calm and loving, without any of our usual family histrionics.

After Christmas we would normally go down to St. Bart's in the French West Indies. My mother and I had visited it once and she had then got instant "houseitis" and immediately bought an apartment. St. Bart's was conducive to her writing, and there was one particular café where she would sit for hours with her notebook and café crème.

I had hoped that possibly we could still go. Surely the weather and ocean swimming would be good for her. But she was much too ill. Although I kept telling her that after a few more rounds of tests and hospital visits I would somehow definitely get her there, instead we stayed in wintry New York.

Cathy thought that she had convinced my mother that hydrazine was the miracle cure. I don't think Mum believed it for a second, but she liked the whole conspiracy theory about the drug industry. It also was much less of an ordeal than radiation or chemo.

Cathy picked us up in her car and took us to the "Penthouse Mansion," a double-width town house just off Fifth Avenue on East Sixty-seventh street. The house was cavernous, artificially lit, its marble rooms decorated with Greek Revival pillars and pornographic statues. Bob Guccione appeared from behind one of the columns. He was a small, energetic man and spoke quickly and effusively about the wonders of hydrazine. It was touching the faith they both had in its powers; the expression *clutching at straws* came to mind.

"And now, Lady Caroline, if you don't mind, I will personally do the honors. I give Cathy her injections every day and she hasn't complained so far!" My mother looked at me nervously, but she nodded in dubious agreement. "I'll give it to you in the behind, seems to work best." He produced a needle and a vial of medicine and made a great show of filling and flicking the needle. Mum looked horribly uncomfortable as she pulled her leggings down and I was struck by the thought that we were in the house of two completely crazy people. I felt if we had tried to leave, half a dozen hefty goons would have appeared to stop us. The injection was quick and seemed to be painless.

Cathy offered us a ride home but Mum said she needed the air. When we were outside, relieved to be in natural light again, Mum turned to me and asked, "Was I imagining it, or was that all rather odd?"

CHAPTER 27

I'm afraid I have had a bit of a blow." It was early in the morning and the phone had woken me up. "They keep taking my months away. They say I have only a few weeks left." Mum was calling from Mount Sinai Hospital. She had been admitted two days before for some more tests.

"Hold on, Mum, don't worry. I am coming right over. Don't move!" As though she was going anywhere. I telephoned Sheridan and told him to meet me at the hospital. As I was leaving, Bob Weinstein phoned. I was hysterical, and he told me to calm down and that he would meet me at the hospital. He sounded cross, as if somehow we were all being incompetent.

Mum was sitting up in her bed. Her skin was now a jaundiced yellow and her face seemed to have shrunk. Dr. Payne was standing next to her. He looked smug. He told Sheridan and me that he had woken Mum up that morning and told her, "Lady Caroline, I suggest that in the last few weeks you have left to live you go home and take care of your affairs."

I wanted to strangle him. What affairs? My mother had never taken care of anything practical in her whole life. She was certainly not going to start now at the very end. Mum just stared pathetically at us, trying to gain some comfort.

Then Bob arrived. He was wearing a well-cut black cashmere overcoat and looked important and strong. I had never been happier to see him. I told him what the doctor had just told us and he went berserk. He insisted on getting a second, third, and fourth opinion. He demanded to see the head of the hospital. He wanted to make Dr. Payne pay for being so insensitive.

Bob also seemed cross with Sheridan and me, as if we had

been inept and that somehow it was our fault things had gotten so bad.

Sheridan and I just sat there. I was shivering, in some sort of shock, I suppose. I let Bob take over. He found out the name of the supposed best oncologist in New York and made an immediate appointment with him. Sheridan, Bob, and I marched straight over to his Park Avenue office.

I remember our sitting across from a kindly man while he explained patiently why there was nothing anyone could possibly do for my mother. He had seen the X-rays and all her test results.

The oncologist was a Trekkie and his desk was crammed with *Star Trek* memorabilia, little figurines of Captain Kirk and models of his starship, *Enterprise*. While we were in his office, he took several calls. In all of them he seemed to be saying the same thing: that radiation and chemotherapy could buy the patient a little bit more time, but perhaps the quality of life would not be good enough to make it worthwhile. One conversation he had was with the parents of a young girl; I think he told us she was only nine. He was trying to be as positive as he could on the phone, but what he was saying was very bad. Bob looked at him and asked him how he could do a job like that. Why didn't he crack up at the end of every day? He just smiled and said, "Because sometimes I can offer hope and that is better than nothing."

After we left the doctor's office even Bob was defeated. We went to a pizza place nearby because we couldn't think of anything else to do. I never eat pizza if I can help it; it just doesn't appeal. But that ice-cold, late-January day, Sheridan, Bob, and I sat in silence, shoving the hot cheesy dough into our mouths.

After that Bob, who was always extremely family oriented, took over ours in an extraordinarily kind way. Mum obviously couldn't go back to Sag Harbor; she would be too isolated.

Why Not Say What Happened?

Bob arranged a suite for her at the Mayfair Hotel on Sixty-fifth and Park. It was grand, with wood-burning fires in every room, a large sitting room, and two bedrooms. Bob sent his car to pick her up from the hospital and bring her to the hotel, where her bedroom was already full of flowers and gifts and cards from friends who had heard what was happening. We arranged round-the-clock nurses for her and specified Irish ones as my mother felt their accents and manner would be comforting.

Evgenia and Julian arrived from Los Angeles and took a suite of their own just down the hall. Evgenia's pregnancy was putting a terrible strain on her back, and she limped around in agony.

And there we all camped out, trying to be as cheerful and helpful as possible. We adopted our own roles. Julian was log and injection man, seeing that the fires in the hotel rooms were always lit and also administering Mum's daily hydrazine shots. I, of course, was in charge of the champagne and food, making sure that every visitor was given a large glass and offered something to eat. Evgenia, having always been the most tidy and organized member of our family, made sure that the maids kept everything clean and that the nurses had whatever they needed to ensure our mother's comfort. And Sheridan bought Mum her newspapers and magazines and sat holding her hand and reading articles or pieces of news he thought would amuse her.

She had a constant stream of visitors. And then just as we had all settled into the routine, we received an announcement that my grandmother was arriving. When we told Mum she didn't say anything. She just rolled her eyes and gave herself another boost of morphine.

My grandmother flew in on the Concorde, and arranged to stay in another suite on the same floor as my mother. She arrived at the hotel wearing a floor-length mink and with so many suitcases in tow that I wondered how long she was planning on staying. To the bitter end perhaps.

When we first took her into Mum's room, Mum pretended to be asleep, but Maureen settled into the chair next to the bed and finally my mother had to feign waking up. She also tried her best to seem as though she was pleased to see her mother. I could tell that Maureen was shocked at her daughter's appearance. We all had become used to her skeletal body and mustard-colored complexion, but my grandmother was visibly upset.

We left them alone in the room and they talked for a surprisingly long time. They hadn't spent any time together for years, and I have no idea (although my sister and I did try to eavesdrop at the door) what they talked about. But when I saw my mother later that evening I got the impression that she was secretly glad that my grandmother had come.

I had forgotten how demanding and spoilt my grandmother was. I had hoped that under the circumstances she would be less selfish than normal, but she still wanted to be "cherished," and because of the situation, she expected us to be more attentive to her than ever. My sister used the excuse of her pregnancy to get her out of Maureen duty and my brother just played vague, so it fell to me to ensure that she didn't feel neglected.

I didn't know how I was meant to entertain her. I showed her how to work the hotel in-house movie system in her room and she seemed amazed and pleased by it. Like every other English visitor, she was fascinated by the number of channels you can get on the TV in America.

I arranged for a shopping expedition together with my friend, the brilliant young writer Andrew Solomon, and his great-aunt Bea. Aunt Bea was as demanding and spoilt as Maureen and an immediate rivalry struck up between them. Aunt Bea was a couple of years older than Maureen—I think she was eighty-six—which she felt gave her the upper hand.

We took the two ladies to Bergdorf's in a chauffeured limousine. Upon arrival, we arranged for them to be wheeled around the store. They both sat regally in their voluminous mink coats and complained bitterly about everything—the store, the quality of the merchandise, and especially about each other. The trip was a nightmare. I couldn't believe we were wasting our time shopping, when Mum was dying back at the hotel.

Maureen's visit to New York didn't last long. I know that she was glad she had made the effort, but after she had had a few little goodbye chats with Caroline, she felt there was nothing else for her to do.

When she had left to go back to London, my mother told me that my grandmother had asked her to seek out all Maureen's old friends and relatives up in heaven. "Please make sure, darling, that when I get there you will organize a wonderful party for me. We will have so much fun!"

THE MAYFAIR HOTEL became headquarters for operation "Lady Caroline Dying." My sister got angry with me because she felt I was allowing too many people to come and visit. "It should only be our inner circle, Ivana, you're turning it into a circus." But Mum seemed to enjoy the attention, and I felt that her friends and a lot of mine who had come to love her, or at least be fascinated by her over the years, really wanted the chance to say good-bye. For me, the whole situation was unreal. I started drinking round the clock just so I wouldn't really have to acknowledge what was happening.

The morphine made her sleepy and she would doze off for

long spells day and night. She said when she nodded off she "went to Morocco." I had been there with my mother and Sheridan and we all had loved it. Mum had particularly liked the bright colors of the flowers, houses, and souks. She had adored the blue that Yves Saint Laurent had used in his famous garden in Marrakech. So when she said she went to Morocco I sort of understood what she meant and I knew she was having a pleasant time there.

Because she was sleeping and waking at weird hours, actual time had no relevance anymore. I slept when I could, napping in the spare room, and Sheridan, Evgenia, Julian, and I would take turns sitting by her bed.

We wanted to make sure there was always someone there in case she should wake up and need something, or simply wanted to talk. We all felt the need to tell her how much we loved her, something that didn't come naturally to a family usually embarrassed by outward displays of emotion.

Every day Dr. Payne would breeze in to give us an update. One day he brought in X-rays of Mum's stomach. He held them up to the window and seemed to relish pointing out the numerous black holes. "That's the cancer," he said. "Looks just like Swiss cheese, doesn't it?"

There was a lot of talk about her bilirubin count. I never quite understood what that was. Julian called it her Billy Baldwin, referring to the actor. "How's her Billy Baldwin today, Jeff?" he would tease Dr. Payne.

My sister was right about its all becoming a bit of a circus. The presence of my friends and the members of our family who came to see Caroline did create a sort of party atmosphere. When Mum's rooms became too crowded, everyone would disperse (or be ushered away) to the plush, circular hotel tearoom and bar. At any time a group of them would be downstairs, drinking and smoking and talking about my mother. They would wait for me in case I needed to get out of Mum's suite to talk or cry—or have a drink. The situation was one of such heightened intensity that I remember laughing much harder than I normally would have.

One day the singer Marianne Faithfull came to visit. My mother had known her for a long time and had even written a song that Marianne had sung on one of her albums, appropriately titled "She's Got a Problem."

Marianne was giving a concert in New York and arrived at my mother's bedside wearing tight leopard-skin trousers and a black leather jacket. She was extremely ebullient (maybe even a little unnaturally so), and she sprawled across my mother's bed, dislodging all her tubes and causing her to wince.

There were already a number of visitors in the room and so Marianne had an instant audience. "I am going to sing for you, Caroline," she announced in her famous cracked, deep voice. She then rose up on her knees on the bed and starting singing, loudly, "Surabaya Johnny, I loved you Johnny, surabaya Johnny, I hated you Johnny." She then changed the lyric to "Surabaya Caroline, we all love you, Caroline, but now it's time for good-bye." She then kissed my mother and wiped the tears from her own face. "I really can't bear long good-byes, my darling," she announced theatrically, and swept out of the room.

After she had gone, everything was silent for a while; no one knew quite what to say. During the entire performance my mother had just sat upright with an expression of total amazement. She finally looked around at all of us sitting and standing at the foot of her bed and sounding perplexed but in a strong voice, asked, "Was that rather wonderful or was it really, really awful?"

Lucian Freud telephoned. My mother looked slightly surprised, but she took his call. I don't know how many years it had been since they had last spoken. We left her alone and they ended up talking for a long time. We could hear her, through the door of her room, laughing, and she suddenly sounded young and girlish. After that Lucian called her often.

She told me that he had explained to her why she "went to Morocco" when she slept. He said that morphine originated in Morocco and she was just going back to its roots. It was a completely mad explanation. I don't think morphine comes from Morocco at all, but my mother seemed delighted with his theory.

Mum reconnected with all her old lovers. Bob Silvers visited nearly every day, bringing books she might like. And Ivan Moffat telephoned her often.

One of my mother's closest and oldest friends, the writer Anna Haycraft, flew over from London to be with her. Anna's husband, Colin, owned and ran the small London publishing house Duckworth, which had published my mother's first books. Under the name Alice Thomas Ellis, Anna had written some very successful novels, and she also had a regular column in *The Spectator*. Anna, like Mum, loved to smoke and drink, and she often came over to the flat in Redcliffe Square for dinner. She would stay late into the night and never once did they actually eat any dinner. Vast quantities of "vod" was drunk and tons of "ciggies" were smoked, but not a morsel of food was ever consumed.

The one topic my mother and Anna disagreed strongly on was religion. Anna was a strict Catholic. She had contributed to *The Tablet* for a while and wrote columns on religion for numerous British publications. My mother was completely irreligious. She didn't believe in any type of God or the power of prayer, or in anything at all remotely ecclesiastical. She couldn't understand her friend's extraordinary faith.

When Anna came to visit Mum on her deathbed, she asked

her if she could read from the Bible and my mother adamantly refused. "It would just be too hypocritical of me to suddenly pretend to start believing now," she told her.

Anna had brought a flask of holy water that she had especially blessed for Caroline in Lourdes. When she thought Mum was sleeping and far away "in Morocco," she sprinkled the water all over her head. My mother sat up as if she had been stung. Shivering, she said crossly, "That will be the death of me!"

DURING HER LAST FEW DAYS, my mother was unbelievably sweet and considerate. She never complained about anything, and even though we knew she was very frightened she tried to not let her children see it. "I just can't believe I am not going to be here anymore," she said to me, matter-of-factly, and I knew exactly what she meant. It is too odd a concept to contemplate.

"How will I know that you are all right? Do you promise you will be all right?" she asked me. She seemed to want assurance desperately. I promised I would, but I didn't feel or sound very convincing. I wasn't at all sure that I would be all right, in fact I knew I was going to be far from all right, but I didn't want her to know I felt that way.

It was Valentine's Day, of all things. New York was sunny and the streets were full of men carrying bunches of red roses and chocolates for their loved ones. I left the hotel just to get some fresh air and maybe buy a magazine or two. Bob Weinstein had stayed the night (or rather grabbed a few hours of sleep) to keep me company, and he and my brother were sleeping when I got back to the suite.

The night nurse told me that my mother's breathing had slowed. When she did exhale, a ghastly choking crackle came out of her mouth. She was permanently in Morocco now. Her room had the sick, sweet smell of deterioration. Her face was solid yellow and seemed to have caved in on itself. Now when I held her hand, although it was still warm, I knew my mother had gone. There would never again be any little jokes between us, never any laughing about us being a "couple of clowns." This really was "too bad even for us," and yet I couldn't share it with her.

Her hands felt bony and small. I grasped her fingers and looked at her rings. I didn't want to ever let go. Her hands felt so familiar, loaded with thousands of memories of experiences and moods and reminders of all the different reasons why I had held them throughout my life.

The nurse said that her organs were shutting down. Like lights in a house. The kidneys, the liver, the lungs, and of course the heart.

WHEN SHE HAD STOPPED BREATHING for good, we opened the window in her room. It's an Irish tradition to let the spirit of the dead fly out. It was such a beautiful clear cold day that I thought my mother wouldn't mind going out into it. Certainly it wasn't as balmy as Morocco, but I thought that under the circumstances a bit of fresh air may have been a relief.

It was decided that she would be cremated at Frank E. Campbell. I couldn't bear to go to the cremation. Julian and Sheridan tried to describe it to Evgenia and me. We had bought her a nice coffin. Not the really really fancy top-of-the-line mahogany one with all the brass trimmings but a solid, dignified, middle-range affair. Handsome, and we hoped comfortable, but not ostentatious.

My brother and Julian wondered if we had been swindled. They joked that as soon as the casket disappeared behind the curtain, the undertakers had quickly taken Mum out, put her into some old cheap pine box to burn, and kept the good one to use again. I thought that Mum wouldn't have minded, really. I mean, as she was into recycling and saving the forests and our planet, she probably would have approved.

Julian gave me one of Mum's rings, the one I had made for her. I was confused at first. "But Mum never takes it off . . ." Then it sank in. And then I cried.

CHAPTER 28

I had Chinese food for dinner the night my mother died. Because it was Valentine's Day, Bob felt he should take me out somewhere nice. I had no idea of what I was supposed to do or what was appropriate. I had no desire to do anything; actually, I thought I probably wouldn't have the desire to do anything ever again. We went to Mr. Chow.

Mr. Chow is an upscale, expensive, and fashionable Chinese restaurant in midtown Manhattan. I used to like the food there, which is a shame because I can never think of it now without feeling overwhelmingly sad and sick.

Bob and I sat in silence as I pretended to chopstick up my fried seaweed and chicken soong. The rest of the restaurant was full of couples drinking champagne and trying to seem as though they were enjoying the most romantic night of the year.

I remember looking at the smiling faces, listening to the noise of excited chatter and laughter, of glasses clinking, and smelling the rich, spicy aroma as trays of Peking duck were whisked round the room. The restaurant felt so alive, so vibrant, and yet it seemed impossible and so unfair.

Only a few hours ago the world should have officially stopped. All the lights should have gone out, all sounds been muted, and life extinguished altogether.

I wanted to be with my mother again, the two of us laughing about the dark side to everything—"Every silver lining has a cloud." Now she had some really good material to work with. We would have made stupid jokes about the last few months, about the hospitals and her visitors, about Cathy Guccione and her injections. "HA! Well, she was wrong, wasn't she?"

She would have laughed about Dr. Payne and his Billy Baldwin, and at the sweet incompetence of her Irish nurses. I especially wanted to have her wry observations about the funeral home and her cremation, and her death, "too bad even for us."

A group of friends of mine were sitting right near our table. They looked surprised to see me out and about when they knew my mother was so seriously ill. "How is your mother?" one of them asked. "Oh she's great," I answered. "She died today." I wasn't being sarcastic; I meant it. She was "great" because she wasn't in pain anymore, and she wasn't frightened and miserable. She didn't feel abandoned and angry and hurt at being left behind. She wasn't wondering how and if she would ever get through this.

MY MOTHER WANTED to be scattered. She asked me to scatter some of her in the garden of the house in Sag Harbor and some in the grounds near the lake at Luggala in Ireland. She had always adored her aunt Oonagh's house and considered the whole property one of the most beautiful places in the world. There is a white monument there, a pagoda-like mausoleum, on the grounds next to the lake's beach.

Three of my mother's cousins are buried there. My mother's aunt Oonagh's children, who all had died tragically young (the Guinness curse), lie underneath those slabs of marble.

It is an extraordinary spot, magical really, a huge, deep lake stretching as far as you can see, nestled in a valley overshadowed by mountains covered in thick black forest and ominous, mossy rocks.

It is the perfect setting for a Tolkien story. In fact, it has been used as the location for numerous films. In one movie, John Boorman's *Excalibur,* there is a scene where the Lady of the Lake rises out of the water triumphantly brandishing King Arthur's sword. The lake at Luggala is perfect casting.

As I am describing Luggala, I realize that I still haven't fulfilled that part of my mother's wishes. I have had endless (of course rather drunken) conversations with my cousin Garech, who owns and lives at Luggala, about the scattering. He is very keen for us to do it and has elaborate ideas for the occasion, complete with Irish musicians, poetry readings, and a tree-planting cere-mony. But like a lot of plans made in Ireland, there has been more talk than action.

We did, however, manage to get Mum out to Sag Harbor. The morning we were to leave there was another huge snowstorm and the roads were all but impassable. I thought that we should delay the journey. I knew how long it was going to take us if we made it at all, but my sister and Julian were determined that we should press on. They had been away from their house in Los Angeles for a while and with my sister's pregnancy on top of everything else, they were longing to get back home.

Mum's ashes were in a wooden box about the size and shape of a large cigar humidor. When we first got into the back of the limousine we all behaved extremely deferentially toward it. We respectfully gave it a good seat and made sure that Mum was secure and comfortable.

The journey turned out to be "one of the worst." Our driver had never driven to Sag Harbor before, and he took us some bizarre route. It didn't help that there was practically no visi-bility and that cars and trucks were sliding into one another ahead of us.

About three hours into the normally two-and-a-half-hour trip, our driver made a pit stop at a garage to relieve himself. By this time Mum's box was no longer being treated with the respect it initially had been and had even become a source of irritation. We put it on the floor so we could sleep on the seats, and Sheridan used it as a footstool.

Another frustrating hour went by, and when I peered out of the frosty window to see which exit we had gotten to on the highway I noticed that all the signs were reading New York City. The driver had gotten confused and turned the wrong way out of the gas station. Now we were heading straight back to the city.

The atmosphere in the back of the car became unbearable. We were all exhausted from trying to deal with our emotions and the need to absorb the shock of the last few weeks. My sister and brother and I started arguing about the most petty things. All the frustrations and emotions that had been building up could no longer be squelched and came spewing out in nasty accusations and personal attacks.

We each had had our own ways of coping during the last weeks. My brother, always quiet and bookish, had tried to be as helpful and solicitous as he could be toward Mum. The situation seemed to confuse him. Though he was trying his best to be "Manly" (the nickname my mother and I had given Robert when he was trying to act "macho"), he seemed completely overwhelmed.

My sister has always been the efficient and pragmatic one. She couldn't stand the general chaos and untidiness that our family left in its wake. She was constantly cleaning up, dealing with ashtrays and empty glasses. She would often take a brush to dirty surfaces around our houses for hours, as though she could scour away all the stains of her upbringing. During the last few weeks she had been a model of efficiency, trying to put Mum's affairs in order, as Dr. Payne had advised Mum to do.

I know my sister reproached me for my more laissez-faire attitude. She felt I was being frivolous, not acting somberly, using our mother's dying as an excuse for drinking and generally having a party. And perhaps I was, but that was the only way I knew how to respond. Whenever something bad happened in my life I tried to hide my pain behind jokes and frivolity, trying to entertain everyone.

The back of the limousine began to feel like a coffin of our own. We were trapped inside it, being suffocated with grief and guilt. Guilt about the mixed emotions that we still felt toward our mother and the frustration at realizing that we would now never be able to address any of our feelings.

It was late and dark by the time we got to the house in Sag Harbor. When I walked through the front door I wasn't prepared for the sheer raw emptiness that permeated the house. Everything was both exactly the same as before and entirely different. Now every piece of furniture, all the old, tattered books in the library, and every photograph of all of us at various stages of our lives, seemed to belong to another time. The house itself had become a piece of history, of the past.

On the coat rack in the hall was an assortment of coats and hats and scarves belonging to my mother. On the floor there was a pair of shabby gold ballet-slipper-type shoes. My mother had wide feet and had always found it hard to get shoes that didn't hurt. Years ago she had discovered some cobbler and he had made these specially for her. I remember how excited she was by her new footwear. "It's like wearing butter on my feet," she had told me excitedly. Now the sight of them was unbearable, they seemed so pathetic and neglected.

We had planned to scatter her as soon as we got to the house, but when my brother and sister were upstairs, Julian took me aside. "I just had a look and it seems that your mother is more chunks than ashes." He took me over to her box and took out a thick inelegant plastic bag. Instead of the fine powder I was expecting, there was a mass of semi-ground-up cartilage and bones. "Don't tell your sister, she's already so upset, but there's no way we can scatter this stuff. Especially in the snow, it's just going to land in messy clumps on the lawn."

We changed our plan and decided to bury her box in the garden. But this proved to be more difficult than we had expected. We chose a spot at the far end under an old pine tree that had served as our Christmas tree one year and that my mother had replanted. We thought she would enjoy the peace and shade. But digging the hole took forever. Poor Julian and Sheridan hacked away for what seemed like hours using small gardening trowels and trying to make a dent in the frozen ground.

When they had dug a hole big enough to accommodate the box, we finally put her in. We found some stones that looked suitable and placed them around the little makeshift grave. The four of us stood in the snow and tried to think of something fitting to say for the occasion. Julian said a prayer, although we knew Mum would have hated it. And that was that—she was gone.

PART
FOUR

CHAPTER 29

They say that after a major loss or shock you should not make any big decisions or changes for at least a year. But after my mother died I had no idea what to do, where I should go, or what the point of doing anything at all was anymore.

I knew I had been very close to my mother, "unhealthily so," some people, including my sister, had warned me. But I wasn't prepared for the absolute, icy cold feeling of bereftness, of suddenly being a stranger in my own life. Nowhere seemed safe or normal or recognizable anymore. I no longer had any sense of home, because in her own shambolic, heartbreakingly inadequate way, Mum had always been home.

SHE LEFT THE HOUSE in Sag Harbor to me. She had told me she was going to because I was the one who lived in New York and would use it. I had already spent so much time there that I knew both its quirks and the eccentricities of the team of people who helped her run it.

But I couldn't face going to that house. I didn't want to be in New York anymore either. I didn't know where I wanted to be. I didn't want to be anywhere, in fact. Yet I packed up and went back to London. The job at Miramax had been put on hold while my mother was ill, and Bob and I didn't know where, if anywhere, our relationship was going. He was continuously blowing hot and cold, and I was in no state to be able to deal with his moods and needs.

London seemed like as good a place as anywhere to be. I had all my old and close friends there. And of course there was my grandmother, still a very large and alive presence.

LONDON DID FEEL FAMILIAR, slow, and manageable in a way that New York never does. I rented an overly decorated flat in a redbrick garden square; the drawing room opened out onto the leafy communal gardens. I had never lived anywhere so genteel and normal. One of my closest friends in New York was an Englishman named Mark Simpson—handsome, sympathetic, and comforting. He had worked for a long time at Buckingham Palace, as a "companion" to the then teenage Prince Edward. After that he had drifted around the palace in various roles.

He was living at the palace when Prince Charles announced his engagement to Lady Diana Spencer. Mark was always telling me fascinating stories about how badly the Royals treated the future princess. She was given her own set of rooms in the palace before the marriage but was hardly allowed to leave them or have any visitors. Mark said Prince Charles would abandon her there on her own, and she would just be sobbing with loneliness. Mark and Diana used to spend every evening watching rubbishy television shows. "I would drive off in my little Mini and pick us up takeaways from the McDonald's in Marble Arch and sneak them back to her at the palace. One evening Prince Charles caught me sitting next to Diana on her bed and was enraged. But she just seemed so in need of company."

Mark showed me the letter that Princess Diana had written him later on. It was written in girlish handwriting and was very sweet and simple. She said that those evenings with him had been some of the best fun she had ever had—before and definitely since her marriage.

I would learn firsthand the kind of comfort he must have provided her. When Mark decided to move back to London from New York, I invited him to come and live with me. Because of all his training at the palace Mark was the dream flatmate. He kept everything absolutely spotless and was a wonderful cook. In the mornings he would silently prepare a perfect breakfast tray for me: thin slices of toast, a pot of Earl Grey tea, and fresh orange juice would be waiting for "Madam," as he loved to call me.

We settled into the most comforting routine, like an old married couple without the annoyances of any sexual tension. If "Madam" was dining in, then Mark would prepare cozy meals of shepherd's pie or roast chicken.

We gave cocktail parties together and Mark recruited all his old butler friends from the palace to serve everyone elegant canapés and drinks. It was very funny in a way—so unlike me. My friends couldn't believe the transformation from the sloppy drinks and squalid surroundings of our house in Redcliffe Square.

My grandmother of course adored Mark. "Pansies make absolutely the best companions," she always said. She called him Marcoush for some reason, and he would often go over alone to her house in Hans Crescent on Sunday nights to have a glass of sherry, watch *Antiques Roadshow,* and gossip about the royal family. He actually seemed to enjoy it, and it meant that I didn't feel guilty about not going myself.

For a while, things trundled along nice and smoothly. I still had no clue what I was doing with my life, but I settled into an easy rhythm. I found a very sympathetic therapist. I told him I was worried that I drank too much. He told me that that was nonsense. He said I was just a very good person whom some bad things had happened to; once I worked out my issues, all my depression and the drinking would go away. Of course I loved hearing that. He was giving me the ultimate cop-out and permission to carry on.

AT LEAST ONCE a week I would go over for lunch at the Chester Square house of the Southern American socialite, Marguerite Littman. She had been a close friend of my mother's—they had once shared a house in California when my mother was out there trying to be an actress.

Marguerite is pretty, petite, vivacious and extraordinarily funny. She is always immaculately dressed and knows everyone, especially famous people. She taught Elizabeth Taylor how to talk "Southern" for *Cat on a Hot Tin Roof*. She had been a very close friend of "Tenaahsee" as she pronounced the famous playwright's first name, and she worked on many of his plays and the movies that were made of them.

Listening to Marguerite tell a story you have to fill in the blanks because she just assumes you know who she is talking about. "Ah was having lunch with Rock [Hudson] at the Bel Air when Betty [Lauren Bacall] stopped by with Bianca [Jagger]. We all were dressed in Bill's [Bill Blass] clothes and going to go to a party Sam [Spiegel] was giving for Liz [Taylor] and Elton's [Elton John's] AIDS charity."

It's hard to keep up with her stories told in that infectious wonderfully Southern drawl, but she is captivating and able to laugh at herself.

There's a story she loves to tell about how she was sitting with Tennessee Williams by the pool at the Cipriani Hotel in Venice one afternoon, when an excruciatingly thin girl walked by. "Oh my God!" Marguerite exclaimed, "That's Anorexia Nervosa!" Tennessee turned to her in admiration and said, "Gosh, Marguerite, you know everyone!"

Marguerite had also been a very close friend of my mother's brother, Sheridan Dufferin. My uncle seems to have been universally adored. He was handsome and funny and clever and charming. He was also a wonderful mimic and a very good tennis player. Sheridan had extraordinarily good taste and when he married his wife, our distant cousin Lindy Guinness, the two of them, much to my grandmother's consternation, transformed Clandeboye into a haven for their artist and decorator friends.

My uncle started an art gallery with his close friend John Kasmin in the 1960s, and it soon became the most fashionable place to show and be seen. David Hockney was one of his discoveries. Tragically, my uncle died of AIDS when he was still very young, in the early eighties—further proof that the Guinness curse was still alive and kicking. The newspapers made a fuss of his being the first member of the House of Lords to contract the disease, but I am sure there were far more who were just not brave enough to admit it.

After he died, Marguerite was so upset she decided to set up her own AIDS charity. Back then it was still a disease with a stigma. No one wanted to go near it, just as they literally did not want to touch anyone who had it.

Marguerite had no such qualms and plunged headfirst into fund-raising. Her great friend Rock Hudson had also been ravaged by AIDS and so she galvanized all her Hollywood connections into doing something for the cause. She immediately roped my mother and me into helping out. This consisted of our going over to Chester Square for lunch and then afterward taking several bottles of champagne into a back room where she had established a makeshift office.

My mother and I were not very good at fund-raising. As we

never talked or understood much about money or business, we had no idea what to do. "Call our cousin Benjamin Iveagh; he's really rich," I would urge my mother.

"Oh, but I couldn't. I haven't seen him in ages. I wouldn't know what to say to him," she would reply. And then add, "Why not call that rich banker you once dated?"

"No, Mum, I told him to piss off. I couldn't." We were pathetic. But as the champagne emboldened us and as we listened to Marguerite's charm-filled encouragement, we managed to get the hang of writing pleading letters and making begging phone calls.

My mother had of course been devastated by her younger brother's death. "You never think that they will go before you. I always think of us as children scampering around Clandeboye," she told me in tears.

Marguerite's AIDS Crisis Trust would soon become one of the biggest and most fashionable AIDS charities in the world. The Princess of Wales became its honorary chairwoman. She personally donated not only a great deal of her time but also some of her most famous dresses to be auctioned off for the cause.

AFTER MY MOTHER DIED, Marguerite took me under her wing. Her house in Chester Square became a welcoming second home to me. Her husband, Mark Littman, is an eminent queen's counselor in London and spent long hours at his chambers in the City of London. I would go over to lunch with Marguerite and stay well into the early evening with her and whatever assortment of guests she would have assembled that day.

Marguerite has a man who works for her named Victor. He is what would be described in P. G. Wodehouse as "a treasure." Victor is charming and polite, and he takes meticulous care of Marguerite and her husband. He is also an exquisite chef and

Marguerite is famous for having some of the best food in London.

One afternoon the phone rang and the familiar voice of Marguerite purred over the line. "Hi, Vaanaah, can you come for lunch tomarra?" I said of course—one of my favorite recreational pastimes was having lunch over there, and I was already thinking about Victor's fluffy, cloudlike cheese soufflé. Then she added, "Ivan Moffat's over here from L.A. and ah know he would lurve to see yoooo." And she hung up.

I felt an immediate wave of dread. I remembered the strange feeling I had when I had last seen him. A feeling he was playing some kind of game with me, a game I didn't know the rules of and probably wasn't interested in playing anyway.

I had just been beginning to feel a little bit okay with my life. Things were going quite well in London. I had just bought a beautiful flat in Onslow Gardens in South Kensington, and I had started seeing the man I was later going to marry.

No. Everything was really not so bad. Only I now had a feeling that seeing Ivan was going to upset me. I considered calling Marguerite back and making up some excuse about why I couldn't come to lunch. But then I thought of Victor's food, and I decided I was just being silly.

After all, Ivan was an old friend of Mum's, and even though he could sometimes be difficult I had known him my whole life. He was a friend of the family. It might be quite nice to see him again.

Nonetheless, I was still feeling nervous the next day as I rang Marguerite's bell and waited for Victor to open the door. As I went up to the second floor, I self-consciously checked my appearance in the mirror. I could hear voices and I wondered how many people she was having today. Ivan was popular and he didn't come to London often so I knew there were a lot of people who wanted to see him.

When I walked into the long drawing room, however, Marguerite was standing next to the lit fire with her usual glass of champagne in hand. Only Ivan was sitting on the white sofa, smoking a cigarette and clutching a glass of beer.

He jumped up when he saw me, and Marguerite bustled over to the white-tableclothed drinks table to get me my champagne.

Ivan looked older, and a little bit seedier, than when I had last seen him. His face was still handsome and intelligent, but he was thinner, as was his grey-white hair. He was always beautifully dressed, but today his suit seemed a little bit shiny from too much use and there were flecks of dandruff on the shoulders.

He looked pleased to see me and beamed his slightly mischievous, captivating smile at me as we hugged and kissed each other's cheeks. Marguerite seemed nervous, but then she always did. Ever the consummate hostess, she buzzed around the room making sure there were enough logs of fragrant wood burning in her fireplace—even though it was spring, she kept a fire lit—and that the sticks of her adored Aqua de Palma incense were not spilling off too much ash. She called down to Victor to bring some caviar.

Both Marguerite and Ivan told me how well I looked and I was pleased because I knew from Mum that he always noticed (and cared very much) how one looked. In fact, I was trying to make an effort. I had been to the hairdresser that morning and I was wearing a new blue-and-white polka-dot Marc Jacobs dress. I felt I looked pretty and was gratified that it wasn't going unnoticed.

"It's just the three of us for lunch today." Marguerite announced. "Ah just thought that would be nicer, don't you?" We both agreed with polite acquiescence, but I did think that it was a bit strange because usually it was a full house at Marguerite's table.

Victor came in with the caviar served with all the requisite bits, chopped egg white, onions, blinis, toast points, and wedges of lemon. He offered us little glass shots of vodka, which I was tempted by but declined. Ivan teased Marguerite and told her that this was all frightfully common, and that all good caviar really needed was a spoon. Then he greedily scooped up a large mound and popped it into his mouth.

I had two glasses of champagne upstairs and was feeling relaxed and hungry. The three of us sat underneath the blue-and-white-tented ceiling of Marguerite's dining room. Victor served us plates of warm artichokes stuffed with crab salad. It was one of my favorite dishes of his, and I had included the recipe in my aphrodisiac cookbook.

I had only managed two mouthfuls before Ivan turned to me and put his hand on mine and said in his deep upper-class gravelly drawl, "Darling, there is something we really have to talk about." Marguerite jumped up out of her chair and muttered something about having to go and consult with Victor in the kitchen. I instinctively recoiled and pulled my hand out from under his.

"You see, I am fairly sure I am your father. Caroline made me promise that I would never tell you. But now she's dead, and, well, it hardly seems fair not to say something. I am very proud to be your father, darling. I hope you don't mind."

I wanted to run out of the room, but I felt stuck in my chair. I wasn't sure my legs would support me anyway. I wanted to say a million things, but no words came out of my mouth because I couldn't think of exactly *what to* say.

Ivan was looking at me and his face seemed concerned and expectant. I think he hoped I was going to burst into tears of joy and cry, "Daddy." After all, he had lived and written in Los Angeles for so long, I think he imagined a sugary Hollywood scenario for us. We would hug and waltz off hand in hand into the sunset, father and daughter reunited at last.

Instead I downed whatever wine was left in my glass. When I was able to speak, I said, "I don't believe you." I allowed myself a dramatic pause and then continued, "And even if it is true, I don't care. It's too late. Don't you see it's too late? I hardly know you. I don't know if I even *like* you." Now tears were streaming down my hot face, but they were most definitely not the joyful ones he was hoping for. He looked sad, pathetic really, and he tried to take my hand again, but I felt repulsed.

"I don't believe you," I repeated. "And I want to do a DNA." My voice was hard and I knew I was hurting him but I didn't mind. I wanted to hurt him. I wished I were a man and could have punched him and knocked him out.

"Well, darling, of course I will do the DNA if that will make you feel better. But I am fairly certain it is true. Why do you think you were named Ivana? When you were born, Caroline even phoned to ask if it was all right if she called you after me."

This was getting worse and worse. Now he was suggesting my mother had been in on the plot. I wanted to kill her too, if she hadn't already been dead.

Ivan realized how upset I was and tried to calm me down. "You see, Caroline left Israel for a period during their marriage, and she came back to me. You have to know that we loved each other. You were born and made out of love."

Oh no! Another wave of nausea came over me. This really was sick-making, "too bad even for us."

He continued. "But although we loved each other very much, we couldn't live with each other. I also believe that Caroline felt that Israel would be a better father for you. You had your two sisters, and Israel agreed to bring you up as if you were his own child. Of course I always wanted to say something to you, but Caroline was absolutely adamant that I never tell. And you know how Caroline was."

I suddenly felt very tired. This was all far too much to absorb and I still didn't believe it. I certainly didn't *want* to believe it. But then why would he lie about something so important? My mind felt overcrowded with a million questions.

I thought of Evgenia and how close we were and how much alike we looked—and on Dad's (Israel's) side, not Mum's. We were both dark and Slavic looking, with wide faces and prominent high cheekbones. I couldn't have got that from Ivan.

I couldn't bear the thought that now Evgenia and poor Natalya were not my full sisters. It suddenly seemed incredibly important to me that they were.

The rest of that lunch passed by in a confused haze, as though I were sitting there anesthetized, as though breathing nitrous oxide in the dentist's chair. That unreal feeling where you know that what is happening to you is incredibly painful, but fortunately you can't feel it. You also know that it is going to hurt like hell later.

I just kept gulping down glasses of wine, trying to dilute the reality of what Ivan had said. I remember that Marguerite came back to the table and attempted to salvage the rest of lunch by being her chirpy and normal self. I snapped at her because I felt she had set this trap for me. I felt that she was in cahoots with Ivan in this dastardly plot to complicate my life.

The truth was, I was furious at my mother. I felt such a sense of betrayal and hurt. The world didn't seem safe anymore. I was catapulted back to the place where no one could be trusted. Where adults lied to you and molested you and almost killed you with their carelessness—a world of excruciating pain and fear. I had always sensed that nothing was quite what it seemed. Now it seemed all my suspicions had been confirmed.

Even if Ivan turned out not to be my father, the fact that he believed he could be was bad enough. The fact that he had voiced the unspeakable meant that we could never go back to how we were before. I didn't know my mother had left Israel to go back to Ivan—why didn't she tell me?

God knows I am the last person to be a moral arbiter. I certainly wouldn't have judged her. Why wouldn't she have trusted me enough to tell me? I thought we told each other everything. I certainly told her, well, perhaps not everything, but damn near. I couldn't believe she could have lied to me about something as important as this.

After lunch, Ivan offered to share a cab with me and drop me home, but I made up some excuse about having to go to Sloane Square to run an errand and said that I wanted to walk. I couldn't stand to be in his presence for a moment longer. I also really did want to walk. I wanted to walk for miles and miles to get away from him and from what had just happened.

I ended up walking home. I was still a bit drunk from all the champagne and wine and I felt like I was floating down the street, like one of those cartoon ghosts made out of wispy sheets, flimsy and bodiless.

We had left it at our awkward good-bye, standing on the steps of Marguerite's house, that Ivan would do the DNA as soon as he got back to California—although the more I thought about it, the less certain I was that I wanted him to. I wasn't sure what purpose my knowing would serve me. Talk about an identity crisis. I had gone along to lunch thinking I was the product of a naturalized American, Jewish, Polish musical genius, and now God knows what I was.

I WAS VAGUELY AWARE of Ivan's background. Aside from the fact that his grandfather was the famous theatrical impresario Sir Herbert Beerbohm Tree, I knew that Sir Herbert had also founded RADA, the Royal Academy of Dramatic Arts. I recalled that they had turned me down. I was among the final six in the audition process, but rejected nevertheless. And then I thought, maybe that's where I got my acting genes.

Evgenia played the piano beautifully and was musically gifted. I had always enjoyed singing and playing jaunty piano pieces from musicals and easy to listen to composers such as Scott Joplin and Nöel Coward. But my sister was serious about music and had studied piano with the highly respected teacher Natasha Spender, wife of the poet Stephen. There was always an intensity and concentration in my sister's playing. She would rock back and forth, to and fro, making strange facial gestures, as though the music had taken over her soul. I envied her her talent and wondered why I hadn't inherited such musical ability from our father.

Now it was all beginning to make some sort of horrible sense, yet at the same time it didn't feel right. There were too many missing pieces. Why did I not feel the slightest connection with Ivan? I thought you were meant to have some sort of instant empathy, a Hallmark card moment where suddenly everything falls into place and you feel that you are home at last. I wasn't experiencing any of that. I just felt unsettled, abused, and confused. As though some creepy alien had just come and tried to take over my body and identity.

I thought about Bob Silvers and all the rumors I had heard over the years about his being my father. I hadn't taken much notice of them, but now all the comments his old friends from his *Paris Review* days had made—remarks that at the time I thought were just playful and teasing—came back. At the *Paris Review* book parties given by George Plimpton, George and Peter Duchin would exchange glances when I was talking to Bob; then they'd comment on how we looked a lot like each other, silly remarks that I hadn't taken seriously at the time.

Since Israel was dead, and Robert was dead, and my mother was dead, and now Ivan was claiming paternal rights, I thought perhaps it might be quite nice to have a living parent. But not Ivan!

After Robert had died, Bob Silvers had been the most paternal person in my life. He was the one who had taken an interest in my education and had helped me with my acting career. He regularly sent me presents when I was growing up. Bob had been constant and kind. And now I began letting myself have little hopes that perhaps he was my father. I respected, trusted, and loved him.

CHAPTER 30

Two days after that lunch at Marguerite's I was driving down Pall Mall with my boyfriend, Matthew. I had of course told him what had happened that day, and he was as angry and confused as I was. He had never met my mother and was trying to understand the complicated world I had grown up in. He was from a solid Catholic family. They went to church regularly, did traditional things like golfing and fishing, and had roast lunches after church on Sunday.

He had had the "normal" things that I craved as a child, and yet Matthew ended up with me and was somehow as damaged and even more addicted to substances than I was. But when I met him and started to date him, he was twelve years clean and sober. He was adamant about his sobriety, and I thought he would be a good influence and some sort of rock to attach my needy limpet-like self to.

Matthew and I had been to lunch in Soho and were chatting away in the car when we saw a man standing on the corner outside the Davidoff cigar shop, looking for a taxi. It was one of those wet days in London when all the taxi drivers shut off their For Hire lights and go home and have tea.

"Oh my God, it's Ivan," I said to Matthew. "Quick, I have to hide." I scrunched down as low as I could in the car seat. Matthew said, "But look at the poor man, he is getting soaked. We should stop for him." But I said, "No, no, drive on, I can't face him right now." Matthew accelerated and we drove off.

Two days later Marguerite called me. "Hi, Vanah, I have bad news. . . . Ivan's in the hospital; he's been in a hit-and-run accident. He's really bad. He's in Chelsea and Westminster Hospital.

I think you should go see him. I know he would particularly love to see yoooo."

My first reaction was of complete guilt and panic. "When did this happen? Where?"

"It happened two days ago," said Marguerite.

I immediately was imagining the scene, Matthew and I cavalierly driving by and then—boom! He's hit and run down by some maniac in the West End of London, and it's all my fault.

Marguerite continued, "He was having dinner with a friend in Fulham, and he stepped off the curb and some driver just hit him and sped off."

I was relieved that at least it hadn't been the afternoon I had so selfishly ignored him, but I was worried and still felt guilty. I went straight to the hospital. I now felt a tremendous concern for his welfare. We still had to do the DNA. He couldn't die on me now. I didn't want him to be just another unanswered part of my history.

I arrived at his hospital bed bearing the traditional sad-hospital-visit grapes and flowers. He looked awful—his face was purple, swollen, and bruised. He was unconscious. I felt a surge of sadness, not just the pity that I had expected to feel but something much more.

How do you describe looking at your "possible" father lying in a hospital bed and not knowing whether to love or hate him? He was also the man who was the keeper of the keys to my identity, and I didn't know whether I even cared anymore.

When he woke up and saw me he grinned his charming, lady-killing grin. I joked that the hospital setting was a very convenient place to do the DNA. He said, "But when we do the DNA they said they needed to take a photograph of me. I'm afraid I am not feeling my most handsome or father-like best to be photographed right now." We both laughed and that was nice.

I realized then that he was as confused and upset as I was. It was not just my identity that was at stake but to some degree his as well. He himself wasn't sure if he was my father, and he was very possibly as ambivalent as I was. Maybe the thought was even repellent to him. I knew he felt that my mother could easily have been leading him on, offering little teasers to keep him entangled in her web.

Even though he was badly beaten up by his accident, I think my visit to the hospital was comforting to both of us. There seemed to be a mutual understanding of the completely absurd nature of the situation. And of course neither of us was averse to a little theatricality.

As I was sitting by his bed offering him the grapes that he reflexively sneered at—they were dusty and limp—Ivan's nurse came bossily scuttling in and asked us if I was the next of kin. It was perfect timing as Ivan and I were attempting uneasily to make small talk, trying to avoid saying anything too inflammatory.

We both were silent, pausing like characters in a Pinter play. The nurse looked at me and then at Ivan in irritation as we sat dumb. "Well, are you family or not?" she snapped. There was another pause. I finally mustered up a strangled "We don't know." And then I felt a surge of anger against this woman. I didn't like her mean dried-up mouth and the tone of what was coming out of it. Who was she to barge into our personal lives? So I stood up and said haughtily, "Anyway, why do you need to know?"

She then started on a list of complaints about Ivan's behavior. He had too many raucous visitors, refused to eat the hospital food, and had been sneaking drinks of alcohol and smoking cigarettes.

I certainly didn't want to stop his fun, and anyway I was in no position to. I told her he was a very distinguished man, and he had earned the right to do anything he damn well pleased.

Ivan was grinning away as I told her off. "She's the Wicked

Witch of the West nurse. I can't bear her, none of the patients can," he hissed, pretending that he thought she couldn't hear. We both knew she heard because she pulled the door shut loudly behind her as she left the room.

We looked at each other with glee and we both relaxed. He told me that there was some whiskey and a split of champagne hidden in his bedside cupboard. I went to get a couple of plastic cups from the water cooler in the hall and poured him out some whiskey. He said he didn't really care for champagne, "too acid," so I popped the bottle all for myself.

We drank to his health, and to whatever else we could think of. And, oh yes, of course we raised a glass to Mum.

OUR MUTUAL FRIEND Don Boyd had introduced me to Matthew. We were both at a party given by Krug Champagne and it was a crowded, noisy, and hot affair—"a bum fuck," as people in England like to call those kind of occasions. Don suggested we all get out of there and go to some new club he had just joined. So a group of us piled into taxis and I started talking to Matthew.

He was tall and thin with reddish hair and was wearing a blue velvet frock coat and winkle-picker-style shoes. He resembled a slightly more modern version of a 1950s rockabilly.

At the club, we talked until late into the night as others variously drifted off home. I noticed he wasn't drinking (I was, but not out of control). Finally he told me he hadn't had a drink in twelve years. That impressed me.

When he told me he was an interior decorator it surprised me as he was totally unlike all the other decorators I knew. I also couldn't imagine him looking at bolts of chintz and choosing wallpaper designs for rich ladies. He appeared to be far too cool and groovy for that.

It turned out he mostly designed offices for places like MTV and Virgin Records. He was then working on a new club in the West End called Soho House, a trendy hangout for movie and music business people.

I had often been to Soho House and had liked the way it looked; it was laid-back and comfortable, like a shabby country house. There were hunting prints on the walls and big old worn sofas everywhere. It had an easy atmosphere, and reminded me of the houses I had grown up in.

I mentioned to him that I had just moved into a new flat in Onslow Gardens and needed help with it. I told him straight off that I didn't want it all highly decorated. Just painted and new bathrooms and a kitchen put in.

Matthew fairly jumped at the opportunity. "When should I come by to have a look? Tomorrow morning? I can be there at ten." I thought that sounded optimistic as it was already two in the morning. These were probably just late-night ramblings anyway and he wouldn't show up.

At nine thirty I was woken by my phone ringing and a voice with a strong South London accent said, "Hi, it's Matthew from last night. I'm in the café opposite your flat. Shall I come up?" I had to blearily piece together the night before. Then I remembered my long conversation with him, and my annoyance at being awakened quickly turned to a more pleasurable feeling.

I was surprised that he was prompt, actually early. Then I recalled he didn't drink so his head wouldn't be feeling as though it was being pierced with pins by mean little dolls.

He looked around the flat and we both had similar ideas on what to do with it. More important, I liked him and thought we could have some fun together. I hired him that morning.

We did have fun together. Matthew lived in Notting Hill Gate, and we spent hours nosing around the Portobello Road market together, buying objects, and in bathroom and kitchen shops looking at chrome fittings. We would take a break and go and have long lunches in good restaurants and I would sit having glasses of wine while he watched me and sipped his water.

We were acting like a newlywed couple who had just bought their starter home, but the reality was we were not anything more than a client and her decorator. There were inevitably a few stirrings, lying together on rugs in the window of the Persian-rug shop in Knightsbridge, or testing the springs of a Duxiana bed, but we were not having any kind of relationship. In fact, I set him up on a date with a girlfriend of mine as I thought he was her type.

Matthew told me later that he had fancied me from the first, but that I was his client and it seemed too unprofessional. I don't believe that. I think he was just too nervous to make a pass.

When my flat was officially finished, he invited me to dinner to celebrate at the restaurant in Soho House. By now we had become good friends, having bonded over brass, light fixtures, and curtain material. And over the course of all the time we had spent together, I learned a lot about his history with drugs and alcohol. He been to many treatment centers and AA, he said, had saved his life.

At the time I thought his stories all sounded exciting—his run-ins with psychotic drug dealers in places like Harlem and Bombay and his narrow escapes with the law. And after having all those dangerous adventures, he seemed sober, self-aware, and honest.

If only I had known then what I do now, about drug addicts and alcoholics. If I could only go back and scream at my younger self. I would scream at her, "For God's sake, Ivana, look out!"

With Matthew I was staring, without knowing it, at a big box of poison with a huge warning sign written all over it. There might just as well have been a black skull and crossbones and red letters: POISON. DO NOT INGEST.

But of course I ignored the sign. As though it were as innocent as a box of chocolates, I greedily delved in. After our dinner that night, Matthew and I went back to his flat.

Over the next ten years I got pregnant, and we married, separated, and divorced. He was in car accidents, in and out of rehabs and hospitals. He was escorted from Sardinia by the U.S. Marines for terrorizing me and some friends with whom I was vacationing on the island. He was abusive, and in a drunken drug-crazed rage he smashed the furniture in my house—the very furniture he had lovingly selected with me. We had fights that made the couple in *Who's Afraid of Virginia Woolf?* seem loving, sober, and companionable. I took out restraining orders and there were countless visits from the police. Finally, he was taken to the Riverhead jail for a short stay.

But—and it is a very big but, in fact the biggest but of all—we also had Daisy, our extraordinary beautiful daughter. She has my mother's huge eyes. But whereas my mother's seemed frightened, as if all they could see was the sadness and pain in the world, Daisy's are sparkling, shiny, and hopeful. For both of us, she makes it all worthwhile. She is a great teacher, and because of her I can't regret any of it.

CHAPTER 31

W hile Ivan was recuperating in Chelsea and Westminster Hospital, I did a lot of thinking. About him and also about Israel and Robert and Bob Silvers. And everything that my mother had told me about all of them. Why was she so keen that I take Robert's name? He obviously wasn't my real father. Why didn't she want me to keep the name Citkowitz like my two sisters?

I also remember many conversations I had with her about Bob Silvers. She had hinted, and sometimes not very subtly, that he might be my father. I remember once after we had lunch with Bob at Claridge's, where he was staying with Grace, Countess of Dudley—the witty, elegant, and cultured woman with whom he'd shared his life and still does—my mother and I took a taxi home. "It's funny, you know. He so wants you to be his daughter."

I was rather flattered and said that in some way I did see him as a father; he had always been so kind to me. But then my mother continued, "Actually, I think he does believe that he really is your father."

This was news to me and I started to feel slightly uneasy. I asked nervously, "Why, Mum? Why would he believe that?" My mother was in one of her most annoying and dangerous moods. She had a gleeful expression on her face and her big eyes were mischievously flashing. She had had a lot to drink at lunch and had barely touched the Dover sole she had ordered and now I could tell she wanted to cause some trouble. Maybe the fact that Bob and Grace seemed so happy together could have had something to do with it.

Over the years I had grown extremely proficient at dealing

with my mother—I knew her moods as if they were my own. I could tell by the way she said hello on the telephone exactly how many drinks she had had, and whether it was worthwhile to continue with the conversation.

My sister and I did imitations of her phone voice. If she had had a lot to drink and you called her up, it could be as early as ten in the morning, and a deep, husky, male-sounding voice would answer and whisper with great emphasis on the *h*, "Hiiii." When she answered like that I would just hang up because I knew I would be in for trouble.

I had learned, the way a fox learns how to stay away from a hound, how to avoid confrontation with my mother when she was in one of her drunken attack modes. I would steer the conversation to something neutral, or divert her attention onto some other subject that she was obsessed by at the time. Anything to deflect the attention away from me.

Sometimes I would escape and just leave the house when I could tell she was spoiling for a fight. Then she would have to find a new target, someone weak and unprepared for her attacks.

But beside her in the back of the taxi stuck in traffic near Hyde Park corner I was a sitting target. "Well, he doesn't have any children of his own. I mean apart from Grace, the most important relationship in his life has been with *The New York Review of Books*. But as far as family goes, you're it." I had had enough now, another one of my mother's drunken theories. But I loved and respected Bob far too much to engage in one of Mum's mad philosophical rants about his personal life.

"Oh shut up, Mum," and I quickly steered the conversation toward some other topic. And so the subject was dropped—for the time being.

I hadn't forgotten that conversation and there had been others like it, but I hadn't taken that much notice because I was still so certain that Israel was my father. However, now that the question of my paternity had been seriously raised, everyone was fair game.

I called Bob up at his office. I wasn't quite sure what to say. There isn't really a tactful way of asking someone if they are your father. I approached the subject cautiously. "Bob, Ivan Moffat is here in London and I had lunch with him at Marguerite Littman's. He seems to think he's my father—do you know anything about this?" There was a pause and Bob said, "That's not true, sweetie. Caroline told me, and I am fairly sure that it's true, that I am your father. I was there with you when you were growing up, living on West Twelfth Street. I was there with you from the beginning until Caroline left London."

Now I was really confused. I thought that it was Israel who had been living with us in the house in Greenwich Village, but Bob sounded so sure. I must have only been two or three so I had no memories of it. I just had always believed what I had been told. I was also surprised that Caroline had told him that I was his daughter. She had never told me that she had actually told him that. But then again, it seems my mother lied to everyone and anyone whenever it suited her.

I could imagine her enjoying the power that she had over these men, using my paternity as some sort of cruel leverage, a juicy piece of bait to keep them bobbing around her.

I started to feel hot and angry and once again ashamed. Ashamed that my identity had been used so flippantly—tossed around like a plastic beach ball.

Also, if they were all so sure that they were my father, and all so keen to *be* my father, why hadn't they come to me before? Why had they stood on the sidelines? The reason, Bob later explained, was that that was what Caroline wanted, what, in fact, she had insisted on. Before I was born she told him she wanted the three girls to have the same father and Israel had agreed to act as though he were mine. After Caroline went back to England, Bob offered to pay for my education. He sent her checks she never cashed. He asked if we could spend more time together. She said no.

It seemed so unfair that at that moment I wanted to hate them all. How dare they? How dare they treat me so cavalierly? I tried to hate them but I couldn't. I couldn't because I still wanted to believe that their motives were pure and that they had had good reasons for their behavior. I started to make excuses for them because I just didn't want to believe that I had not been loved.

It sounds pathetic, but I also blamed myself. Of course it made sense that they should want to be only partly in my life; after all, wasn't I damaged like some precious stone with hidden flaws that render it worthless?

I was ready to forgive everyone for treating me badly. It was completely understandable—it was my fault and I deserved it. Perhaps my mother knew how unlovable I was and that was why she had kept my identity hidden, to protect me from getting hurt.

Then I began to wonder if all this subterfuge and mystery had not somehow contributed to my feelings of inadequacy. Apart from the abuse and the burns, I had always sensed that something else was not right—perhaps the reason that I had never felt at ease in my own skin was because the skin I was trying to fit into was the wrong skin. Like the ugly duckling that didn't realize that she was really a swan: she would have been a perfectly good swan but she made a lousy duckling.

Bob Silvers had volunteered to do a DNA test, but I wasn't certain that I wanted it. I had spent thirty years on this planet without knowing the truth—why should I shake up my world now? What difference would my knowing for certain make anyway? I would still be the same person with the same mixture of worries, flaws, and problems.

If Bob *was* my father, I wouldn't turn overnight into a Jewish intellectual. Nor, if Ivan was my father, would I suddenly become a suave and sophisticated writer of screenplays. I doubted anything would change at all.

Neither of these men had been able to properly act as my father, so why try to scientifically prove a point? I had done quite well without them—well, no, I hadn't actually. But having an "official" father wasn't going to change anything now. It was "too late"; the two saddest words in the English language, and I felt them acutely.

I decided that I would just let it go, I didn't need to know. I was in a comfortable relationship with Matthew, I was enjoying my life in London, I had lots of friends, and—as much as my mother would have hated it—I had become close to my grandmother. I had come to appreciate her and all her eccentricities. I actually enjoyed going over to her house in Hans Crescent and spending weekends with her at the Owl House, her country place near Tonbridge Wells in Kent, named after her huge collection of everything owl.

My grandmother remained vibrant, demanding, and troublemaking right up to the end. She adored litigation, and whenever I visited her in Hans Crescent, her bedroom would be strewn with legal papers pertaining to all the lawsuits she had going. She was a lawyer's dream, spending untold pounds suing the Guinness trustees (of which she was a very vocal one herself) and anyone else she felt had done her an injustice.

She died of a stroke in 1998 but not without ensuring her place in heaven first. On her deathbed she converted to Catholicism. Having lived what can only be described as a selfish and pam-

pered life without much in the way of spirituality, she prevailed
upon a priest and her old friend, the radical Catholic Lord Long-
ford, to smooth her transition into the next world. She was even
given a Catholic name, Sister Mary something or other and, age
ninety-one, she passed on.

Although she had been married twice since his death, my
grandmother insisted on being buried at Clandeboye alongside
her first husband, Basil, and all the other Marquesses of Dufferin and Ava, including her son, Sheridan.

Maureen had also insisted on retaining her title. She claimed
that one of the last things Basil Dufferin said to her as he left
on his fatal mission to Burma, was "Please, darling, if anything
should happen to me and even if you marry again, *please* promise
me you will keep the title." So, although legally she should have
been Mrs. Buchanan and then Mrs. Maude, she was always the
Marchioness of Dufferin and Ava.

CHAPTER 32

For my grandmother's ninetieth birthday, Evgenia and I had given her a grand ball at Claridge's, the venerable and, to Maureen, reassuringly expensive hotel in Mayfair. When I say we had given it, I meant it was suggested to us very heavily by her lawyer, business manager, and confidant, Ludo de Walden, that she wanted to have a big bash and that we should bloody well be the ones to do it.

I was actually happy to oblige. I love a good party, and my grandmother was a deserving beneficiary, having spent most of her time and energy attending and giving them. The occasion went from being dubbed Maureen's Ninetieth to becoming Maureen's Tiara Party, because the creamy engraved invitation read, "White Tie, Tiaras, and Medals may be worn." There was a lot of frantic searching through old jewelry boxes as tiara-less friends and relatives looked for sparkling ornaments for their hair.

The organizing and prospect of being the belle of a big ball gave my grandmother in her extreme old age an enormous boost. We had fun going over the menus at Claridge's with her. Maureen had never been a foodie; in fact, her lack of interest in either eating or serving it was a point of dismay for her many houseguests.

The food she served at her twenty-room pink villa in Sardinia—which my uncle Sheridan had nicknamed Villa Costalotta—was legendarily awful. First of all, there wasn't nearly enough of it, and then what there was, was pretty revolting. Because she didn't care about food herself, and loved to eat lots of stale white bread smothered in soft, half-rancid butter and great gobs of cream, she never paid the slightest attention to what her guests were being served.

The couple employed to look after her in Sardinia were straight out of a bad comedy act. Gino and Maria and their seemingly endless number of children and grandchildren occupied "Casa Maureena," and were a law unto themselves except for the months of July and August when the "Marchesa" and her pals moved in in a big splashy way.

As my grandmother had never set foot in any kitchen anywhere, she gave them complete control of that domain. Gino was a gnome-like man, with a huge, red, hooked nose, a big round stomach, and an uneven temperament. His wife, Maria, was an equally intimidating and small creature, with a head of dyed jet-black hair who wore vast amounts of eye and lip makeup and a sly expression. They stubbornly pretended not to understand any language that anyone addressed them in, particularly Italian, which was what one assumed Sardinians spoke. Instead they preferred to talk (and apparently only take orders in) some strange uninterpretable dialect of their own.

It was frustrating to watch Maureen in her bedroom in the morning using her ancient English-Italian phrase book, painstakingly trying to explain to Gino what he should buy and make for lunch and dinner every day. Although she really had no interest in these matters, she liked to behave as if she did. No matter what instructions he was given, the meal produced would be the same, "Gino's famous pasta and sauce," a disgusting concoction of spaghetti and frozen meatballs smothered in a lumpy and weirdly sugary tomato sauce.

I used to walk down to the local market and stare longingly at the delicious ripe figs and peaches, smell the fragrant herbs and wonderful Sardinian cheeses, and ogle the glistening fresh fish, all just begging to be cooked and eaten. It was disappointing to return to the house and sit on the terrace overlooking the beautiful Mediterranean and have Maria grumpily plunk down the same old inedible bowl of heavy, hot pink mush.

One July some titled Scottish friends of Maureen's arrived to stay for a week, and they were keen fishermen, who routinely caught and smoked their own salmon from a river on their estate. As a house present they proudly presented my grandmother with a huge sealed package of their home-smoked salmon—a gift she was pleased by as smoked salmon was one delicacy that she actually did enjoy and consequently consumed vast quantities of. My grandmother sent it to the kitchen with instructions (actually, strange translations from the Italian dictionary) that it be served that evening as she had guests coming for dinner and bridge.

The mood was optimistic that night and her hungry guests anticipated that for once they might actually get something good, or at least edible, to eat. We heard the familiar (and for me dreaded) sound of Maria's flip-flops clopping down the marble hall. She appeared at the dining room door carrying on a large platter what had once been a pink and succulently oily salmon but had now been rendered a grey, dried-out, sad relation. As if cooking it to death wasn't bad enough, Gino had also smeared it with his disgusting pasta sauce.

My grandmother seemed to find this mistake amusing and enjoyed the look of dismay on the faces of her guests. "Oh, silly Gino. Well, as there is no food, it gives us all more time to get into bridge playing. Ha Ha!" Her starving prisoners didn't find it so funny. And of course I suspected that Gino had done it on purpose.

Often in the morning I would surprise him in the kitchen. He would be sitting watching an Italian football match on a blaring TV (there were no televisions anywhere else in the house), a huge bowl of fresh peaches, cheese, and a great big vat of red wine in front of him, none of which was ever offered at our stingy meals. I would hopelessly beg him please, please, as I didn't eat meat, could I be allowed to make a salad, using those plump tomatoes, that redolent basil, and that fresh mozzarella that I knew were in the pantry? Or could I go and buy some things and just be allowed to use the kitchen for a second? Or even just borrow a bowl?

The reaction would always be the same, Maria's painted eyebrows raised in anger at my suggestion and her husband gruffly saying, "No no, Gino make you very good meal. Gino make his famous pasta." He would kiss his fingers and pound his chest to indicate how *fantastico* it would be, and then push me out of the kitchen.

I suspected that the only things that they managed to cook successfully were the books, but because they had been with my grandmother for so long and had developed their own complicated and eccentric way of running the house, it would be all but impossible to prove anything. They had made themselves appear to be indispensable, and for the two months she used her house in Sardinia, my grandmother did indeed depend on them.

I didn't even really want to get rid of them—they were by now part of our increasingly crazy extended family—but I didn't want them to fleece my grandmother, either. When I asked to see what they were doing with the lire my grandmother doled out every morning, I was presented with a tiny notebook filled with numbers scrawled in pencil beside a list of what were supposedly grocery items but were completely indecipherable and definitely not in any recognizable language. I knew that to challenge him would have been pointless.

When Prince and Princess Michael of Kent came for a visit, they were so dismayed by the food, and lack of it, that they snuck off after dark to the nearby pizzeria in Porto Raphael. I had often done the same, pretending I was going for an after-dinner walk and instead ducking inside a trattoria for a big plate of fried calamari.

I knew my grandmother enjoyed the drama and tyrannical power with which her employees seemed to reign over her house. She encouraged their rudeness and used them to manipulate her houseguests and keep them in a constant state of discomfort and fear.

Maria was her spy, flip-flopping down the passage first thing in the morning, a grim look on her face, dying to tell tales of her guests' misdemeanors. "Oh, Marchesa, there was a big, huge lot of sand and water on the marble floor in the white bedroom, because Lady So and So"—or whoever was the culprit at the time, sometimes the "Americana" (all American guests were dismissed as Americanas)—"came up from the beach and make big big dirty mess." Or "Senorita Ivana out very late last night. She wake us up because we hear her climbing in through window." It was curious how her English greatly improved when she was telling tales on us.

Actually, it was true about my climbing through the window at night. When I wanted to get out to go down to the local piazza, it was just easier to slip in and out of my bedroom window. I would half-close the shutters and leave the window open. That way I didn't have to explain or ring the front doorbell and wake everyone up. The house was circular, one story, and built around an inner courtyard, with the main bedrooms all facing out with open views of the Mediterranean.

Maureen's green shuttered bedroom windows opened directly onto the balustraded front terrace, which was the most-used space in the house as the steps and paths down to the beach led from there. This arrangement allowed her to see and hear everyone's comings and goings without being observed herself. I would be peacefully reading and sunbathing when her shutters would fly open and a black hat and rhinestone sunglasses would pop out. "Darling, can I have a word with you in my bedroom in ten minutes." I knew I was in trouble.

Usually when some crime (a house rule broken) was committed, my grandmother would hurriedly pen a nasty note written on blue Marchioness of Dufferin and Ava notepaper, complete with coronet, and give it to Maria to post under the transgressor's bedroom door.

I would sometimes have a huge pile of them waiting for me after breakfast, all written in the same injured tone, varying only in degrees of nastiness. "Darling Ivana, it really does pain me to learn that you have been sneaking out of the house and leaving your window wide open for bandits to enter and kidnap us all. Also, I hear that your room is <u>CONSTANTLY</u> untidy and that you tried to interfere with the kitchen staff over the food that I expensively and painstakingly took a lot of trouble over organizing. It really is too too path [pathetic] that you have grown up to have such bad manners, just like your poor mother. Love from a broken-hearted and sad Maureen."

My mother had told me that growing up she and her siblings had learned to live with these vitriolic notes. She also said that as there were so many of them, Maureen felt entitled to consider herself a "woman of letters."

THE TIARA BALL was the highlight of Maureen's twilight years. All her friends and family that were still living (although some of them were so old it was questionable whether they really were still with us) turned out for her.

She looked marvelous. Her shamrock tiara was perched

proudly on her white hair and she wore a black taffeta gown with a high ruffle around the neck and big puffy sleeves. On the bottom of the ruffle she wore a huge diamond pin that my sister and I nicknamed the Monster Brooch.

Because her feet and ankles were weakened by arthritis, she chose to greet her guests sitting down. Claridge's had organized a white platform on which a blue-and-gold satin sofa was perched, and there she sat regally. An enormous bower of her favorite flowers—lilies and roses—formed an arch around her, completing the elaborate tableau.

She clearly enjoyed every moment of the evening, particularly the arrival of the Queen Mother, who sweetly explained to us why she hadn't worn a tiara. "It's my hair, you see. It's just too thin these days and I find those things so painful because they dig into one's head, you know?"

There was, of course, a big band that played tunes of my grandmother's era. A rousing rendition of "We'll meet again, don't know where, don't know when . . ." brought tears to her eyes, as did many other songs all carefully selected by her, and there were speeches and toasts given in tribute.

I gave a speech but I totally forgot everything I had planned to say. Instead I choked up and blurted out passionately, "We just love you so much." I quickly handed the microphone to someone else. Maureen told me afterward that she had found my fumbled words very moving.

I was glad that we were able to do that for her; we promised that for her one hundredth birthday we would try to find a way to top her ninetieth. But we never got the chance.

CHAPTER 33

My grandmother suffered a mild stroke at age ninety and spent a week in the hospital. After her release, we employed a string of private nurses (they all had to be Irish as they made her feel like she was back home).

She did physiotherapy to learn to walk properly again. The nurses would escort her to the local garden park and make her walk, with her stick and their support, a few painful steps at a time. I watched as she had to do at ninety-two exactly what I had done at age six. Although she used fruitier language than I had to express her displeasure. "One, two, three, *fuck*. One, two, three, *fuck*," she would scream, much to the surprise and consternation of the families picnicking nearby.

When she had recovered enough, she declared that before she was "a goner," she would like to return for one last time to Clandeboye, to see the house and pay a final visit to the graves of her son and her husband.

It was a request that would fill my aunt Lindy, who had inherited the house, with dread and horror, since the two had never really seen eye to eye. But it was a request she could hardly deny. To her credit, Lindy was gracious about it, although she rang me up in complete panic and begged that I accompany Maureen to Belfast and, she firmly stipulated, *back*.

The idea of being in the middle of two strong-willed and dueling marchionesses terrified me.

THE FINAL WISH of a dying old lady to return to her home country, to her ancestral house, and to the place where she said she had been happiest was operatic in its pathos. She wanted to pay one last visit to the final resting place of her son and husband and where she herself had (firmly) requested to be laid to rest.

As we set off in the ambulance from Hans Crescent with her favorite Irish nurse, Eileen, accompanying us, I felt we were embarking on some kind of religious pilgrimage. The usual quick and easy trip over from London felt interminable, with Maureen crying out in pain every time there was a jolt in the vehicle or something nudged her bad side. It took forever as we waited for her wheelchair to make it through security—no matter the personal nature of our visit, we were still going to Northern Ireland in the midst of the "troubles."

We were all exhausted and drained by the time we bumped up the familiar driveway to Clandeboye in the ambulance. Maureen was sitting upright on the stretcher bed trying to peer out the tinted windows at the sight of the greystone portico. Tears began to trickle down her cheeks.

I suddenly felt incredibly sorry for her and hated myself for being inconvenienced and irritated by having to make the trip. I took her hand—it was trembling uncontrollably, but she managed to give mine a weak squeeze. I knew how hard this was for her. Ireland was the country she had grown up in and loved, and Clandeboye the home that she had restored, lived in, and, as she would put it, "cherished." It was the house where she had raised her three children (although my mother might dispute who had actually brought her up) and where she had been widowed young.

What emotions and memories she must have experienced as Robert John, the butler once loyal to her, now to Lindy, and the other members of the staff rushed out to greet her and help the ambulance men slowly carry her wheelchair through the stone hall and up the enormous staircase.

Why Not Say What Happened?

For her, the house must have felt like a museum full of memories. She was probably thinking of Uncle Sheridan, Aunt Perdita, and Mum as young children, laughing as they slid down the banisters and played dangerously with the ancient swords. I too started to imagine that I could hear the sound of their childish laughter echoing down the years. I began to cry for the loss, and for my mother.

Lindy had gone to some trouble to make her mother-in-law feel welcome. The fires were all lit, although it was spring, because Maureen had always kept it like that, and I noticed she had quickly put all the portraits of my grandmother that she had previously taken down back up in their original places of honor.

Maureen had requested that she be put in the bedroom called Burma, ironically named after the country where her husband had been killed. Lindy had filled it with flowers and books (not that Maureen was reading anymore) and old family photographs. Maureen looked carefully and, I knew, disapprovingly around the room, her still-judgmental eyes noticing every little change that had been made since she had handed over her crown to Lindy.

Her nurse and the various servants fussed around her and managed to get her settled as comfortably as possible into the canopied mahogany four-poster. Lindy chattered nervously away at her, and tried to explain all the wonderful projects and plans she had lined up for the future of the house and estate.

Maureen steadfastly ignored her, a method she often used on people she didn't approve of. Instead she addressed Robert John directly, saying coldly, "I won't be wanting any dinner tonight, thank you, Robert John. I just would like to be left in peace." And then she added, "I would like to visit Ava," her name for my grandfather, "first thing in the morning." And with that we were dismissed.

Lindy had invited three other people to stay, all close friends of hers. She hoped they would be able to support her through the ordeal.

At dinner that night, in the dining room but at a much smaller table than the one I was used to eating at when Lindy had her house parties, we drank a great deal of good wine and tried to act as if everything was all perfectly normal, chatting and gossiping as usual. But we all knew what was really happening. In a last act of sheer obstinate will, like Lord Marchmain in *Brideshead Revisited*, Maureen had come back to Clandeboye to die.

The following morning, straight after breakfast, we set off on the long walk up to the family Campo Santo. Maureen was very quiet, and her face was shrouded by a big, floppy black hat. We had decided that Robert John and a strapping young local boy who worked part-time for Lindy should push her wheelchair as far as they could and then carry her from there.

There was a gravel path that led from the house and over two bridges, allowing us to cross the streams that ran from the lakes. The path took us to Brenda's Garden, a lush and immaculately groomed spot named for my mother's beautiful but mentally fragile grandmother, Brenda, the third marchioness.

From there it was uphill, over rocks and wildflowers, and through some marshy woods. Maureen was carried regally, taking in all the scenery but remaining silent. Nor was there anything for anyone else to say; the occasion seemed to call for quiet.

We finally arrived at the moss-covered crumbling stone mausoleum, where the viceroy, his wife, his mother, and various other Dufferins were buried. I had always found this spot so spooky and had never wanted to linger. It was in a particularly dark and eerie part of the woods and felt cold and damp.

Behind, in an open and sunny clearing, was the large circle

where, among various friends and relatives of our family, the flat rectangular tombstone of Grandfather and Uncle rested.

England's poet laureate John Betjeman, who had been at Oxford with my grandfather and who everyone thought was in love with him, had helped Maureen design the memorial stone. It was Betjeman who wrote the inscription:

IN MEMORY OF
BASIL SHERIDAN
4TH MARQUESS OF DUFFERIN AND AVA
CAPTAIN ROYAL HORSE GUARDS
A MAN OF BRILLIANCE
AND OF MANY FRIENDS

I felt that Maureen should be left alone, and so I stood back from the clearing. It was chilly, overcast, a typically Irish day, and I watched my grandmother as she stood looking at the stones of her husband and son. She lingered for about ten minutes, lost in a world of memories and emotions.

As she stood there, the clouds seemed to slide apart like curtains opening on a stage, and the sun came beaming out and lit up the circle, filling it with warmth and otherworldliness.

I am not particularly religious but at that moment I felt quite spiritual, caught up in the momentary beauty of the graves, the trees and flowers all sparkling in the sunlight. Maureen looked up from under her hat and her face seemed more relaxed and peaceful than before. She even managed a little smile. "I think I'm ready now."

After that, she took to her bed and refused to come down for meals and barely saw anyone. Her body, always small, now seemed tiny huddled up in the enormous bed. The window shutters and heavy blue Indian silk printed curtains were all closed.

By the fifth day we were all desperate. I felt extremely uncomfortable acting as a go-between knowing that Lindy was longing to get us both out of there. She probably resented my presence as much as my grandmother's. At least Maureen wasn't eating anything, but Lindy was obliged to feed me three meals a day. We had always gotten along and she was doing her bit not to make me feel unwelcome but she had her own life to lead and the thought of being left alone indefinitely with Maureen horrified her. Having her niece moping about must have been a drag.

Luckily, Aunt Perdita was around. She lived on a farm where she ran a riding school for thalidomide children, about fifteen minutes from Clandeboye. She was being her usual wonderful, funny, and jolly self. She didn't seem at all surprised by her mother's stubborn insistence on being able to die in a house that she had turned over to her son and now his widow. I think she had long ceased being surprised at anything her mother did.

On the sixth or seventh day of the standoff, when I visited Maureen's room for my morning update, I sensed that something had shifted. I think she realized she wasn't going to be able to will herself to die—strong-willed as she was, her body was stronger still. She finally allowed that she would like to go home. However, she felt she was too weak and ill to make the journey the way we had come.

When I reported this new development to Lindy she lit up and said, "I will make enquiries." Lindy had always been a woman of strong determination and when she set her mind to something, it usually was accomplished. She was an excellent shot, tennis player, equestrian, painter, and businesswoman. Within the hour she had arranged for an air ambulance to come to Clandeboye the following day.

When Maureen was told that she would be carried on a stretcher straight from her bedroom at Clandeboye to her bedroom at Hans Crescent, she perked up a little, and so did I.

Why Not Say What Happened?

The helicopter landed on the front lawn. I felt as though I was in a scene from *M*A*S*H* as the skilled medics carefully placed Maureen into the aircraft and I ducked under the blades and clambered up beside her. Inside, the place was kitted out like the other ambulances we had been in, except this time I had a jump seat next to her stretcher. I had never had an aerial view of the house before and it was thrilling to see clearly the shamrock shape that the three lakes and river formed. It made me appreciate even more my great-great-grandfather the viceroy's vision when he had laid out the estate.

The journey was quick and Maureen seemed relieved to be going back to the comforts of her own home. When our final ambulance pulled up outside the blue door of Number Four Hans Crescent and her maid, Mariana, and her chauffeur, Ben, and secretary, Sally, all came hurrying out to meet her, she looked happy.

I left them all to it to make a fuss over her; no one seemed to notice I was even there. It was late and I was tired, so I grabbed my bag, walked up to Sloane Street, and went home alone to my flat.

A YEAR LATER we both were back at Clandeboye, only this time I was there to bury her. She is next to Ava and near Sheridan. Lindy sweetly told me that there is a spot for me, too, when my time comes. I don't really want to think about it, but I suppose it's an option.

CHAPTER 34

Not long after my grandmother's death, I found out I was pregnant. I was euphoric. I loved being pregnant and naïvely hoped that all my troubles would evaporate with the arrival of a child. I prayed that this innocent embryo would now replace the black wasp's nest of anxiety and fear that had taken such a strong hold over me.

I believed Matthew would make a good father. I honestly thought that he was winning his battle with drugs and alcohol and that he would be a good role model for our child. I still can't believe I could have been so blind. I don't like to think that I am a stupid person, but sometimes I wonder.

I hadn't planned on marrying Matthew, but now that I was pregnant it seemed a natural progression. I had dinner in New York with Bob Silvers, Grace Dudley, and their good friends, Sid and Mercedes Bass. When I was living in New York I had become quite close to Mercedes. I was introduced to her by Jayne Wrightsman, who had been a great friend of Uncle Sheridan.

Jayne is a superb hostess, and although her dinners were formal and grand affairs she somehow managed to make everyone relax and enjoy themselves. Everywhere you looked in her vast apartment overlooking Central Park, there was an exquisite object or rare English, French, and Italian drawings and paintings of her impeccable choosing.

The dinners were often black-tie affairs. After canapés, Cristal served in delicate pink crystal glasses and caviar, we would be seated in the dining room. There was always a fascinating mix of people, ranging from Henry Kissinger to Jackie Onassis (Jayne

Wrightsman had advised her on the furniture for the White House) to museum curators, artists, and writers.

The first time I attended one of these dinners I was intimidated and shy. I was by far the youngest person in the room and felt that I had nothing of interest to say to all these worldly and glamorous people. Jayne was wonderfully welcoming and instinctively took me over to Mercedes, who instantly took me under her chic wing.

From a distance, Mercedes looks unapproachable. Reed thin and beautiful in a dark-eyed, exotic way, she is full of fun and seems to have boundless energy. She quickly became an important person in my life, giving me advice and showing a familial interest in my well-being.

One night over dinner, I announced my pregnancy to Sid, Mercedes, Grace, and Bob, all of whom received the news with much excitement. Champagne was immediately ordered, and the good news toasted gleefully. In that moment I almost felt that I was their daughter giving them the blessed news. Of course, at that point there was the very real possibility of Bob being my father, and I felt proud that I was doing something right for once. I was having a child and everything was going to be fine.

After that dinner it was obvious I wasn't going to be allowed to elope or have a small, quiet wedding in a registry office, which is what I had discussed with Matthew. Mercedes and my friends would never let me get away with that. And finally I, too, got swept up in the fantasy of a big, white fairy-tale wedding.

I phoned Matthew in London and broke the news that when we married in March, it would be at the Rainbow Room on the top floor of Rockefeller Center. He took it quite well; why shouldn't he? I spent the next three months in New York in escapist heaven, growing fatter and planning my Cinderella wedding.

I have to admit I enjoyed it all immensely. Mercedes orchestrated most of the details, from the beautiful invitations to my exasperating (due to my expanding waistline) dress fittings with Oscar de la Renta. Accompanied by the wedding planners she had found, Mercedes and I rode around New York, visiting florists, caterers, and cake makers. I was doing all the frivolous things that giddy brides dream about, and I was loving every silly moment of it.

Guiltily, I thought about how different it all would have been if my mother had been alive. She would have scoffed at this extravagance, and somehow, in the way that only she could, she would have turned what was ostensibly a joyful time into one of "the worst." I knew that if she were alive I wouldn't be doing any of this. I probably wouldn't even be bothering to get married.

When Evgenia had bravely held her wedding at Mum's house in Sag Harbor, my mother had very nearly ruined it. A week before the event something (trivial, I'm sure) had upset her and she drunkenly telephoned everyone, including my sister and her fiancé, Julian, and told them that the wedding in Sag was off. It took huge amounts of pacifying and persuasion to get her back on board, but in the end, although their plans for having it in the garden were thwarted by rain, the wedding was touching and simple and loving. Instead of coming down an aisle, Evgenia descended the stairs followed by her bridesmaids, actress Glenne Headly, screenwriter Jenny Lumet, and me.

So I was feeling strong and happy and invincible, the luckiest girl on the planet. I knew it couldn't last, and of course it didn't.

On my first visit to my gynecologist after I found out that I was pregnant, I had had an awkward moment. She had asked me for a complete history of my family's health. On my mother's side I had all the answers: she had died from cancer; my grandmother had lived till very nearly one hundred; alcoholism was rife in the family; no epilepsy that I knew of; yes, some mental problems, actually quite a lot of mental problems, one of my sisters had died of a drug overdose. But when she asked me questions about my father, I faltered. I began to act defensive and confused. "Umm, I don't know which father you mean." She looked at me quizzically and then said slowly, as if she were talking to a rather backward four-year-old, "I mean, naturally, the father whose genetics your child will inherit."

AFTER IVAN WAS DISCHARGED from the hospital in London, he had returned to California, and the question of whether or not he was my father was dropped. Not forgotten, not at all, but postponed, like a teeth-cleaning appointment at the dentist. Something nagging that you know you will have to do at some point, but not so urgent that you can't put it off for a while.

I had decided to take the path of least resistance—that is to say, I had copped out. I had tried to convince myself and anyone who would listen that genetics were unimportant and overrated. I was who I was because of my upbringing and life experiences, not because my mother may or may not have drunkenly received the bodily fluids of some particular man one night.

It was a flawed argument, of course, and seemed particularly so now when we were trying to establish whether my child would be prone to some hideous illness or genetic defect. I realized how selfish and careless I had been in not finding all this out before I became pregnant. I knew it wouldn't change anything regarding my feelings toward my baby. But it seemed irresponsible not to find out early about any lurking dangers so we could be prepared and perhaps avert them.

Bob Silvers agreed to do the DNA immediately. My sister, as she was in California and in close touch with Ivan, offered to arrange for him to get it done there. Ivan was still quite shaken up from his accident and he was not leaving his house much, so Evgenia managed to procure a DNA kit from somewhere.

Bob found the supposedly best DNA specialist in New York and we met one rainy afternoon in his office on Central Park West. The waiting room was filled with photographs and newspaper articles about him.

A fat, red-faced man wearing a bright yellow suit welcomed us jovially into his office. He immediately gave us a long talk explaining why he was the best-known DNA man in the world. He told us that he made frequent appearances on *Jerry Springer*, surprising unwitting fathers with children they never knew they had. He reeled off a list of celebrities whose paternity suits against them had been dropped thanks to his vital evidence. He told funny stories about his clients and produced his card, on which his phone number read 1–800-P-A-T-S-U-I-T or something of that nature.

Bob and I sat opposite him feeling increasingly embarrassed. This man was making wisecracks about something that was really not the slightest bit funny to us. Perhaps his whole flamboyant act was really just a clever tactic that he employed to diffuse what must be an intensely awkward situation for everyone who came to see him.

With great showmanship, as though performing a thrilling magic trick, he theatrically produced a couple of tongue compressors that looked like the sticks we used to lick ice cream from. Then he took hefty swabs of skin from the cheek inside our mouths. That's where you get the juiciest example of the entire genetic makeup of your body, he explained.

He put the samples into two plastic pouches labeled with our information. My fate was literally sealed inside an envelope ready to be sent to the lab. It was a strange sensation knowing that everything that I had believed about my life up till now was contingent on three slimy bits of cheek flesh, smeared on undignified-looking wooden sticks.

The doctor smugly informed us that the results of the DNA test were practically infallible; whatever the outcome, it would be 99.9 percent accurate. We both agreed that those were pretty acceptable odds, and that was that. All we had to do now was wait.

Although the situation in the doctor's office had verged on the comical, something happened while I was there that I hadn't expected. As I had sat watching Bob stoically undergo the indignity of the proceedings, I caught his eye for a second and we looked at each other and smiled. Instead of feeling awkward or shy, I felt unbelievably proud of the fact that he was doing all this for me.

In that moment I knew, and could physically feel, that he loved me. My entire body reacted almost with a feeling of shock. The closest sensation I can think of is when you first know you are deeply attracted to someone and that the feeling is reciprocated. At that moment you are connected and there is no turning back.

In the doctor's office it was almost as if I had fallen in love with Bob, in the way that you love your child or, dare I say, parent. I also felt deep compassion for him. Until then, I had been so concerned with myself and what this meant to me and how it would affect my baby, I hadn't considered what Bob must have been going through.

My mother had led him along and encouraged him to believe he was my father and then told him he couldn't act as my father. Now he had to go through this humiliating process. He was as much a victim in all of this as I was, and he was behaving remarkably honorably.

OUTSIDE THE DOCTOR'S OFFICE on Central Park West, there was an obvious sense of relief between us that we had got that over with. I felt lighter, as you do when you complete an exam or difficult interview. Bob and I parted ways effortlessly. There was easiness and a new sense of closeness between us— we had just shared an experience that was ours alone and it had brought us closer.

"'Bye, kiddo," Bob had said, hugging and kissing me on both cheeks. "I will call you when I get the results."

Afterward, in the cab on the way home, I began to feel sharp pricks of anxiety. Before I had gone to the appointment I had felt sure that Israel was my father and that I wanted him to be. That was what I had believed all my life. It was what made the most sense.

If Israel was my father, it would mean that nothing would be any different. Evgenia and Natalya would still be my full sisters. I would still be half Jewish, Polish/Russian, and my wide face and dark eyes would make sense. And my dad would still be safely dead.

But now I dangerously began to allow myself to fantasize about Bob being my dad. It would be as though I were given a second chance at having a father. I started to think of ways in which I could make him proud of me. But then I realized that if Bob was my father, very soon I was going to make him a grandfather. Surely that was the best possible thing you could do for a parent.

When I got back to the hotel I was staying at while I planned my wedding, I felt a desperate longing to share what had just happened. But I couldn't think of anyone to call. Once again, the only person I would have wanted to speak to was my mother. The ironic thing was, maybe she would have been just as interested in finding out the outcome of the test as we were.

I couldn't talk to Matthew—he scoffed at anything to do with feelings. All his years of drug and alcohol abuse had left him detached and emotionally sterile. I hadn't realized it at first, but he was also a narcissist. Perhaps that's why we got along so well at the beginning. We were both so self-absorbed, we couldn't recognize how damaged we both were.

At the beginning of our relationship I had mistaken what I now know to be obsession for love. Matthew was extremely attentive and wanted to be with me all the time. His life seemed to—and, looking back, I realize did—revolve around me. This in its way was irresistible. I believed that I had found someone who really loved me and would be a good father to our child.

My sister would have tried to be supportive and helpful, but she had been living in Los Angeles for a long time and I knew she had become close to Ivan. After all, she was the one who had had to go to his house to do the "swab," and I knew she felt sorry for him. Also, the outcome of the test was important for her too. She had been lied to as much as I had. Growing up, she had believed, just as Caroline wanted, that I was her (full) little sister—a Citkowitz. I knew that our relationship was as important to her as it was to me.

So, instead of talking things over with Evgenia and Matthew or with a professional or friends, I did what I had always done with my feelings—I stuffed them. I stuffed them as far down and as far away from the surface as I could. My first reaction would have been to liquidate them away with alcohol, but I was pregnant. It would have been too reckless to drink the way I would have liked to.

Normally, I would have arranged to meet some friends and we would have had a great excuse to drink. I could have wallowed in my situation and enjoyed being the center of attention in such an unusual drama. I would have drunk enough not to care about the outcome of the test and I would have just gone home and passed out. But that was no longer an option.

The idea of my baby was the only pure, untainted, and innocent thing in my world. She would need to have fortitude to fight her way through life, and I prayed she would be able to navigate an easier path than I had managed.

But then I began worrying, how could I look after a tiny baby when I hadn't the slightest idea how to look after myself? In six months I was going to be a mother, and I still didn't have the slightest clue how to be me.

I started panicking. What on earth had I been thinking by getting pregnant? I had spent my life blaming my mother for all my problems, and now I could turn out to be a far worse mother than she ever had been.

CHAPTER 35

I didn't allow myself to dwell on the outcome of the test. Between my Lamaze classes, dress fittings, and wedding arrangements, I was running all around New York.

And then in the middle of all this frivolity, I got Bob's call. His voice sounded distant.

"Seems it's not me. It's that Moffat fellow who's your father." I don't remember much more than that about the conversation.

I found it hard to connect his words to their meaning and I couldn't take them in. It was as though we were talking via a bad satellite link and it was taking a while for the feed to get through to me.

I wasn't expecting this piece of news at all. I don't know what I was expecting but it absolutely wasn't this. I felt I was somehow playing in a funny game that my mother had orchestrated from the grave. Only it wasn't funny anymore, and the joke was on me.

After I put the phone down I still couldn't fully comprehend what Bob had told me. "That Moffat fellow is your father." I tried to think calmly about what that actually meant, but it didn't feel right. Who was I, really? Just a made-up person, a mishmash, a cobbled-together excuse for a person. Ivana Lowell—even my last name wasn't rightfully mine. It was just something that had been stuck on me as an afterthought to make me feel as though I had an identity. But the truth was I didn't.

I think that all the pregnancy hormones surging inside instinctively formed a protective layer around me. I didn't feel like getting upset and brooding. I decided that I was going to take the high road and try to embrace my new situation.

I knew I should telephone Ivan, but I felt nervous and shy. I wasn't sure how he had taken the news or what his reaction had been when he had found out the results. What did he feel about me? Did he even like me? It was a little bit late in life for him to have another daughter suddenly thrust into his life.

Ivan already had three children. His oldest child, Lorna, was from his first marriage, and he had two sons from his second.

And Jonathan! An uneasy feeling crept over me. Jonathan Moffat was my brother! I had flashbacks of Jonathan's many visits to the house in Redcliffe Square, of locking him in the cupboard, and of his puppy dog expressions when he looked at me. I remembered my mother's seriously troubled reaction to my friendship with him.

Jonathan was all grown up, married with children of his own now. I remembered uneasily a curious evening I had spent celebrating his thirtieth birthday. Ivan had come to London from L.A. and had taken Jonathan, his younger brother, Patrick, and me to the London nightclub Annabel's. Ivan had been a member of this once glamorous and exclusive club since its inception, and he made a big show of taking us to dinner there.

At first Ivan was enjoying himself, showing off by ordering Dom Pérignon and discussing the menu in French with the maître d', whom he said he had known for ages.

Jonathan got a little tipsy, and he had stood up a bit unsteadily to ask me to dance. Ivan flew into a rage, accusing him of behaving inappropriately and embarrassing all of us. I had defended Jonathan and said that I didn't mind, and that in fact I would love to dance.

When we returned to the table, Ivan was in a vile mood and remained so for the rest of the evening. He was hypercritical of both his sons and generally dismissive and sarcastic. Patrick had just finished art school and was struggling to be an artist. Ivan ridiculed his efforts and questioned his talents. He was even nastier to Jonathan. We were discussing children's names, and Jonathan made a comment that if he were ever to have a daughter, he would like to name her Ivana as it was such a pretty name.

I was about to say what a lovely idea that was, when I saw that Ivan's face had turned the color of the red-lacquered bar at Annabel's. "That's the most ridiculous thing I have ever heard," he spluttered, leaning in menacingly toward Jonathan, his tie scraping over his Dover sole. He noticed our shocked expressions and backed off a little. "I mean, Ivana's a Polish name. Caroline and Israel gave it to her. Why would you want to choose a Polish name?"

The subject was dropped, but he continued to be cruel to his boys for the rest of the evening. I remember feeling sorry for them both and relieved when the evening was over.

NOW OF COURSE I know why Ivan had been so upset. The possibility that a son of his had a crush on a daughter of his would have been appallingly creepy. And, as my mother had sworn him to secrecy, he was having to suffer in silence.

I can only thank God that I hadn't reciprocated Jonathan's feelings toward me. I once again realized what a complicated and dangerous game my mother had been playing.

She had managed to persuade Israel to raise me as his daughter and then Robert to adopt me. She had convinced Bob that he was my father and Ivan that he was too, and then forbidden them to say anything. In yet another bizarre twist she ensured that the connection between two of her men was eternal by having lines from a Lowell poem to the dying engraved on Israel's tombstone.

Somewhere your spirit
Led the highest life;
All places matched
With that place
Come to nothing

I'm surprised that Lucian hadn't somehow been dragged in just to complete the circle. Then I remember the nice irony of Robert clutching one of Freud's portraits of my mother when he died. I suppose that sort of ties Lucian into the proceedings. I really have to admire her. It was quite an impressive display of duplicity on so many levels.

My new situation started to seem interesting. I was sad that Bob Silvers wasn't a blood relative, but I knew that he would always remain as close to me as anyone in my life. Anyway, I had an entire new family now. A brand-new father (well, actually he was quite old, but new to me) and three new siblings. I didn't know his daughter, Lorna, at all; all I knew was that she was beautiful, eccentric, and lived somewhere in California on a boat with a duck. I already liked Jonathan and Patrick, and now that Jonathan was a father I also had a couple of new nieces to get to know.

I decided it was time I found out more about my dad, Ivan Moffat. Doing research on Ivan turned out to be easy and much more interesting than I had imagined it would be. I knew that Ivan's grandfather Sir Herbert Beerbohm Tree had over his long career produced and starred in more than ninety plays. D. W. Griffith, Ellen Terry, and Oscar Wilde were among his friends. His younger brother was the popular writer Sir Max Beerbohm.

It seems my new great-grandfather, Sir Herbert, was as prolific in siring children as he was at producing plays. He had three daughters by his wife, five sons and a daughter by his longtime mistress, and (at age sixty-four) another son by a young actress he met in New York. One of his sons was to become the movie director Carol Reed.

Sir Herbert Beerbohm added "Tree" onto his professional name after his father, Julius, warned him about how hard an actor's life would be "unless he rose to the top of the tree." Herbert retorted, "But that's where I'm going" and the name Tree stuck. The theater he built in 1848, Her Majesty's, in the Haymarket, is still one of the best known and most popular in the West End of London.

Ivan told me that he adored his mother, Iris Tree. She had grown up in a large Walpole House on Chiswick Mall in London, built by Charles II for his mistress, the Duchess of Cleveland. Her parents frequently entertained at home and patrons from high society and "High Bohemia" would attend these theatrical evenings.

Iris was educated by a series of governesses, but her real education came from the stage. She learned history through Shakespeare, and she and her two sisters were allowed to stay up late waiting backstage at Her Majesty's, peeking out to watch their father's performances.

With her large blue eyes and flaxen hair worn in a bob before the style became fashionable, Iris cut an unusual figure. She captivated several members of the Bloomsbury set, including the art critic Clive Bell and the painter Augustus John, who did several portraits of her.

She was a wild and free spirit. Determined to become an artist, at the age of sixteen, against her parents' advice, she enrolled at the Slade School of Fine Art. There she discovered poetry and began writing her own poems.

I have had 28
Lovers, some more
Some less—
I have Greek feet.

Perhaps rather misguidedly, if that example is anything to go by, she decided she was a better poet than an artist.

Her two best friends while growing up were Nancy Cunard and Diana Manners, who married Duff Cooper. Nancy's father was the shipping magnate Sir Bache Cunard, and Diana was the daughter of the Duchess of Rutland. Together they formed an inseparable high-profile trio of beauties, and they would remain close for the rest of their lives.

When her father was contracted to make a film of *Macbeth* for D. W. Griffith's film company, the eighteen-year-old Iris traveled with him to Los Angeles and New York. She stayed with the actress Constance Collier, who introduced her to Charlie Chaplin. He was intrigued by her; in his autobiography he wrote about their first encounter. "She was a model of Mayfair sophistication, tall and attractive she entered with her characteristic swagger and carried a long cigarette holder. 'How do you do, Mr. Chaplin?' she said in her deep sonorous voice. 'I suppose I am the only person in the world who has not seen you on the screen.'" He was charmed and the two became close friends.

After the movie was finished Sir Herbert took Iris to New York, where he was playing Shylock in a production of *The Merchant of Venice*. At the opening-night party she met an attractive young American painter named Curtis Moffat. After a courtship lasting only a few months, and against the wishes of her parents, who thought she was too young, they married.

As I uncovered more and more about Ivan's background, I found it at once fascinating and disconcerting. Iris intrigued me, and the more I learned about her I realized what an exhilarating character she was—eccentric and witty, with a gift for mimicry. She liked to dress theatrically, almost as though she were in costume: bright Gypsy-like dresses; hats without the crown, only the brim; harlequin stockings. In fact she didn't sound very different from my grandmother Maureen—more bohemian perhaps, but equally theatrical.

And then I had to keep reminding myself that Iris was also my grandmother. It felt odd to think how closely we were related and yet she seemed as though she was from another world—and in a way she was. She seemed exotic, like an extinct animal you have heard of but are not quite sure whether it ever really existed.

I studied all the photographs and portraits of her I could find, and scrutinized her features to see if I could spot a likeness between us. I discovered a photograph of a bust of Iris by the famous sculptor Jacob Epstein. Her bobbed hairstyle fits like a helmet around her head and makes her resemble a Roman gladiator. One of her huge eyes is closed, the other hooded. She has a turned-up nose and a full mouth like mine.

In the photographs she had a strange kind of beauty; she looked even more like my mother than like me. Ivan had said that he adored his mother, and perhaps their similarity is what first drew him to Mum.

Then I realized that the resemblance between my mother and Iris didn't stop with the physical. The trajectory of their lives was also strangely similar. Both were unconventional beauties from privileged backgrounds. Both had artistic temperaments. Both of them eloped at the age of eighteen with handsome and "unsuitable" artists. And both went on to have many intense and complicated entanglements with men, many of which took place while they were still married to someone else.

I found out that my mother had actually known Iris long

before she met Ivan. My mother's aunt Oonagh had introduced them in Ireland. Caroline had found in the older woman a kindred spirit.

I like to imagine the two of them back then, neither one imagining how intimately they would one day be linked. Through me.

CHAPTER 36

When I started planning the wedding, I had asked Bob to give me away and he had agreed. It had then seemed the most natural request. Now I was faced with a dilemma. What should I do about Ivan? There was definitely no protocol here. I didn't even know if he wanted to be part of my family. Until now we had both existed happily autonomous from each other. Did the fact that he was now revealed to be my father mean I had to rearrange my wedding plans to incorporate this new development?

Bob and Grace were giving my rehearsal dinner at their apartment and the invitations had already been sent out. We hadn't sent one to Ivan. It hadn't seemed important to have him there, and now it would just be weird. I mean, how many fathers could be there? I could always justify not inviting him by pretending that it was in his own best interest, that I knew he would have felt uncomfortable.

Then I started to feel guilty. What were my motives in not inviting him? I knew exactly what they were—and they were not pretty. I didn't want him there because it suited me much better for Bob and Grace to give the rehearsal dinner and for Bob to give me away and give the toast at my wedding.

All I had ever craved was a normal life—I was terribly bourgeois in that way. I hoped that having Bob by my side would somehow legitimize me. I wanted everything to be tidy and pretty. Ivan being there would have spoiled the picture.

I didn't consider Ivan's feelings. I was so concerned about trying to make myself look and feel good, I didn't consider how much I might have been hurting him.

I wish I could excuse myself by saying that it was my way of getting back at him. Ivan had hurt me by not coming forward earlier, and now I was returning the favor by snubbing him. But it wasn't that simple. I didn't want Ivan there because it just didn't suit me. So I didn't invite Ivan to the wedding.

ON THE AFTERNOON OF MY WEDDING, I arrived early at Rockefeller Center and ascended the sixty-something stories to arrive at the Rainbow Room. Evgenia, my maid of honor, and her daughter, Natalya, who was the flower girl, were to meet me there and we were all going to get ready together.

I was already busy deciding with my hairdresser, Joseph, exactly where we should place the little diamante hairpins in my chignon when Evgenia finally showed up. I was about to exclaim how beautiful she looked, but then I noticed her odd expression; she looked all flustered and her face was pale, as though she had been through some ghastly ordeal. Little Natalya was close to tears.

"I have never crossed a picket line before," Evgenia said, her voice shaking. "It was really scary. They were screaming and shouting, 'You should be ashamed of yourselves!' They yelled 'Scum!' at us when we went past. Poor Natalya was absolutely terrified!"

I had no idea what she was talking about. I wondered for a minute if my wedding had sent my sister over the edge. Just then Mercedes arrived, looking glamorous as ever. But she also appeared shaken. She was trying not to let me see it, but she was obviously disturbed.

"I managed to find another entrance, one they weren't blocking," she said. "I think the police are trying to disperse the crowds."

As more of my friends began to trickle in I got a clearer picture of what was happening. The unions were picketing Cipriani and my wedding. It was the first big event that Cipriani had catered since they had taken over the Rainbow Room, and they had managed to make a lot of people angry by unfairly dismissing some of the staff.

When Julian arrived, he took Evgenia and me aside. "You won't believe this," he whispered, "but your brother Sheridan has joined the picket line and is refusing to come up for the wedding! He's out there in his black tie shouting at your guests."

This was really too much. It was one thing for my guests to be terrorized, but it was insufferable that my brother should have joined the picketers. I knew that he had become a card-carrying member of the Communist Party, but I thought that perhaps he could put aside his beliefs for one day. "Well, please get him out of there and up here," I hissed back at Julian. "Tell him I want, no, I *need* him to be at my wedding. Beg him. Do anything."

A moment later my cousin Desmond Guinness rushed up to us, his face flushed with excitement. "It was too marvelous," he exclaimed, blue eyes flashing. "I came in a car with all these grand ladies, and when we saw the commotion we all thought it was the paparazzi waiting to get photographs of us. We were frightfully disappointed when we realized it was just a mob of protesters. I haven't seen a crowd this angry since my mother married Oswald Mosley!"

As more and more guests arrived, the string quartet began playing one of the Schubert pieces I had selected. The guests took their seats on both sides of the area that we had decorated and arranged to resemble a church aisle. Bob and I waited nervously in a back room, occasionally peeking out from behind the door to see when we should make our entrance.

I had my veil down, and we were about to step out when I

heard a commotion taking place in one of the rows of seats. I poked my head out and saw two ushers and Matthew in the aisle trying to grab hold of a woman who was seated in one of the front rows. She was protesting loudly.

I lifted up my veil to get a better look. It was Lady Stewart. She was now in the aisle, flanked by the ushers and Matthew, but was still angrily trying to shake them off.

"What's she doing here? I didn't invite her," I exclaimed to Bob. He looked at me in bewilderment.

The entire congregation was now engrossed in the drama as Lady Stewart refused to leave. She insisted, "I'm a friend of Ivana's, and I'm staying." She looked pleadingly around the room as if to try to rally support from the other guests, but they all turned away uncomfortably.

Managing to break free from Matthew's grip, she quickly darted back to where she had been sitting. Defiantly, she sat down again.

I could see that Matthew was really angry. I wanted to tell him that it didn't matter and to just let her stay, but he was too far away to hear me.

The arguing continued for another five minutes or so, until she finally acquiesced. Holding her head up with as much dignity as she could muster, she stomped back up the aisle headed toward the elevators.

At last the musicians struck up the chords of the "Wedding March," and we were off.

After Matthew and I had exchanged vows, I turned to face the audience. I was relieved and happy to see my brother sitting next to Julian. But when I looked for Sheridan during predinner drinks, he had disappeared again. Julian confirmed that he had gone back to join the picket line. He explained that he had, with much difficulty, been able to persuade my brother to come to the ceremony, since it had nothing to do with Cipriani. It had been a huge gesture for Sheridan, as it meant he had to cross a picket line. But his allegiance to the Communist Party and his conscience simply wouldn't allow him to attend the drinks and dinner. I was disappointed, but I knew that by attending even the ceremony, my brother had made a huge sacrifice for me.

Sheridan confided later that he had been given a really nasty reception by the union members when he returned. Of course, he had felt horribly ridiculous in his tuxedo. Worse, the other picket-line protesters kept taunting him about the way he was dressed. In spite of those incidents, the wedding was a success. Everyone drank a lot and danced on the revolving dance floor to Peter Duchin's orchestra late into the night.

By one o'clock I was exhausted. But every time I tried to get Matthew to leave, he rushed off to find someone else he just had to talk to. When I finally cornered him, I realized he was completely high on something. His face was sweaty and the pupils of his eyes were enormous. He was talking manically, but his rushed words didn't make any sense at all.

I had never seen Matthew like that. Since I had known him he had seemed totally "clean." I was annoyed but also curious to see what he would be like when he let his inhibitions down. Matthew was usually reserved and guarded. When we were dating he had been careful not to let me see this wilder side. It also meant that he no longer could be so sanctimonious and critical of my drinking.

On our wedding night I suppose he felt that there was no point in hiding himself from me anymore. He zoomed around the party, laughing raucously and cracking miserable jokes. He didn't want the party to end and insisted that everyone come back to our suite at the Carlyle to carry on.

At the hotel, the hard-core partyers stayed up all night in the living room of our "honeymoon suite." I went to bed as soon as we got back. I didn't even bother asking Matthew to join me; he was having too much fun. He seemed to have completely forgotten that it was our wedding night. So really, from the first I never had great expectations.

MY BABY WAS DUE IN JULY. I found out I was having a girl and I thought that it would be lovely to take her out to the house in Sag Harbor and for us all to spend the summer there. The house was perfect for a young family. There was plenty of room, and my mother had made the garden pretty in a very English way, with lots of roses, honeysuckle, rhododendrons, and wildflowers.

One of the happiest times of my life was preparing for my baby's arrival. There was something so joyful and pure about picking out the crib and the wallpaper and gazing longingly at the adorable baby clothes.

I wanted everything to look like the pages of a catalogue. I couldn't believe that it was really possible to have rooms look normal. I had always thought that matching curtains and bedspreads and carpets were part of a rarefied world to which I could never belong.

Because my rooms as a child had been so ramshackle and higgledy-piggledy, I had always fantasized about things that my mother considered really bad taste, things like wall-to-wall carpeting, frilly curtains, and pouffy cushions. I used to love to wander around the furniture rooms of Harrods and dream of one day having a house that looked just like the showrooms.

In my daughter's room I could finally let loose my vision of what a baby girl's room should look like—everything in pink with lots of bows and flowers. I felt positively defiant as I picked out pillows to match the pattern on the curtain, which in turn matched the furry carpet and the decorations on the crib. I felt as though I were five years old and choosing things for my doll-house. I found it hard to believe that I was a grown-up now with a credit card, a house, and, soon, a baby.

My mother had always had such mad theories, particularly about what was expensive and what was affordable. She had grown up so out of touch with the rest of the world, surrounded by staff and suffocated by wealth, and yet also a product of wartime rationing and deprivation. I felt she never was able to grasp what was normal and what was extravagant. She absolutely detested shopping and preferred to just hand me her credit card rather than face the hell she considered any store to be.

My mother's phobia of stores could be quite contagious. When we were still living at Redcliffe Square, a few days before I was to start my new drama school, I begged my mother to come shopping with me for the dreaded items required by the school. It was a particularly boring list of things to get—tap, ballet, and jazz shoes; leotards and footless tights; and comfortable trousers. We had typically left it to the last minute and now we were having to race around the shops in London desperately trying to finish the task.

The final straw was the name tags. The school insisted that you have the sewn-on kind, the ones you are meant to order with your name printed on in advance. Of course we hadn't ordered any, and now we couldn't find them anywhere. We ended up in the haberdashery department of Fenwick. It was overheated and overlit. My mother was at her wit's end, sighing and moaning at the nightmare of it all, her blue eyes clouded with frustration at what she perceived to be the salesgirls' ineptitude and their blank expressions as we tried to explain what we needed.

"Oh I just can't do this anymore," my mother practically screamed. She looked at me pleadingly. "Please, can't I go home?"

I don't quite know what happened, but suddenly I felt faint and panicky. My head felt as though it was cracking open. I leaned on the counter, but I couldn't stand up. I collapsed on the floor of the shop and started bawling my eyes out. I felt that everything was completely hopeless, that somehow if I didn't have the correct name tags I could never have a reasonable life and would be forever condemned to live in chaos. I just lay there sobbing and repeating, "I don't know what to do. I don't know what to do."

By now there was quite a crowd around us as shoppers abandoned their search for ribbons and buttons to stare at the deranged girl and her not much saner-looking mother. I don't remember much else until I was lying in a bed in a private room in Priory Hospital in Roehampton.

I remember my mother, and for some reason her and Robert's great friend the writer Jonathan Raban, sitting on the end of my bed with a big bottle of champagne they had snuck in. Mum said that she completely understood why I had broken down so pitifully. She promised I would never have to go back to that dreadful shop, Fenwick, again.

I felt a bit foolish but also hugely relieved to be somewhere safe and not having to go shopping anymore. I never did get those name tags.

HOME DECORATING definitely fell into the way too extravagant category for my mother; therefore modern kitchens and bathrooms were out of the question. Because she didn't drive, my mother also considered cars a waste of money. I remember one day trying to persuade her to buy a new car. The one we had was decades old and decrepit. It was not only noisy and uncomfortable but also dangerous, with bits of mirrors stuck on with masking tape and broken windscreen wipers. When I pleaded with my mother to replace it, she replied, "Don't be ridiculous, no one has cars anymore!"

This became a joke in the family. "No one has cars anymore." Every time we went out I would marvel at the extreme lack of cars on the road. She eventually gave in and bought an impractical maroon-colored vintage Mercedes. She had spotted it for sale on the side of the road somewhere and had liked the color. Aubergine, she called it proudly.

As she didn't drive, she would get people to chauffeur her around while she sat grandly in the back. Her house in Sag Harbor was right in the village, so she only used the car to go to the liquor store or the farm stand. "Driving Lady Caroline," we teasingly called this.

CHAPTER 37

It feels very strange to be sitting here in my mother's house in Sag Harbor writing about the past like this. I thought I could be entirely detached, but remembering everything, especially how my mother looked and how uncomplaining she was at the end, has bought up a torrent of feelings. Feelings that I have spent my life trying not to feel. But this time I am just sitting with them. I tell myself that it's okay, that these are just emotions and they are not going to kill me. My immediate reaction when I have an uncomfortable feeling is to do anything to squelch it, preferably with a chemical of some kind.

This time I made a conscious decision to allow myself to feel. I am alone in the house, and I go into the room that was my mother's bedroom. I sit on her bed, and for the first time in a long time I look around and think about her. I look at all the funny little pieces of furniture she had picked up from second-rate antique shops in Sag Harbor. "Pathetic little Sags" she would call them. I notice that the photograph of me—one of my old acting head shots, which she had up on the wall across from her bed—has turned sepia, its edges and corners wrinkled.

I look through the books she had on her Egyptian-style bookcase: a bizarre mix of obscure Latin poetry (Robert's), a book called *Getting the Part* (mine), and one on transsexuals, which she was reading as research for a book she was planning to write on the subject.

Of course I start crying and I allow myself to. I feel such a huge array of things. Sorrow, self-pity, love, and then a huge wave of anger. "Why, Mum? Why did you have to bloody lie to me? Why didn't you just tell me."

Why Not Say What Happened?

I sit in her room for a long time, half-thinking that I will find some kind of answer. I think about every conversation I ever had with Mum about my paternity. How she had sometimes been evasive. But also how adamant she had been about my changing my name to Lowell. Even in her most drunken and usually candid moments she had never told me the truth. Finally I get up, leave her room, and close the door behind me. I would like to say that I feel light and that it had been a cathartic experience, but all I feel is incredibly drained.

WHEN I FIRST INHERITED the house from my mother, I wasn't sure that I would ever want to live there. There were so many memories and her presence could be felt in every room, in every object, and in every piece of furniture, all of which she had moved around with her over the years. It was the stage for so many different scenes that she had played out in her life.

There was the set of heavy Venetian streetlamps that I remembered had stood like bright sentinels in the houses in Redcliffe Square, Kent, Ireland, and even in Condo. Sheridan had once managed to pull one down on top of himself, and when he was older my mother always teased him that he probably wasn't "quite right in the head" as a result of his collision with the lamp.

The lamps had all landed here, and I had inherited them along with their stories. My daughter would someday be burdened with them and an entirely new set of problems. It is strange how everything can still look exactly the same yet feel so completely different. The old books and photographs were just things before. Now they were memories.

I knew that my mother had left the house to me because she loved it, and she hoped that I would someday want to live there. She had always felt that a house that size needed a family. She was right. When I had first taken Matthew to the house, I hadn't set foot in it for two years. I wasn't at all sure how I was going to feel about it. I thought that I would probably find it creepy and sad, full of far too many memories and associations. I thought I would never be able to feel comfortable there. I would probably want to sell it.

I imagined that my mother's presence, or lack of it, would be felt in every room. There was also the possibility that she would be haunting the place; remember, she was buried in the back-yard. If she were there as a ghost, she would be restless and annoyed that the peace that she had searched for in life, and thought she had finally found, had been so rudely disturbed.

The first day I went back to visit, I went into the kitchen; this was the room we had used the most. I looked out through the bay window into the garden and remembered the night we had buried her. It had been so cold and we had been physically and emotionally drained. I suggested that we go down to the village to get a restorative drink. Julian and Sheridan agreed. But my sister, who doesn't drink and to her great credit hasn't for decades, said she was tired. She would rather stay home.

It was a blistery, snowy night. After we left the house in search of some good cheer, Evgenia made herself a cup of tea and sat down on the sofa in the kitchen. The naked stems of the climbing roses tapped eerily on the panes of the bow-shaped windows. My sister looked out into the misty white garden, and to her horror she saw a ghostly figure coming down the path. All she could see was a shock of white hair moving toward her.

My sister hoped she was hallucinating, but then the ghostly apparition put its visage to the window and started knocking on it. Poor Evgenia screamed hysterically as the creature found its way round to the kitchen door and came fully into the light. It was only then that she realized that the white hair belonged to our next-door neighbor, the late, well-known monologist Spalding Gray. He had come to offer his condolences on our loss.

AS I SAT IN THE KITCHEN, I thought of a million silly and actually happy times I had had in this house with my mother.

How many late-night discussions had taken place around the simple pine kitchen table? A cast of houseguests had come and gone, each one unaware of playing a part in the long and surreal tragicomedy of our family life.

I remembered summer weekends with my friends, most of whom my mother immediately took hostage and turned into her friends. After a few hours of being in the house, even the more conventional ones would abandon their previous reserve and gleefully take part in the surrounding madness, as if suddenly liberated by the informality.

Meals were produced at strange times, if at all. There was no order to the weekend activities. But if you were staying you had to play along or risk condemnation for "not getting it." I watched friends who rarely if ever got drunk, drink far too much. They would behave in strange and uncharacteristic ways when they were staying with us.

A highly regarded Irish Catholic priest and theologian from Boston named Maclaren came for the weekend with a friend of my mother, a poetry lecturer at NYU named John. When he arrived early Friday evening, Maclaren was soft-spoken and polite, but he seemed nervous and in awe of my mother and somewhat intimidated by her and the house. Besides being a priest, he was a writer and a big fan of my mother's books. And of course, coming from Boston, he idolized Robert Lowell.

My best friend, Charlotte, was also staying with us that weekend. It was a hot July evening, and Charlotte and I decided to make caipirinhas. After school, before we had both gone to drama colleges, we had spent six months together in Brazil, falling in love with not only the country but the men and the way of life there.

We had gotten a taste for the national cocktail, a delicious mixture of the sugarcane liquor cachaça and lime juice, to which we added mint. We had been thrilled to find that the local Sag Harbor liquor store sold cachaça and immediately bought several bottles along with lots of limes and mint.

We made a particularly strong batch to offer as a welcome drink to our houseguests and at first Maclaren coyly demurred. "I'm not much of a drinker," he explained and asked for a club soda. But after Charlotte, my mother, and I feigned hurt and dismay that he was refusing such a labor of love, he broke down and agreed to try one of our concoctions.

Charlotte and I quickly grew bored by the religious conversation the two men had managed to get my mother engaged in. We snuck upstairs to watch a movie. We were nearing the end of our film when we heard a commotion outside in the garden. We tried to ignore it, but soon my mother burst into the room, turning on the light we had shut off for movie viewing.

"You have to help. Maclaren has gone quite mad," she declared. "He's had too much to drink and he's started fighting with John. I think they might kill each other."

We ran downstairs and out into the garden, where the two men were indeed involved in a furious brawl. A couple of garden chairs had been knocked over and Maclaren was sitting on his friend, shouting profanities that I was surprised were part of a priest's vocabulary. He had his hands around John's neck, while John was struggling to break free from the death lock position.

My mother began making shooing noises at the men, halfheartedly attempting to break them up. "Go and get some cold water and pour it on them," she told Sheridan excitedly.

"Mum, that's for dogfights," I said impatiently. But then I reconsidered. Perhaps it wasn't such a bad idea, and so I ran inside and helped Sheridan fill a bucket. Then we sloshed it over the raging fighters.

It had the desired effect. Maclaren stopped. He let go of his grip on John and jumped up from him in shock. He looked at us, his face scarlet and bewildered. He seemed to have no idea who we were or where he was. He swayed from side to side as he tried to comprehend the situation. Then he walked unsteadily to one of the deck chairs and, shaking the water from his head, collapsed. Immediately he fell into a drunken slumber.

John, meanwhile, was trying to straighten himself up with as much dignity as he could manage and apologize to my mother. "I don't know what came over us. I promise I have never seen Maclaren behave like that. He never normally drinks anything. Now I know why! I don't even know what I said to make him so angry."

My mother assured him that it was quite okay and told him not to worry about it. We all went into the kitchen to make some sobering coffee, but Maclaren reappeared and drunkenly informed us that he was leaving. He went out to the hall to try to find his bag and coat but we managed to intercept him. We told him not to be so ridiculous and that he must stay the night.

"Get his car keys," I told John, to which Maclaren responded with another outburst of angry cursing, this time at me. We had to use all our persuasive powers to convince him. Finally he let us help him upstairs and onto the bed in one of the attic bedrooms.

We were tired from the excitement and decided to abandon the rest of the movie and go to bed.

When my mother said goodnight to us she was clearly in good spirits. I think she had been rather dreading the idea of the priest's coming to stay, thinking that he would be dull and she would have to be on her best behavior. But he had turned out to be far more entertaining than anyone could have imagined.

I hadn't been asleep for very long, maybe a couple of hours, when I heard a timid tapping on my door. "Ivana, it's John. I am so sorry to disturb you, but Maclaren has disappeared." I felt a twinge of annoyance. This priest was becoming a proper nuisance.

I was now wide awake and turned on the lights. "What do you mean disappeared? I thought you had hidden his car keys from him."

"I did. His car is still here but he has gone." I looked at the clock on the cable box and it was almost 3 a.m. Where could he have gone so late?

"What's happened?" My mother popped her head around her bedroom door. "What's everyone doing?" She came excitedly out into the corridor and I noticed she was wearing a blue shirt and sheer panty hose but no underwear. "What have I missed?"

"Mum, go put some clothes on. Please."

Charlotte now was standing with us in her bathrobe and John was trying to explain the situation. He had gone into Maclaren's room to check up on him only to discover that he had gone. His overnight bag was still there, but he wasn't anywhere to be found.

My mother had now pulled on a pair of baggy leggings and was hopping around enthusiastically. "Well, he can't have gone very far without a car. We have to find him. It would really be too awful to lose him. He is my guest, after all." I agreed with my mother it would be a shame to lose him, so we decided to form our own little search party.

Why Not Say What Happened?

We went into the kitchen and tried to find a flashlight, but of course none of them worked. My mother pulled some white tapered candles from the holders in the dining room and we each armed ourselves with one.

It was a pleasant, warm night and the village was completely silent. There was not a soul on the roads, and all the houses were dark. Slowly, we began our procession down Main Street. "Maclaren, where are you?" we called softly. We peered into the neighbors' backyards and into the alleys between the stores.

As we proceeded on, our calls became louder and bolder. "Maclaren, come out, come out wherever you are."

With its gingerbread houses and old white churches, Sag Harbor was looking particularly genteel and picturesque in the moonlight. We, however, were a motley crew. Mum, John, and I led the party. Charlotte and Sheridan were holding up the rear in their nightclothes, chatting away as though they were just on a nice summer's evening walk. They had grabbed a towel and draped it around their shoulders.

We walked down to the end of Main Street and onto a pier that jutted out into the bay. There were huge handsome yachts dotted around, and although their masts were lit up their decks were deserted.

"Maclaren, Maclaren, are you there?" my mother called loudly out to sea. A dog barked but otherwise nothing.

"You don't think he's done a suey, do you?" my mother asked John. She sounded more hopeful than concerned. "What do you mean?" he looked perplexed. "You know, done a suey. Committed suicide," Mum replied, emphasizing the last two words in a mock whisper, apparently annoyed that he hadn't understood. "He may have jumped off the bridge. You know, Spalding Gray tried to do it once. But it was too shallow, and he just ended up knee deep in mud feeling a bit foolish."

"Is he the type who likes to go to bars?" I asked helpfully. "I know there is a rather rough and seedy Irish bar called Murph's that stays open all night. Do you think he might have gone there?"

"I told you he doesn't normally drink, that's not his thing at all," John snapped back at me. "He's usually very quiet and shy."

"Well, he certainly managed to put away the caipirinhas," Charlotte said. "I warned him they were strong but I think he drank a whole jug on his own. He could have saved us some for tomorrow."

"Where is Murph's?" My mother perked up. "I have always heard about it. Let's go and look for him there."

"Oh, Mum! You just want to have a drink," Sheridan complained.

We walked over the bridge, looking over the edge to make sure there weren't any "floaters." We walked right around the outskirts of the village until we had completed a full circle and were back near our house. Our candles were all out and we were cold. The sun was starting to come up.

"I'm exhausted and am going back to bed." I declared. "I am sorry, John. I am sure he will turn up sometime." I felt we had done enough. It wasn't our fault his friend was so maddening.

At eight thirty there was a sharp knock on the front door and I peered over the banister. There was a police car outside. My mother was already rushing to see who was there; she was still in the same clothes as earlier that morning and I guessed she hadn't gone back to bed.

Maclaren was standing outside with a policeman. The priest looked awful, disheveled, and pale. His clothes were rumpled and covered in brown and green stains.

"A neighbor found him passed out on their lawn. He didn't seem to know where he was," the officer explained, looking at my mother. I thought he was smirking. "He says he's a friend of yours, ma'am."

I looked at Maclaren and his face was crumpled with mortification. He didn't know where to look so he just looked down at the doorstep. I hoped he wasn't going to start to cry.

My mother was still asking the policeman questions, pushing for all the gory details. "Did you have to arrest him? Is he in trouble? What's going to happen now?" You could tell she was trying to squeeze every last embarrassing incident out of the situation. I could already imagine her retelling the story, innocently reveling in the "appalling behavior" of her guest. Of course, she'd milk the Catholic priest part.

I felt horrible and ashamed for us all.

What was it about my mother that made people around her act so uncharacteristically? Did she just draw out sides of them that had always been there but needed a little prodding from an expert? Or perhaps she just attracted those who sensed a kindred, damaged spirit, and felt at home with her.

Whatever it was, sometimes I actually felt scared. I was so close to her, I felt that if I wasn't careful I could become just an extension of her. It was so easy to become caught up in it all.

CHAPTER 38

On that first visit back to Sag, I had looked out onto the pool, now full of leaves and dead or still-struggling bugs. It had the lonely feeling of a room or a nightclub in the harsh light of the morning, empty and tawdry now that the party was over.

I thought about how excited I had been when I first saw it. Of course we had never had a pool—that was considered far too extravagant—but like everyone else I had always longed for one.

When we had lived at Maidstone Park, in Kent, we had some neighbors, the Every-Greens, I'll call them, who lived in a big mock Tudor house at the beginning of our driveway.

The Every-Greens were snobbish and took great pride in their immaculately maintained garden. They had an enclosed tennis court, and an electronic garage that housed two cars—a silver Jag for visits to town and a Land Rover for the country. But their real trophy, the sign that they were Somebody-Greens, and the object of my intense envy, was their kidney-shaped swimming pool.

It was situated close to the hedge that bordered our driveway, and so I had to pass it every day. As we drove by in our rickety old car, it glinted at me importantly and seemed to gloat. It somehow knew that it represented a world I longed to be part of. A place where the dads wore blazers and ties and went to work in town every day and the mums were on the school and village committees and had genteel parties around the pool that even the local vicar would attend.

When my mother first bought "the big house," these neighbors had been excited. Perhaps a little jealous that someone else was going to be living in the grandest house in the area, but happy that it was at least a titled Guinness heiress.

A week or so after we first moved in, Mrs. Every-Green invited us all for drinks. I had noticed the children's gleaming bicycles stacked neatly next to the garage and the expensive-looking wooden slide and swing set that was set up pristinely in their garden. And I had also noticed one of their blond daughters as she roller-skated by in her white lace-up boots. She had smiled at me as she did a little twirl, extending a long straight leg behind her.

I desperately hoped that we would become friends, she and her brothers and I, and that they would ask me over to play every day. Perhaps in the summer they'd even invite me to swim in their fancy pool.

With both my sisters away at boarding school, I was lonely. The size of the house and its distance from the other houses only accentuated my feeling of being cut off. I had felt both elated and a little surprised when Mum and Robert told me they had accepted the neighborly invitation. I prayed that the visit would go well. But a few hours before we were due to leave, I knew that it was going to be a disaster. My mother was in a restless and contrary mood. She had already decided that the Every-Greens were going to be ghastly.

I tried to plead their case, saying that we didn't know them and that their house looked awfully nice. I said it was important that we should all be friends. But my mother was already calculating excuses to get out of it. And my heart sank further as I followed her into the kitchen and saw her pour herself a huge beaker of "vod."

"Let me get you some tonic, or at least some ice," I offered as she took her first swig. Even as an eight-year-old I knew the right measure for a drink and what it took to dilute it.

I realized that I wasn't going to get very far with my mother so I sought out Robert to try to explain how important it was that we make a nice impression on our neighbors.

He was lying in his usual position, in the large, corner spare room on the top floor that he used as his study. His lanky frame was stretched out on the blue velveteen-covered bed, surrounded by his manuscript pages, all annotated with his spidery pencil marks. His silvery head rested on his right hand and elbow.

To my annoyance I noticed that my dog, Lulu, was lying contentedly next to him. She had taken to creeping up there recently, and Robert and she had developed a cozy companionship. I was irritated by their secret little bond, and Robert knew that and teased me about it.

However, apart from his stealing the affections of my dog, in Robert I knew I had an ally. I felt comfortable and at ease in his presence. He seemed so childish himself, it was as though I was with one of my contemporaries. He told the silliest jokes. And he particularly liked reading me cautionary tales about the vile things that happen to children who misbehave.

I knew he would most certainly be on my side—if only I could get him to understand the importance of the situation. He could sometimes act so vague, and the way he had of teasing me— going off on no doubt amusing, but to me incomprehensible, tangents—could be frustrating.

Of course he had no idea that we were meant to be going over to any house whatsoever to meet anyone at all. He hadn't the slightest idea what I was talking about. But he listened to me and I think sensed my concern. He eventually agreed that we should make an effort to be friendly. He said, "Good fences make good neighbors," a remark I didn't understand because we didn't have any fences anywhere near their property, but I didn't want to ask him what he meant. I was just glad he was on my side.

Why Not Say What Happened?

I knew from the disappointed look on Mrs. Every-Green's face when she opened the door that we were not what she expected, and definitely not what she was hoping for. We had walked up the driveway from our house and were rudely late. My mother had already had far too many vods and her black eyeliner was panda-like around her eyes. Robert was acting peculiar, overly chatty, excited, and hard to follow. He was muttering things to himself and finding his own remarks extremely amusing. I could tell he made Mrs. Every-Green nervous and that she wasn't at all sure how she was meant to react, if at all. I knew that he was going to behave really inappropriately, and I think my mother sensed that he was entering one of his manic phases. Maybe that's why she seemed even more anxious than usual.

I was taken off to be shown around by one of the children, and so to this day I am not sure exactly what happened among the grown-ups. On the way home my mother seemed upset. Not drunk, just worried.

Robert was walking with us, but he wasn't really with us. I took his hand, and he squeezed mine and peered down at me through his specs. "Tell your mother that she's your mother," he insisted. He looked serious, as though he were telling me something really important. A couple of nights later he was taken away on one of his "trips."

I was only invited back to the neighbors' to swim a couple of times, and I didn't enjoy the experience because although the water was warm, my welcome felt frigid. I could sense how suspicious and mistrustful the family was of me. I felt that they felt that I was somehow going to contaminate their precious, heavily chlorinated pool.

Later on events took a wonderfully farcical turn. Our beloved cart horse, Paddy, broke out of his paddock. He boldly clopped up the driveway and into the Every-Greens' garden, where he proceeded to munch happily on some plants among the rose beds. One of their gardeners spotted him, and his angry shouts startled poor Paddy so much that he fled in the opposite direction and plunged straight into the swimming pool.

He was a large and sturdy horse. Although he was retired from cart pulling (he had actually once belonged to the queen), he was still impressively strong. In his frantic attempt to get out, he kicked his huge shaggy, fetlocked hoofs, managing to smash most of the delicate ornamental tiles that sided the pool.

The firemen were called, and the two families stood on opposite ends of the pool watching anxiously as Paddy was carefully hoisted out by means of a sling-like harness and a crane. He was a little shaken but otherwise unharmed. He instantly became a hero in our family.

Robert was particularly tickled by Paddy's little adventure. He became a huge admirer of what he now referred to as "our magnificent steed." It ended up costing my mother a fortune in repairs, and from then on my swimming was strictly limited to the icy-cold river at the bottom of our field.

WHEN MY MOTHER FIRST SAW the house in Sag Harbor, the pool was oddly one of the things that had attracted her. She usually hated the look of them and felt that they were eyesores in sometimes otherwise pretty gardens. But this one, with its dark royal blue tiles and sitar shape, met her approval. She liked the way the surrounding green trees and pink and red rhododendrons were reflected in its dark blue water.

I couldn't believe it when she bought the house and we finally had our very own pool. I felt that we had suddenly been elevated into the class of pool-owning gentry. Now when I invited my friends in England to come and stay, I could casually drop, "Oh, and don't forget to bring your swimming clothes." I really pushed my luck with my mother, though, when I suggested we put in a heater. "No one has heating anymore!" she scoffed.

The first thing I am going to do is put a heater in the pool, I thought, feeling liberated and rebellious. I am also going to buy a nice *new* solid American car. And when my daughter is ready to go off to camp or school, she is going to have every article of clothing marked with a beautifully sewn-in name tag.

I decided to be disgustingly normal. Everything would be kept spotless and orderly. Of course I had no idea how I was going achieve this, or even what it meant really. I just thought, or hoped, that if I could keep everything on the exterior looking all nice and tidy, then perhaps I wouldn't feel so jumbled up inside. I started to feel excited at the prospect of making a life in Sag Harbor, that maybe I was capable at last of enjoying the gifts that I had been given.

I realized that most of my life I had spent as though I were some lunatic in a maze, going round and round the same destructive path. I would go in a circle that was familiar but always ended up at the same wretched starting place. Round and round I would go, like a blithering idiot, moaning about my upbringing. The crazy and saddest thing is, what was I doing while I complained so bitterly? I can tell you exactly: I was drinking, being difficult myself, marrying an addict, having fights with him, and then divorcing him.

"They fuck you up, your mum and dad," Philip Larkin wrote. Yes, of course they do; everyone knows that. But it would help to know who your parents are so you can blame the *right* ones for the fucking up. I could have learned at least a tiny lesson from the way mine did it and not just copied them. That shows terrible lack of imagination on my part, I'm afraid.

CHAPTER 39

Daisy Caroline Miller was born in New York Hospital on July 16, 1999. She arrived earlier than I had expected, and, wouldn't you know, July 16 is also my mother's birthday. I couldn't believe it when I started having the contractions. It was too strange a coincidence.

We called her Daisy because Matthew had a grandmother Daisy. Throughout the entire birth, Matthew was buzzing about manically. The night before, when I was going into labor, I was pacing and groaning around our rented apartment in New York. He lay in bed and repeatedly told me to "shut up and go back to sleep."

At the hospital he was more interested in my pain medication than anything else. When I finally received an epidural, he had tried to stay in the room because of his fascination with needles, but the nurses shooed him out.

Hours after our daughter was born, I was still in agony from labor and was given some pills for the pain. But before I could take one, Matthew seized them for himself and told me I would be fine with Tylenol.

The evening of Daisy's birth Matthew went out to dinner to celebrate. I was left alone in the hospital with an unfamiliar, helpless little person next to me. I didn't have the slightest clue what I was meant to do with her. I was scared of her, scared *for* her, scared for us both.

I reached over to the flat cot where she was lying. She was wearing the hospital issue white snow cone hat and tiny white socks. She stretched out her tadpole-like legs, and her eyes, although still semiclosed, seemed to register me.

I picked her up carefully, terrified that my touch would frighten her, hurt her even, and she would reject me. I was anxious that I wasn't going to be able to give her everything she needed and deserved.

"Well, darling, it's just you and me from now on. I hope we get along."

I am ashamed to admit, and it is the hardest thing for a parent to admit, that I let my daughter down. I loved her deeply, but that wasn't enough for me to stay sober for her, to keep my marriage together, and not to go under—and not just once but many times. Sometimes I didn't even want to struggle to come back up. I just couldn't be bothered. When I was that far down it seemed like it would be so much easier not to fight for that last gasp of life-giving air. Perhaps it's just pure maternal instinct that has stopped me from sinking to the place where there is no more coming up again.

I wanted so much to give my daughter the sense of stability that I never had, but when you are drowning yourself, how can you keep someone else afloat?

LIVING IN SAG HARBOR, I felt a surge of happy energy around me. I felt enormously grateful to my mother. I had come home.

Of course it felt sad and empty without her, but I knew that somehow if I could make it my own I might be okay. I could raise my daughter in a way that would make me feel proud.

After I had been settled into the house for a while I started doing some "emotional housekeeping," something you are told to do when you leave rehab. I started my cleaning with the messiest, most obvious place there was. I decided to invite Ivan to come and stay in the house in Sag Harbor.

I hadn't seen very much of him since our rather startling "discovery," but he had come to Daisy's first birthday party in London and had been at his best. He was sweet and kind and seemed pleased to be playing the role of doting grandfather. It was as though we had just rented him especially for the occasion. A few of my friends whom I hadn't seen for a while looked a bit confused as Ivan sat beaming and holding Daisy in a very familial way, but it wasn't the time to go into it. I just left them wondering.

I still had, however, very divided feelings about his new role in my life. I hadn't decided how I should react to it. In rehab there is a huge emphasis put on "family of origin." And this was still a great source of confusion for me. When they asked me to talk about my relationship with my father while growing up, I really didn't know whom I should be talking about. Which relationship is the one that affects you most? And the one that either damages or nurtures you?

Is your relationship with the man you thought was your biological father the most important one? Probably. But then I hardly knew Israel. In fact, I didn't know him, never lived with him as far as I can remember, and he died when I was six.

Bob Silvers told me that he was around the most, from my birth until my mother married Robert. He lived with us in the house on West Twelfth Street. He remembers vacations in Jamaica, with us playing on the beach and learning to swim. That sounds so lovely. Perhaps those were the important years.

When I think of my childhood as snapshots, Robert was the man who seems to be in all the most vivid ones. When I was being molested, he was a distant figure somewhere in the house, unaware and incapable of knowing. Yet, while it was happening to me I knew how angry Robert would have been if he had known. I knew he would have wanted to kill Mike, it would have horrified him so much. Perhaps that's one of the reasons I never told anyone; I knew instinctively that Robert's fragile mind couldn't have borne it. But even that knowledge was a strange comfort to me.

I have so many images of him and his sweetness, of his lying stoically on the tiny towel at the burn hospital, his repeatedly getting lost at train stations, liking toast and bacon burnt until black. Memories of just lounging around on a hot summer day on the lawn of Milgate, my mother trying to dye her hair blonder with beer and the wasps swarming around.

I remember reading out loud with Robert the manuscript of his translation of Racine's *Phaedra*. I would insist on taking the title role and Robert would play all the other characters. Of course I didn't understand the grand tragedy of the play at all. I just tried to pronounce and act the words with enough passion to make it seem as if I did.

While we were reading he would often make a correction in his translation and that would make me feel wonderfully important, as though I were contributing to literature. During our readings, or "rehearsals" as we liked to call them, he would light one of his menthol-tipped cigarettes and hand me an unlit one. I would suck on it and pretend to smoke. I enjoyed the cold minty taste of the tobacco air that came through the hole in the filter.

I remember roller-skating around the house with my dog Lulu pulling me by a skipping rope, the rattle of the wheels on the flagstones echoing through the house. Knowing it was disrupting my mother and Robert's peace mischievously made me enjoy it all the more.

These are the images of my childhood, the ones that I miss. The images of a father. *My* father.

CHAPTER 40

With alcoholism, it's your genetics that count the most. After all, your biological parents' DNA gave you the disease in the first place. So for just plain medical reasons, Ivan was the one to focus on. I wasn't even sure if he was an alcoholic. He certainly liked a whiskey or two, and in the Fellini movie *La Dolce Vita,* there's a scene in which Ivan's mother, Iris Tree—my grandmother—appears, and she certainly looks as though she was a heavy imbiber. So I probably had it from both sides.

In one rehab in Arizona, they ask you to write letters to your parents to be read out loud in group. These are meant to be apologies for all the bad things you did to them while you were drinking. Well, that was a total wash for me. My mother was dead, and I had never done anything at all to Ivan, good or bad.

When they asked for family members to visit and participate in Family Week, there was no way I'd invite Ivan. He hardly knew me, and I wasn't going to drag him there to do the embarrassing and hokey things that they make those poor families do. So I told them the truth—both my parents were dead.

That wasn't much better, really, because throughout that week I had to do Dead Chair. It's an exercise in total mortification. The entire rehab faculty sits in a large circle of chairs, and two chairs are placed in the middle. Patient and parent are made to take turns in the hot seats facing each other. They each in turn list their grievances against the other. The format was the same for everyone, and the party on the receiving end is not allowed to make a comment until the other is finished.

First you had to name the grievance, and then you use a "feeling" word, describing how it made you feel.

"Dad. When you . . . slept with my best friend in high school and asked me not to tell Mom about it. I felt . . . sad, hurt, lonely, and angry."

"Katherine, when you stole my favorite diamond brooch that was a present from Grandma and used the money to buy meth, I felt . . . angry, sad, and hurt."

This was riveting entertainment, sort of like bearbaiting or reality TV. You were fascinated and appalled that you were watching, and so glad it wasn't you—until it was.

I had to do it on my own and pretend that my dead mother was sitting in the chair opposite me. I made up the blandest accusations that I thought would sound convincing.

"Mum. When you . . . got drunk at my school and embarrassed me in front of my teachers, I felt . . . sad, angry, and lonely."

That was easy. It was unfair, actually, because she wasn't there to get even with me. I wouldn't have enjoyed trading insults in front of an audience with someone as intelligent, observant, and caustic as my mother, but then again we would have given them a real show. Instead I got all the sympathy, without any recriminations.

It was rather disconcerting, surreal, actually dragging my poor mother back into this situation. I mean, fine if I was in a nice restaurant having delicious wine and perhaps a dozen oysters and she had to make an appearance. But rehab? Everybody sober? In front of all those intense counselors and their earnest concern? It would have been her absolute worst.

My one consolation for this mortifying exercise was when I was asked why I had chosen not to resurrect my dad as well.

I had said because I hadn't known him well enough. But then I thought of the endless opportunities for entertainment I was missing, and I started smiling at the prospect.

Imagine if Israel or Ivan or, God forbid, Robert were really there. What would I say to them?

"Robert. When you . . . allowed me to have wine with you at night and then were carted off to the loony bin for months, I felt . . . happy, loved, confused, and drunk.

"Robert. When you . . . acted bizarrely and thought you were Napoleon, or Mussolini, I felt . . . confused, scared, and amused.

"Israel. When you . . . acted as though you were my father, I felt . . . secure, happy, and loved.

"Ivan. When you . . . told me I was your daughter and I didn't believe it and then it turned out to be true, I felt . . . angry, lonely, sad, hurt, confused, angry, angry, angry."

Now I wish I had brought them all back because after all it was my imaginary family week. I could have put them in chairs in the middle of the room, and said, "When you all lied to me about who my father was I felt . . . fucked up."

Quite fun really. Perhaps that should become a new family parlor game, something to take the place of charades.

IVAN SEEMED PLEASED when I called to invite him to Sag Harbor. He agreed to come for a week, and he repeated that remark about houseguests being like fish; they start to go bad after three days. I joked that I would pretend not to mind when he started to stink as long as he kept his door shut and the windows open, and we both laughed.

It was a lovely day in July when he arrived. I had made quite elaborate preparations for his arrival. I felt a need to please him, although at the same time I was irritated with myself for wanting to make a good impression.

I knew that he was extremely fastidious about his food, and so I had telephoned Marguerite Littman, who knew him so well. He had always praised her food.

"Well, he lurves caviar, of curse," she said with that Southern drawl. "And he always asks for crab salad or potted shrimps. He doesn't really like wine but likes whiskey and a special kind of beer that I have to order from California." She giggled and sounded amused when she said, "Good lurk, Vaana."

I put him in my mother's old room (knowing the irony wouldn't be wasted on him). I bought flowers and made the house look as clean and "normal" as I could.

I ordered the caviar from Caviarteria in New York. I didn't order the beluga, which Marguerite had told me was his favorite (of course), but the sevruga was still shockingly expensive.

I made little toast points and carefully chopped up all the bits of egg white, onion, and parsley that traditionally accompany fish eggs. I made a tomato salad, using the small amount of basil I had grown in my garden. And I neatly laid out pungent and deliciously runny French cheeses and an apple tart I had picked up from the local gourmet food store.

I went to the liquor store (praying no one from the local AA meetings I had started attending would see me) and bought his favorite and, I glumly discovered, expensive brand of Scotch whiskey. I tracked down his favorite beer. This was all in preparation for his first evening. I thought if I made a good initial impression, the rest of the week could take care of itself.

I sent a car to JFK to meet his flight from L.A., and when he arrived he insisted on trying to pay for it. I told him it was taken care of and he looked both embarrassed and relieved. I saw he had gotten much thinner and seemed smaller somehow. He was still limping from his accident and was leaning heavily on a wooden cane. His big boyish smile was exactly the same though and he was very talkative. Best of all, he seemed genuinely pleased to see me.

When Daisy came running out to meet him, I hesitated. Then I introduced him as her grandfather. He liked that. "Gosh, she's beautiful. She looks so like Caroline," he said. I agreed. But I couldn't resist saying, "And you. I bet you think she looks just like you. Don't you?" The question came out sounding sharper and more sarcastic than I had intended, and I started to feel resentment churning in my stomach.

I knew my daughter was beautiful, but I didn't want him to take any credit for it. Before he could reply, I said, "Actually I think she looks just like her father." That ended the discussion.

Ivan and I were both actors by nature and could play the scene any way we chose to. I decided I wasn't going to make it easy for him. Why should I? I was already annoyed at myself for having gone to so much trouble in preparation for his arrival.

When he had settled his things into my mother's room, he came down to the kitchen and I gave him his whiskey. After taking a swallow he produced an assortment of photographs from a torn plastic bag I noticed he had been carrying when he arrived. "These are for you and Daisy."

Beaming, he picked up a wooden-framed photograph of Iris Tree. It had been taken by his father, Curtis Moffat. He showed it to Daisy. "This is your great-grandmother," he explained. He next produced an aged black-and-white photograph of a severe-looking woman dressed in Victorian clothes, with a wide-brimmed hat and long skirt, sitting on a bicycle. She resembled the pictures of the women suffragettes I had learned about in school.

"This is Lady Tree, or 'Mammeena,' as we called her," Ivan told Daisy. "She was my grandmother and your mother's great-grandmother and your great-great grandmother."

Daisy was totally confused. I was glad she was only three and not able to ask complicated questions.

Ivan next took out a photograph of himself as a young man. In the black-and-white photo he is reading a newspaper, the *45th Division News,* and the enormous headline reads "War Ends." His face is boyish, and I am startled by how much he resembles his son Jonathan. Now my brother Jonathan. Over the years we had lost touch, but now I felt uneasy, slightly ashamed, as if we had done something wrong.

I remembered again how angry Ivan had become that evening at Annabel's when Jonathan had said that if he ever had a daughter, he might like to call her Ivana. It might have served Ivan and Mum right if Jonathan and I had fallen madly in love and had ugly, weird, inbred children together. That would have taught them not to be so reckless with their lives.

Ivan explained the photograph to Daisy and me. He had been in Paris when the Second World War ended, with the filmmaker George Stevens. They were members of the small U.S. Army film crew, the "Irregulars," and they were filming the liberation. He said it was the most exhilarating day of his life.

He gave us some other photographs, including a copy of a colorful portrait of himself by the California artist Don Bachardy, and he enthusiastically told a story about each.

I knew that he was trying to be nice and that he wanted us to feel excited about, and included in, our new family, but I didn't want to hear how wonderful and extraordinary his mother and grandmother were. They meant nothing to me—about as much as those impersonal photographs that you see absently stuck in silver frames in antique shops. I resented his trying to impose these equally meaningless people upon us.

I wanted to tell him that I already had quite enough old family photos. Familiar ones, of people I actually knew, or at least had always known were my relatives. Photographs of places I had lived in and been to often. Photographs of Maureen holding her three children. Pictures of my grandfather Basil Dufferin standing on the terrace at Clandeboye, or of my great-aunt Oonagh by the lake at Luggala, or of her sister, Aileen, in the garden at her beautiful house, Luttrellstown. Even photographs of the viceroy in India, or his standing near Helen's Tower, the tall stone monument that he had built at Clandeboye in memory of his beloved mother, Helen. Those photographs held a significance for me.

I had always known that these were my blood relatives and *their* stories, like everyone's own family stories, interested me.

When I looked at photographs of Helen's Tower, I could remember visiting it with my mother, and her pointing out the poems that the viceroy had requested the leading literary figures of the day write to memorialize his mother.

On the walls of the tower on gold plaques are gushing poems by Browning and Tennyson dedicated to Helen. My mother used to love to tell everyone that those were "the worst" poems that any of these great writers had ever produced. She would point at Browning's lines—"Who hears of Helen's Tower may dream perchance / How that great beauty of the Scaean Gate . . ." She'd say, "I mean really, those are not some of his best lines, are they?"

The Tennyson poem also amused her: "Helen's Tower here I stand / Dominant over sea and land / Son's love built me, and I hold / Mother's love in letter'd gold . . ." She laughed as she read the poem aloud and told me how appalled Robert had been when she had taken him there. "Whatever did the viceroy do to those great writers?" he had asked. I never knew the viceroy, of course, but I had heard about him for as long as I can remember.

I didn't try to hide my lack of interest in Ivan's family memorabilia. I casually glanced at the photographs without even the polite show of enthusiasm I would muster for an acquaintance's tedious family albums.

When he proudly gave me a copy of *The Rainbow Picnic*, a biography of Iris Tree written by Daphne Fielding, I just looked at it and said, "Oh yeah, I think we have a copy of this somewhere." Then I put it down absently on the kitchen table.

I knew I was being, if not deliberately cruel, then something uncomfortably close to it, and I was taken aback by my behavior. It was not that I had extended the invitation expressly to punish him—the gesture had been friendly and conciliatory—but now that he was here . . .

The fact that we were pretending that everything was all right seemed hypocritical for both of us. As if it were perfectly acceptable for him to come waltzing into my life, with smiles and charm and family photographs.

He didn't know me at all. He hadn't known me for thirty years. He hadn't helped me through school, with my attempt to become an actress, through my difficult marriage and divorce. At least, Bob Silvers had been part of my life. Where was Ivan when my mother, whom he now claims was the love of his life, was so desperately ill? He never offered to help me when I knew she was dying and was trying to do everything I could to save her.

Now he was old, unwell, and frightened. He was examining his own life and mistakes. He was coming to me, as if I were a priest, for absolution. I recalled reading "The Pardoner's Tale," part of Chaucer's *Canterbury Tales*. It's the story of a bogus man of the church traveling from parish to parish offering to "pardon" sinners in exchange for money. Ivan wasn't offering me money, but he still wanted my forgiveness.

Ivan was making a real effort. He seemed to be enjoying himself, and I think was genuinely enthralled by Daisy, and appreciative of the house and garden. He was affectionate toward me. But all this made it worse. I didn't want him to feel at home. I didn't want him to feel as though he was deserving of a warm welcome. I didn't want him to feel as if he had an attractive ready-made family into which he could comfortably fit.

I served him the caviar. At the back of the cupboard I had unearthed a silver bowl and flat ivory spoon intended for serving caviar; I had no idea where I had gotten it, probably from my grandmother or as a wedding present from someone who didn't know me. But it gave me tremendous satisfaction to present it casually as though this was how I dined every night.

I wanted to give him the impression that I lived a perfect life, with bouquets of flowers everywhere, delicious food, and an adorable and well-behaved daughter. And that I had achieved all this without him. He deserved none of the credit; I had done this alone.

Of course he didn't seem cognizant of my effort or my motives. He just lapped up the caviar, complained that the blinis were too like pancakes, and said that cheese in America just wasn't as good as it was in Europe.

As he downed several beers I, like a martyr, sipped my Diet Coke and pretended not to mind his criticism. When I brought out the apple tart and a tub of ice cream, he sneered, "Elegant presentation." And then refused to have any. "This is far too much food, you know—I don't eat very much."

I briskly put it back in the fridge. And then surreptitiously topped up my Diet Coke with his whiskey. I knew I shouldn't. As

I filled my glass, I could hear the consternation and warnings of the counselors at rehab, my AA sponsor, and everyone else who had been cheering me on. In one easy gesture I was pouring away seven months of hard work. At that moment, though, I didn't care. I couldn't think about the consequences. I just wanted for one minute, for one second even, not to feel anything. I wanted everything to stop inside. I wanted to experience nothing. I didn't even want happiness, just anesthesia.

If a glass of whiskey—which I didn't even like to drink—could stop me from thinking and hurting, if a mouthful of something that burned my tongue and tasted revolting could, for a teeny amount of time, make me feel not even good but tolerable, then why wouldn't I want it?

I can hear the dissenting voices as I write this. "Of course you had a choice. It's only when you pick up a drink that you have no choice. Pick up the phone, go to a meeting, sit on your hands even though you feel your skin is splitting. Wait until the feeling passes. Do whatever it takes, and it will get better."

But the moment the amber liquid was coursing through my body I felt better. Ivan began to seem a benevolent figure, my newfound dad, how lucky I was to have found such a clever and urbane father.

I suggested we sit in the garden so he could smoke (something he had insisted on doing inside the house in spite of my objections). We went outside, and he told me stories about his life and loves and all the famous people he had known in Hollywood.

Every now and then I would excuse myself and sneakily refill my glass with his whiskey. With each gulp, his stories became more interesting and more amusing. I began to relax and enjoy his clever (and obviously well-rehearsed) imitations of James Dean, Elizabeth Taylor, Rock Hudson, Charlie Chaplin, David

Selznick, and William Randolph Hearst—all people he had worked with in Hollywood.

After he had exhausted his repertoire of stories about famous people, he turned the conversation to my mother. He repeated anecdotes I heard him tell many times of their life together in California. Tales of her shyness, awkwardness, and drinking in front of "Hollywood royalty," as he referred to the group of people he had succeeded in ingratiating himself with. He had mastered a fairly convincing impersonation of her, but I minded that he was mimicking her voice and mannerisms in such a condescending and unnecessarily spiteful way.

I started to find his attitude repulsive. What was he trying to prove? I knew my mother better than anyone, I knew her faults and weaknesses. I also knew the anguish that she lived with and struggled against every day. I was the one who had witnessed her frantic nocturnal pacings. The one who had overheard her desperately muttered exclamations of horror to herself when she thought no one was listening.

I had lived with the look of complete terror and panic that consumed her once beautiful face. I realized that whatever she was feeling was unbearable. That is not to say that I understood her moods or wasn't frustrated and irritated by what easily could be dismissed as self-indulgence. But I do know that pain, whether physical or emotional, is something that is all-consuming and very hard for anyone else to understand.

When I had my accident and felt that boiling water scorch every nerve in my stomach, genitals, and legs, I couldn't possibly have described the actual feeling to anyone. How can you convey a physical sensation to someone without actually administering a dose of the same pain?

I believe that's how my mother felt. It was as if her mind was being constantly scalded. That's why she was so drawn to Robert;

his mental illness was such a huge part of him and certainly no secret. Perhaps they had found their own private language for communicating suffering. "My mind's not right." A famous line in one of Robert's poems. In our house we used it as a catch-phrase, one of our little jokes. But we also knew it wasn't funny, not at all.

Now as I sat with Ivan in the garden, my mother's garden, and listened to his callous and cruel remarks about her, I thought of a side of her that was often forgotten. It didn't match the easier and more entertaining perception people had of her. Her discipline and artistry as a writer.

No matter what kind of night she had passed, stomping around, drinking, and "catastrophizing," in the morning she would get up early, pour herself a strong cup of coffee, and sit down with her notebook to write.

While she was working, sitting upright in the red velvet wing-back chair in the living room, she would manage to focus. For several hours she seemed to be able to escape whichever of her "worst nightmares" were troubling her at that time.

In a relatively short career she had written ten books of fiction and nonfiction. One of her novels was runner-up for the Booker Prize and would have won had one of the judges not considered it too "slender." Her hilariously macabre account of the 1979 grave diggers' strike in Liverpool published in *The New York Review* was just one of her funny, sly, and controversial articles.

Her book *The Last of the Duchess,* about the final months of Wallis, Duchess of Windsor, is funny, ghoulish, and sharp. When it was first published everyone thought my mother had made up the whole story of the duchess's imprisonment at the hands of Maître Blum, her autocratic lawyer. It has all proven not only to be true, but even worse than my mother had described.

When Ivan started to criticize one of her novels for having an "unconvincing male protagonist," I wanted to kick his cane out from under him and shove him, along with the chair he had made himself so comfortable in, into the pool. I wanted to watch him sink beneath the surface.

She was worth a thousand of you, I thought. She had genuine compassion and talent and capacity for love. In that moment I missed her so so much and I just wanted her back. I wanted to imagine that she had just nipped into the kitchen to refill her glass and look for the ever elusive match for her ciggie.

That Ivan was sitting there in the chair where she should have been, lavishing attention on the granddaughter that my mother would have loved, being pandered to by a daughter that he had had by accident was really too much to bear.

The fact that he was sitting there drinking and smoking and laughing at my mother's expense (after all, it was her money that had paid for all of this) while her poor ashes were amateurishly buried under some stones a hundred yards away, was quite monstrous.

If Mum could have been there she would have loved and relished the ghastliness of the scene. I could hear her gravelly voice whisper enthusiastically, "He really is awful, isn't he? Don't you see now why I never wanted him to be your father? He really is too bad, even for us."

I tried to make the rest of Ivan's stay as pleasant as possible. I took him to the beach and to various dinner parties. We managed to play our roles of father and daughter enjoying a nice little family holiday together quite convincingly. Yet I couldn't help feeling as if Ivan had been hired for a couple of weeks to play my father and that someone had written a very clever script for us to act.

Or, perhaps it was as if we were starring in one of the movies Ivan himself had written. After all, hadn't he worked on some of the best, *Shane, Giant, A Place in the Sun,* all of them vivid portraits of family tragedy?

On his last evening with me, Ivan and I went over to dinner in East Hampton. Jean Vanderbilt, our hostess and a lovely, funny woman, not only a friend of mine but someone who had known Ivan for many years.

She had a friend from Arizona staying with her, Jimmy Davison, whom I had met often with Marguerite Littman in London and liked very much. Apparently Jimmy and Ivan had also been friends for a long time and so the dinner was a weird sort of reunion for all of us. Of course neither Jean nor Jimmy had been aware of the intimate connection between Ivan and me. Well, we hadn't either, so you could excuse them for that.

They were welcoming and sweet and acted as though it was perfectly normal that their old friend and their relatively new and younger friend should arrive together, Ivan leaning heavily on both my arm and his cane for support.

Before we sat down for dinner, we chatted away in Jean's cozy living room. Ivan was in a good mood. Jean was letting him smoke in the house and had given him a nice big tumbler of his favorite whiskey, so he felt right at home.

The conversation was light and pleasant. Jimmy went on about how wonderful Daisy was and how he'd been smitten with her since she was a baby, and he laughingly told Ivan that he had thought about kidnapping her and taking her away to live with him on his almond ranch in Bakersville.

Ivan loved that and said he felt proud to have such an extraordinary granddaughter, a remark that irritated me but that I let slide. Why not allow him to enjoy this, I thought. Why shouldn't he be allowed to take some pride in her? But even as I was trying to convince myself that I should be gracious and lenient with him, the old resentments came bubbling back.

We sat down to dinner. Jean's food was always delicious—fresh produce grown locally and cooked simply. I was still abusing my no-drinking regimen. I had realized on Ivan's first night with me that there was no way I could remain abstemious while he was staying. His presence was just too unsettling, and he wasn't doing without any of *his* crutches—his cigs, his whiskey, and, I couldn't help reminding myself, a nice new cane, one that I had bought for him in Southampton.

So, I had happily been drinking cold white wine until dinner was served. Then because it was lamb she was serving, I switched to the nice fat red Margaux that Jimmy had brought as a house present. The atmosphere was relaxed and convivial; Jimmy and Ivan were both clever and well-practiced storytellers, and it was easy to just let them talk.

All evening, Ivan and I had been skirting around the most interesting conversation point: us. Were we never going to discuss the real nature of his visit? And were we going to pretend that everything was all fine now? That we were thrilled with the way things had turned out?

I couldn't. I just couldn't. I interrupted Ivan midway into one of his stories. "I wish we had never found out," I blurted out. The room went silent and Ivan looked at me quizzically, shocked at my outburst.

"Don't you see it's all too late?" I said loudly and theatrically. Now I really sounded as though I were in a movie—and not a very well written one, at that.

I didn't know what I was saying because I didn't have any idea what I wanted to say. I just needed to say something. If I kept on stuffing down all my old feelings, I would never have room for new ones. God forbid I could perhaps make way for some good ones for once.

"I wish Bob Silvers was my dad. I much prefer him to you."

My face felt hot, and I could feel my temples and forehead beginning to sweat. I didn't dare look up across the table to where Ivan was sitting. I didn't know what to do so I started to cry.

I thought perhaps that if I shed enough tears they could some-how dilute the impact of my terrible words. As I reached for a napkin to wipe my eyes, I managed to sneak a look at Ivan. He just sat there very still, his body rigid, his face seeming to have shrunk, as though my words had sucked all life out of it.

This was not going to be a Hollywood fairy-tale ending. The unspeakable had been spoken. And now we were out of dialogue.

AFTER IVAN'S DEATH I learned about a conversation he had with an old girlfriend who had dinner with him the night before he suffered a massive stroke.

They had talked about dying, and she asked him if he believed in any kind of afterlife. He said absolutely not. "Dead is dead." She then wondered if he had any regrets. He told her that he supposed "one always has regrets" and then added, "I'm sorry it took so long for Ivana to find out."

When I heard that, I felt sad, but I was incredibly touched. I didn't think that I had mattered so much to him.

TWO MONTHS AFTER IVAN'S VISIT I was still replaying our conversations and unspoken interactions, and the dominant feelings I had when I looked back were of regret and guilt.

The more I thought about it all and about Ivan, the more ashamed I felt about the way I had treated him. Instead of continuing to feel antagonistic toward him, as I had at first, I started to think of him fondly.

I took out all the family photographs he had given me and examined them with greater interest. I put them up in my bedroom and gave Daisy the colorful portrait of her grandfather to put on her chest of drawers.

I read *The Rainbow Picnic*, the book about my new grandmother, Iris, and it confirmed the feeling that we would have gotten on and had some fun together. I reveled in the theatrical achievements of my new relatives, and even began to feel a sense of belonging. I decided that Ivan and I should start afresh. Perhaps it was in some way good and important that I had expressed the way I felt because now the air could be considered cleared. From now on we could try to have a real relationship, one that didn't have a foundation in bitterness and resentment.

I was slowly coming round to seeing a relationship with Ivan as a gift. A challenge, too, but also a gift.

Why Not Say What Happened?

I DECIDED I WAS GOING TO GIVE MYSELF a second chance at having this man as a father. I knew that for his part he was willing to embrace and maybe even love me.

I suddenly felt incredibly lucky. Hadn't I always wished, like everyone who loses a parent young, to be able to have one last moment with them? You would give anything to just have them back for a minute to tell them everything you didn't get a chance to say when they were alive.

I decided that I would call Ivan and invite him and Jonathan to spend Christmas with us. We could have a proper family Christmas together. Perhaps, I thought, I could even persuade Ivan to dress up as Santa. I was excited at the prospect of seeing Ivan again—I needed him to know that I wasn't the cruel and cold woman that he had encountered on his last visit. I looked forward to being able to show him another side of myself, a loving and appreciative one.

As I was sitting in Sag Harbor waiting for it to be nine a.m. in L.A., when I could call and be certain of not waking him, I got a call from my sister, Evgenia. Ivan had suffered two strokes and was in a coma in Los Angeles.

She said, "If you feel you would like to come, you'd better come now because he isn't going to last very long." My immediate reaction was that it was my fault. I had been so vile to him when he had come to stay that I had caused him two months later to have a stroke.

I got a flight to Los Angeles the next day. During the flight I drank white wine. I had been sober the whole two months after Ivan's visit, but I convinced myself that if ever there was a time when a girl needed a drink, this was it. I was losing a parent, and I had lost so many already.

I couldn't help thinking of Lady Bracknell's remark in Oscar

Wilde's *The Importance of Being Earnest*: "To lose one parent, may be regarded as a misfortune; to lose both looks like carelessness."

This was my fourth. I must be a complete idiot.

I went straight from the airport to the hospital. I knew that his daughter, Lorna, was with him, and his sons, Jonathan and Patrick, were on their way from London. I felt uncomfortable as I walked down the hospital corridor toward his room. I had never met Lorna before and I was sure that she would find my presence intrusive.

When I got to his room, I was surprised and relieved to find it empty of visitors. He lay there with all the vital tubes and IVs pulsing away, and he was breathing, uneasily, through a respirator.

His face was grey and his eyes closed. I took his hand and squeezed it gently, "Ivan, it's me, Ivana." He seemed to understand. I am sure I heard him say, "Uh, uh, uh," and I was grateful for that—I just wanted to hear him say one last thing.

I don't think he could hear me, but you never know.

I leaned down and kissed his cheek.

The nurse came in and asked me whether I was family, and this time I said without any hesitation, "Yes, I'm his daughter."

Epilogue

I own two portraits by the well-known English painter Augustus John. The paintings are of two very different, strong, and uniquely beautiful women: my two grandmothers, Iris and Maureen. They seem to stare defiantly down upon the viewer. Both have large, bright blue, heavy-lidded eyes, and slight smiles on their mouths.

A few days ago I brought the paintings from my apartment in New York to the house in Sag Harbor. I asked Daisy to help me decide where they should go and help me hang them. She took the task very seriously. Hammer and hooks in hand, we tried out various places around the house.

We finally settled on the long drawing room, which we didn't use much apart from when we had guests, but it was definitely

the grandest room in the house. Daisy and I had great fun deciding where each one would be positioned. We did not want to give
either a preferable spot, lest the other be offended.

It was interesting how even at eight years old my beautiful and
clever daughter understood the personalities of her relatives.

"We can't put your mum's mother so near the door," Daisy lec-
tured. "She would hate that and she'd feel really left out. I think
she would like to be near your mum."

Above the fireplace in the room hangs a copy of Lucian
Freud's portrait of my mother *Girl in Bed*. My mother had the
Tate gallery in London copy the original, and it looks very close to
the real one. It is the same painting that Robert was clutching
when he died in the taxicab in New York. She is young, only
nineteen, and she already has a look of melancholy about her.
But she still is ethereally beautiful.

Daisy and I decided that we should hang Maureen and Iris
side by side on the wall opposite my mother. After we had finished, Daisy and I stood in the middle of the room admiring our
handiwork. I looked at the various photographs scattered around,
propped up on the mantelpiece and on side tables. There were
pictures of Israel, Robert, Ivan, and a youthful Bob Silvers. There
was Lucian and my mother in Paris, Maureen holding my mother,
Aunt Perdita, and Uncle Sheridan when they were babies.

My family.

And there was the one photograph that I had always found
unsettling. In it Robert, my mother, and baby Sheridan are trying
to pose for a picture taken by a professional photographer. I
don't know what was going on that day but Robert and my
mother look rather menacing. They are both scowling ominously.
Robert's wild hair is scraped back unflatteringly. My mother's
huge eyes look murderous. Neither of them is looking at the

camera. Instead they are staring in opposite directions as if at something horrendous.

Little Sheridan is at the forefront perched precariously on my mother's knee. His plump, round face seems confused.

I looked at the photograph and I started to laugh.

"What's so funny, Mummy?" Daisy asked, wanting to be in on the joke.

I took my daughter's hand, and she beamed back at me waiting for a reply. "Oh, it's nothing, sweetie. Just my family."

Ivana

Small-soul-pleasing, loved with condescension,
even through the cro-magnon tirades of six,
the last madness of child-gaiety
before the trouble of the world shall hit.
Being chased upstairs is still instant-heaven,
not yet your sisters' weekends of voluntary scales,
accompanying on a recorder carols
rescored by the Sisters of the Sacred Heart in Kent.
Though burned, you are hopeful, accident cannot tell you
experience is what you do not want to experience.
Is the teenager the dominant of ache?
Or flirting seniles, their conversation three noises,
Their life-expectancy shorter than the martyrs?
How all ages hate another age,

and lifelong wonder what was the perfect age?

— ROBERT LOWELL

Printed in the United States
by Baker & Taylor Publisher Services